Single-Session Therapy and Procrastination

Single-Session Therapy and Procrastination

Windy Dryden

Onlinevents Publications

First edition published by Onlinevents Publications

Copyright (c) 2024 Windy Dryden and Onlinevents Publications

Windy Dryden
136 Montagu Mansions, London W1U 6LQ

Onlinevents Publications
38 Bates Street, Sheffield, S10 1NQ
www.onlinevents.co.uk
help@onlinevents.co.uk

A catalogue record of this book is
available from the British Library.

First edition 2024

ISBN: 978-1-914938-30-6

Contents

Preface

Single-Session Therapy (SST) delivers therapy services to people looking for immediate help with an issue they are troubled about. While such people may wish to understand their issue better or express their feelings about it, most seek a solution to the issue with which they have become stuck. Technically, SST can be more than a single session. It is an intentional endeavour where the client and therapist contract to help the client leave the session with a solution they can implement to reach their problem-related goal after the session has ended, on the understanding that more help is available to the client on request. By contrast, the single-session work that appears in this book is SST, which lasts for one session (see below).

In Chapter 1 of this book, I will discuss the single-therapy mindset, which is at the heart of single-session work and, in Chapter 2, I will discuss the practice of SST that flows from that mindset. Then, in Chapter 3, I will discuss the nature of procrastination and what can realistically be achieved in a person with procrastination in a single session. In doing so, I will also briefly discuss the insights that I use from Rational Emotive Behaviour Therapy to help clients when it is clear that we both need more than general SST practice to assist the client in getting unstuck from their problem with procrastination.

This Project

As I mentioned above, people who came forward to have a single session with me knew that they would only have one session with me and that the problem they should bring up is one to do with procrastination. Before beginning with all but one of the volunteers,[1] I said the following: 'Before we begin, let's see that we are on the same page. My understanding is that you have signed up for a single session devoted to helping you with a current problem that you have with procrastination for which you are seeking help. You have agreed to

---

[1] The session that I had with Sofia was held during a two-hour workshop I ran for Onlinevents on procrastination. All other sessions that appear in this book were held in private with volunteers who signed up to see me in the month that followed the workshop.

have the transcript of our session in the book under a name chosen by you, and by the end of August this year, you agree to submit a 500-word reflection outlining your experience of the session, what you took from it and what difference it made to you. Is that your understanding as well?' All but one of the people I spoke to confirmed that this was their understanding as well.[2]

---

[2] One person thought that I was offering supervision to counsellors who may be struggling with a client with a procrastination problem. Once I clarified that this was not the case, the conversation came to an amicable close.

PART 1

THE THEORY AND PRACTICE OF SST

1

The Single-Session Therapy Mindset

In this chapter, I will outline the mindset that SST practitioners are encouraged to adopt while practising this mode of therapy delivery. In doing so, I will note differences between SST in clinical practice and SST done for this book arising from the SST demonstrations that I do for Onlinevents and which form the context for this book.

The Single-Session Therapy Mindset

When therapists new to SST attempt to practise this mode of therapy delivery from a more conventional therapy mindset, the results are generally unsatisfactory for both the client and the therapist. The conventional therapy-minded practitioner generally tries to do too much in the session, cramming as much in as possible with the result that the client goes away confused and overwhelmed with little benefit from the session. So what are the major components of the SST mindset (see Cannistrà, 2022)?

One Session or More. Be Open to Both Possibilities

In general SST practice, the therapist strives to integrate two positions: (1) working with the client to see if the latter can be helped in one session, but (2) open to the idea that more help is available. When offering more help to the client at the end of the session, the SST therapist presents the available options to the client in an even-handed way.

Conventional therapy-minded practitioners tend to emphasise the 'more help is available' position with clients because they can always see that their clients have more issues. They find it difficult to go along with want a particular client wants (i.e. help with one nominated[3] issue),

---

[3] In this book, I refer to the problem or issue that the client chooses to discuss with the SST therapist as the 'nominated' problem/issue. This is important

fearing that the client's undealt with issues will take their toll on the client later.

Conversely, when the SST therapist takes their single-session brief too literally, they are reluctant to offer the client more help, thinking incorrectly that if the client wants more help, this represents a failure on their part.

In the SST work that I do for Onlinevents, as demonstrated in this book, the work is limited to the single session for which the person has volunteered. The person is well aware of this before they volunteer for the session. Thus, my Onlinevents SST work lacks the integration of the two positions described above. As there is only one position, there is nothing to integrate.

Help at the Point of Need

If SST were a plant, it would thrive in compost comprising help at the point of need as its primary nutrient. From this perspective, in many ways, the best 'home' for SST is in an 'open-access, enter now' centre[4] since the person can seek help when they want it knowing that it will be provided during that visit.

When SST is offered by appointment, help must be offered to the client as soon as possible after they have approached the agency for SST. In my view, the potency of SST is diluted when a person has to wait more than a week for the session and having a long waiting list for SST is an oxymoron.

When considering the SST work that I do for Onlinevents, in one sense, the person is getting my help with their issue with procrastination as soon as they volunteer for it and from this perspective, it is very much 'help at the point of need'. On the other hand, I am unsure how long the person has struggled with their procrastination problem without seeking help. I view my work for Onlinevents as similar to the situation where a person who has had a problem for a while is given an opportunity to deal with it promptly and uses that opportunity.

---

where the client has more than one problem. In this book, of course, the client's nominated problem is procrastination.

[4] I developed the term 'open-access, enter now', to describe facilities that offer therapy to all who wish to access it, and anybody can enter the facility by whatever means they choose when it is open. The term 'walk-in', while still common in the SST literature, is currently seen as excluding people who are not able to walk into such a facility, due to their disability.

It Is Possible to Conduct a Session in SST Without Prior Knowledge of the Person

An important part of the SST mindset that we, as practitioners, bring to the work is that we can help someone with their nominated problem without knowing much about the person in advance. As I will discuss below, the SST therapist does send out a pre-session questionnaire to their client before meeting them for the first (and possibly only) session of SST. However, their primary purpose in doing so is to encourage the client to prepare for the session so that they can get the most from it. It is not designed for the therapist to collect information from the client that the therapist considers vital to have before the session, which may be nothing of the sort. Even when the client returns the form before the session, the therapist reads it to understand the client's thinking at the time that they were completing the form. Indeed, some SST therapists prefer to see a client without knowing anything about them and will not read the completed and returned form before the session.

When I see people who volunteer for what I call a Ronseal SST session[5] I know nothing about them other than that they are volunteering to have a single session with me on a current problem that they have for which they are seeking help. I also know that they do not mind discussing this issue with me in front of a live audience or if the event is being run by Onlinevents in front of an online audience. If the event is on a particular theme, such as procrastination, then I will also know that the issue for which the person wants help is very likely to be the same as the event theme. Thus, all the volunteers whose session transcripts appear in this book indeed had problems with procrastination given that the event was advertised as one on 'SST and Procrastination' and the sign-up sheet that was posted online for people who wanted a complimentary session with me made it clear that the person was to bring a personal problem with procrastination to their session with me.

View the Session as a Whole, Complete in Itself

---

[5] In 1994, a British company called 'Ronseal', which manufactures wood stain, paint and preservatives, developed a slogan to explain and demystify its products. It was 'Ronseal. It does exactly what it says on the tin'. This caught the public imagination to the extent that the phrase is used internationally and is now a commonly used slogan. The Ronseal approach to the question, 'What is SST?', then, is: 'Single-session therapy is a therapy that lasts for one session.'

From the perspective of the conventional therapy mindset, the first session in therapy is invariably a prelude to further sessions. In that session, the conventional therapy-minded therapist will carry out one or more of the following activities: an assessment of the client and their problems, a case history or a case formulation. All these activities are designed to get therapy off on the right foot when it starts. Consequently, the conventional therapy-minded practitioner does not think of the first session as a whole, complete in itself. The way they think about the first session has been aptly summed up by an American colleague of mine[6] who once said that the purpose of the first session of therapy is to encourage the client to come back for the session. This contrasts with the single-session therapy minded practitioner who does view the first (and perhaps only) session as a whole, complete in itself, with a beginning, a middle and an end. For them, the purpose of the first session of therapy is to work together with the client to help the latter leave the session with what they have come for, on the understanding that more help is available if requested.

Potentially, Anyone Can Be Helped in a Single Session

When I give a presentation or a workshop on single-session therapy, one of the most frequently asked questions is, 'Who is suitable and unsuitable for SST?' (Dryden, 2022a) My answer is anyone who wants it. What we have learned from the experiences of those who have worked in 'open-access, enter now' services is that as the heading of this section makes clear, anyone *can* be helped in a single session. This is not to say, however, that everyone *will* be helped in a single session. The position that is taken, therefore, in SST is that the best time to answer the question, will your next client benefit from SST is to have the session and to see if they have benefited from it at the end.

This is the position that I take in both by SST practice and in the demonstration and other 'one-off' sessions that I do for organisations such as Onlinevents.

Focus on the Person, Not the Disorder

Whenever I am asked questions such as 'Can someone with "x" disorder benefit from SST?', my response is 'What is the person's name and what do they want to take away from the session?' My response shows that in SST we focus on the person and not on any disorder the

---

[6] Dr Michler Bishop.

person may have. Another way of considering this issue is to think that if ten clients with 'x' disorder seek assistance from SST, then, while not all will be helped, some will. Who will be helped will depend on a number of factors, including what they want to achieve from the session. The more realistic their goal, the more likely they will benefit from the session.

In my work for Onlinevents, there is no need for me discover if any of the volunteers that I see have a disorder as we will work together on their nominated problem, e.g., procrastination.

The Therapeutic Relationship Can Be Established Quickly in SST

Another concern that conventional therapy-minded practitioners have about SST concerns the therapeutic relationship. Such therapists are used to developing this relationship over time and cannot understand a good relationship can be developed in such a short period. Research carried out by Simon, Imel, Ludman and Steinfeld (2012) found that clients who had been helped in the first and only session that they had, developed a better working alliance with their therapists than clients who had not been helped in that session.

In addition to showing that I understand the client from their frame of reference and being transparent about the nature of SST and about what I can and can't do as an SST therapist, the best way I can develop a relationship with the client is to do the following. First, I endeavour to help them to set an achievable session goal and work with them to achieve it. Another alliance-strengthening factor is for me to help the client to select a good solution to their problem that they can integrate into their life and regularly implement.

SST is Client Led

In contrast to what occurs in conventional therapy, where the therapist largely determines what kind of therapy is to be offered the client and how often the client is to be seen, in SST the client takes the lead on these matters. Thus, the client determines such issues as what problem to nominate to discuss in the session, what they want to achieve from the session, what type of help would best suit them and how much therapy to have. The SST mindset helps the therapist to work in this client-led way, whereas the conventional therapy mindset would interfere with it. While in the latter, the client's view is sought, it is not generally prioritised as it is in SST. For example, in NHS Talking

Therapies for anxiety and depression agencies, all clients are assessed on entry to determine which therapy services best suit them. This is largely determined by the agency. When SST was piloted in such an agency, people were assessed for their suitability for SST. They were not allowed to self-refer to this service. The consequence was that only people with mid issues received SST. This is in stark contrast to the client-led nature of agencies that offer 'open-access, enter now' services. Here, clients refer themselves to these agencies and people with a whole range of problems can be helped and report finding the therapy they receive beneficial (Hoyt & Talmon, 2014; Slive & Bobele, 2018).

The Power of Now

When an SST therapist is with a client, all they know for certain is that they are with them *now*. Given that, the therapist will ask themself, 'How do I want to use the time that I have with this person to their maximum benefit? Do I want to assess the client, take a case history, carry out a case formulation, or do I want to offer them help with their stated wants for the session?' The SST therapist will, almost without exception, give the latter as their reply. The therapist says this and acts on this point because they do not know for certain whether the client in front of them will return, even if they assure us that they will. In the conventional therapy mindset, the power tends to be ascribed to the future rather than to now, i.e., what is predicted to happen in future sessions is deemed to be more powerful than what happens in the first session.

In the work I do for Onlinevents, the client and I meet for the first time when they volunteer, and we have the session, so since they want to tackle their issue (in this case procrastination), we get down to the business of doing this straight away.

Less Is More

Practitioners who bring a conventional therapy mindset to single-session therapy struggle to do the work in several ways. One way in which this issue becomes manifest is in the therapist trying to do too much in the session and sending too much material to the client after the session. This has two results. During the session, the client becomes overwhelmed and confused and, in consequence, takes little away from the process. After the session, the client becomes bemused by the amount of material the therapist has sent them and ends up using little of it going forward. It is as if the conventional therapy-minded practitioner is guided by the principle 'more is more', given the limited time that they may have with the client.

By contrast, practitioners who bring a single-session mindset to SST, use the time that they have at their disposal to help the client focus on their stated wants and to take away a solution to their nominated problem, if requested. The important point is that they are cautious in the amount they cover in the session with the client. Also, they do not routinely send clients material after the session but will do if requested and when they do so, they will send one or at the most two pieces of material. In short, they are guided by the principle, 'less is more'.

I apply the principle of 'less is more' to my sessions that I do for Onlinevents which, I hope is evidenced by the transcripts that appear in this book.

Take Nothing for Granted

I have pointed out above that the best way of discovering if a client will benefit from SST is to offer them a session and to see at the end if they find it beneficial. This is why we do not spend time figuring out in advance who may and may not be helped in SST. We have learned to take nothing for granted. Consider these four scenarios, which illustrate what I mean:

- An SST therapist meets a client at the outset who is keen to engage in SST, has a clear session goal and has a good history of self-help, The therapist thinks that it is likely that they will be able to help the person. Yet, at the end of the session, the client reports no benefit.
- An SST therapist meets a client who is willing to engage in SST but does so reluctantly, is not clear what they want to achieve from the session and does not have a good history of self-help. The therapist thinks that there is little they can do to help the person under these circumstances, and yet at the end of the session, the client reports finding the session very helpful.
- An SST therapist leaves the session very pleased with the work that they have done with a client. The therapeutic dyad collaborated on finding a focus, co-created a solution which the client rehearsed, developed a doable action plan and identified potential and formulated a way of dealing with these. Yet, a week later, the client returned seeking SST from

another therapist, claiming that they received no help from the session with the first therapist.

- An SST therapist leaves the session despondent about what just transpired between them and the client. The therapist struggled throughout the session to keep the client focused on their nominated problem, failed to help the client set a session goal, could not assist the client to develop a solution, and the client struggled to articulate what they got from the session at its end. Yet, a week later, the therapist received an email from the client thanking them for the session, which they found very helpful and stating that they are well on the way to dealing effectively with their problem.

Taking nothing for granted means that the therapist acknowledges that while they will make inferences about what may happen or has happened in a session, they will hold conviction in these inferences lightly, knowing that they may well be wrong. Consequently, the SST goes into a session with the mindset that they will give their all to the client despite what they think may happen and despite there being few signs of a good outcome.

2

The Practice of Single-Session Therapy that Stems from the SST Mindset

The single-session therapy mindset not only orients practitioners to SST it also suggests ways of practising this mode of therapy delivery (Dryden, 2023a). In this chapter, I will outline the practice of single-session therapy that stems from this mindset.

Single-Session Therapy Practice

Eliciting the Client's Informed Consent

As in other forms of therapy delivery, one of the SST therapist's initial tasks is to elicit the client's informed consent. This involves the therapist making sure that the client has an accurate understanding of SST as well as agrees to the practicalities of therapy such as confidentiality, the therapist's or agency's cancellation policy and the payment of any fees. The therapist should also outline any risks involved in SST and how they can be addressed. Finally, the therapist should elicit any concerns the client may have about SST and answer any of their questions about the SST process.

As outlined in the Preface, before I carried out the sessions I did for this book, I said this to the volunteers, 'Before we begin, let's see that we are on the same page. My understanding is that you have signed up for a single session devoted to helping you with a current problem that you have with procrastination for which you are seeking help. You have agreed to have the transcript of our session in the book under a name chosen by you, and by the end of August this year, you agree to submit a 500-word reflection outlining your experience of the session, what you took from it and what difference it made to you. Is that your understanding as well?' Once the person confirmed that this was their understanding, we began the single session.

Helping the Client Prepare for the Session

Once the client has given their informed consent to proceed and a date has been agreed for the session, the therapist sends the client a pre-session questionnaire. This form is designed to help the client prepare for the session so that they can get the most from it. The therapist makes it clear that completing the form is not a mandatory part of the process and informs the client that if they choose to complete it, then it would be useful to return it to them before the session so that they can also prepare for the session.

Here is an example of questions that I use in the pre-session questionnaire I send out in one of the settings I work where most of the work is SST.

1.   What is the issue that you want to focus on in the session?
2.   Why is this significant?
3.   What do you want to get from the session?
4.   What do you think I need to know about the issue to help you with it? Summarise in bullet points.
5.   What steps, successful or unsuccessful, have you taken so far in addressing the issue?
6.   What are the strengths or inner resources that you have as a person that you could draw upon while tackling the issue?
7.   Who are the people in your life who can support you as you tackle the issue?
8.   What help do you hope I can best provide you in the session? Please check the *main one*.

- Help me to develop a greater understanding of the issue.
- Just listen while I talk about the issue.
- Help me to express my feelings about the issue.
- Help me to solve an emotional or behavioural problem; help me get unstuck.
- Help me to make a decision.
- Help me to resolve a dilemma.

I do not use a pre-session questionnaire in the demonstration and other work I do for Onlinevents.

Beginning the Session

SST therapists begin the session in different ways, and I will briefly review these here (see Dryden, 2022b).

Purpose

Some therapists begin the session by ensuring that the client understands the purpose of the session and that they share an understanding with the client on this point. This is particularly important when there has been no contact between the therapist and the client before the session, and the client has not completed a pre-session questionnaire. An example of this beginning question is as follows:

- *'What is your understanding of the purpose of our conversation today?'*

As you will see, this is the way that I begin all the sessions in this book.

Problem

With the exception of single-session therapists who have an allegiance to solution-focused brief therapy (e.g. Ratner, George & Iveson, 2012), many SST therapists begin the session by asking for the client's nominated problem. An example of this beginning question is as follows:

- *'What problem, concern or issue would you like me to help you with?'*

Goal[7]

Since SST is goal-directed, many SST practitioners prefer to begin the session by asking about the client's goal. An example of this beginning question is as follows:

- *'What would you like to achieve by talking with me today?'*

Type of Help Sought

The final way in which an SST therapist can begin the session is to ask the client what help they are seeking from the therapist. An example of this beginning question is as follows:

- *'What help would you like from me today?'*

---

[7] See also the section entitled 'Helping the Client to Nominate a Goal' below.

In my experience, the therapist will often have to clarify what they mean here and the best way of doing so is to outline the possible types of help they can offer the client.[8]

Helping the Client to Nominate a Goal

When thinking about a client's goal in SST, it is important to distinguish between a goal related to the client's nominated problem (which I refer to in this book as the client's problem-related goal) and a goal related to what the client wants to achieve by the end of the session (which I refer to as the client's session goal). If the client mentions the former when asked about their goal, then the therapist can ask them about the latter. Then, the therapist needs to assist the client to understand that the achievement of their session goal is an important step towards the achievement of their problem-related goal.

In the work that I do with the volunteer clients seeking help for procrastination, I am interested in learning what they think are healthy alternatives to their procrastination issues and strive to help them set these as their problem-related goals, Then, I help them to identify a way of doing this by the end of the session.

Discovering What Help the Client is Seeking from the Therapist

While most clients access SST for help with finding solutions to emotional and behavioural problems, other forms of help are available. These include:

- Helping a client to understand an issue.
- Helping a client to express their feelings about an issue.
- Helping a client to talk about whatever they want in an unstructured way.
- Help a client to make a decision.
- Help a client to resolve a dilemma.
- Offering a client a professional opinion.
- Helping a client with signposting to other services.

---

[8] For more information see the section entitled 'Discovering What Help the Client is Seeking from the Therapist' below.

The important point here is that the therapist offers the client the type of help that they are looking for and do not foist on the help that they do not want even if the therapist thinks they need it.

The work that I do for Onlinevents tends to be helping people to solve an emotional/behavioural problem with which they feel stuck and this is certainly the case with this book.

Creating a Focus and Maintaining It

Apart from when a client wishes to use the session as an opportunity to talk about whatever they wish in an unfettered work, SST works best when the client and therapist co-create a focus and remain with this focus. The exception to this is where it becomes clear to both client and therapist that the original focus is not the most important one and, in that case, a new, more central focus is agreed and kept to.

In working to create a focus, this could be based on the client's nominated problem, problem-related goal or the session goal. Once established, the therapist is responsible for ensuring that the therapeutic dyad keep to the agreed focus. This may involve the therapist interrupting the client if the client goes off track. Therapists are not used to doing that and some are reluctant to do so because it goes against the principles that they learned in their professional training course. However, when the therapist fails to interrupt the client it may mean that the client will not get as much from the SST process than they would have got if the therapist had interrupted them.

In my experience, the best way to interrupt a client is to take the following steps:

- Give the client rationale for interrupting them.
- Seek and get the client's permission to be interrupted.
- Ask the client how you can best interrupt them.

Understanding the Problem[9]

Once the client has nominated a problem which they and their therapist have agreed to focus on, the next step is for the therapist to help themself and their client to understand the problem. The SST therapist has two tasks here: eliciting the client's view of the problem and how

---

[9] SST therapists who practise solution-focused brief therapy would tend not to do this.

they unwittingly maintain it and offering the client their view of the client's problem and maintenance factors.[10]

In my view, understanding the problem is best done by assigning an example of it. This is the case because the important variables are likely to be best remembered in a specific example of the problem. Such an example might be:

- A recent example
- A vivid example
- A typical example
- An anticipated example

In my view, any of the above examples are acceptable if they pass the 'Cluedo'[11] test. Cluedo is a murder mystery game where the players' task is to guess the identity of the murderer, in which room the murder took place, and the implement used to commit the murder.[12] In my opinion, there are two advantages of working with an anticipated example of the nominated problem. First, this is especially useful where the dominant theme of the client's problem is avoidance, as is the case with procrastination. In avoidance-based problems, assessment is difficult because the problem does not appear since it is being avoided. With procrastination, the person is asked to select a precise time to do the task that is being avoided and where they would do it (e.g., 2 pm, writing my essay in my study) and to imagine what they would experience at the point just before avoiding doing the task. This provides the missing experience, and this experience can be assessed and understood by therapist and client alike. The second advantage of working with an anticipated example of the problem is that any solution identified can be applied to the same situation. Thus, the person can be asked to imagine implementing the solution at 2 pm when sitting down to write their essay in their study before doing this in actuality.

Searching for a Solution

Much of the work that an SST therapist will do will be on helping clients to find solutions to their emotional/behavioural problems. A good

---

[10] See Chapter 3 for a discussion of the framework I bring to understanding procrastination and how to deal with it in SST.

[11] Known as 'Clue' in the USA.

[12] For example, *Colonel Mustard, in the Library with the Candlestick* (Hamley, 2015).

solution is one that addresses the client's nominated problem effectively and helps them to achieve their problem-related goals will be demonstrated in the transcripts in Part 2.

Types of Solutions

As I have noted elsewhere, the client can be helped to develop a variety of solutions. These are:

- *A reframing solution.* Here the client is helped to put the problem into a new, more helpful frame.
- *An attitude change solution.* Here, the client is helped to change their attitude to the adversity that lies at the heart of their problem.
- *An inference change solution.* Here, the client is helped to change a distorted inference relevant to their problem to a realistic inference rendering the problem non-problematic.
- *A solution based on a change in the person's relationship with the problem.* This often involves the therapist encouraging the client to accept (but not like) the existence of the problem rather than struggle unconstructively with it.
- *A behavioural change solution.* Here, the client is helped to change their behaviour which has helped maintain the problem.
- *A situational change solution.* Here, the client is helped to change the situation in which the problem occurs.
- *A combination of solutions.* Here the client is helped to use a combination of the above-mentioned solutions.

Factors Relevant to the Selection of a Solution

There are several sources that may contribute to the client's selection of a good solution. These include:

- The opposite of the factors that serve to maintain the client's problem.
- What the client has done in the past that has helped in dealing with the problem.
- What the client has done that has led to the solution of related or unrelated problems.
- The internal strengths that the client has that can contribute to the solution being developed and implemented.

- The external resources – both interpersonal or organizational – that the client can call upon to develop and implement the solution,
- The client's role models.
- The client's view of a good solution.
- The therapist's view of a good solution.

It is important to note that a good solution can be drawn from these sources. Not all of them may be relevant.

Encouraging the Client to Rehearse the Solution

Once the therapist has helped the client to select a solution, it is important that the client tries it out to get a taste of what it may be like to implement it. This is akin to taking a car out for a test drive before you buy it. Common ways of rehearsal include roleplay, chairwork and imagery work (see Dryden, 2023a). After the client has rehearsed the solution, they may decide to accept it, change it or reject it. In the latter case, the search for a new solution is undertaken. The client and therapist work in this way until the client has found a solution to which they are willing to commit themself.

Helping the Client to Develop and Implement an Action Plan

Once the client has committed themself to a solution, the therapist then helps them to develop an action plan that will facilitate the implementation of the solution. It is important that the client should be able to integrate such a plan into their daily life, otherwise no matter how effective the solution has the potential to be, the client will not carry it out. In this plan the client should do some or all of the following:

- State what the solution is.
- Give clear reasons why the solution is to be implemented.
- Specify where the solution is to be implemented.
- Include the people who need to be present, if relevant.
- Specify when the solution is to be implemented.
- Make clear how frequently the solution is to be implemented.
- Identify potential obstacles to the implementation of the solution and detail how these can be prevented from occurring or dealt with if they do occur.

Ending the Session

In my view, once the therapist has helped the client to develop an action plan, this signals that they are approaching the end of the session. Frank (1961) argues that while people come to therapy with a range of different symptoms, they all, to a greater or lesser extent experience a sense of demoralization. Consequently, ending a session well contributes to the restoration of the client's morale. The following are important elements of how the therapist should bring the session to a satisfactory conclusion. They should:

- *Ask the client to summarise the session.* Doing this encourages client autonomy and prioritises the client's views on this point over the therapist's views. The client's summary should ideally reference the solution and the associated action plan.
- *Ask the client what their takeaways are from the session.* These may include both the solution and other points that the client found meaningful.
- *Encourage the client to think about how they may generalize the solution and other takeaways to other relevant situations in their life.* While some clients will naturally think about this issue the majority need the client's active help to do this.
- *Tie up loose ends.* Here the therapist encourages the client to say anything about the issue that they may have wished they had said or to ask anything about the issue that they may have wished they had asked later that evening.
- *Outline options for the future.* Here the therapist encourages the client to choose from the following two options:
  - Decide that they have got what they have come for and end therapy.
  - Opt to reflect on the solution, digest what they have learned, take action and let time pass. Then, decide whether or not to seek further help and, if so, choose from services that the therapist or agency offers after being informed of waiting times to access each service.

Following the Session

After the session, a number of contacts may occur.

- Directly after the session, the client may be asked to provide feedback on their experiences of the session (see Dryden, 2023b).
- In some agencies, the client is contacted two or three weeks after the session and is asked how they are getting on and whether or not they require further help.
- About three months after the session, the client is contacted to give feedback on (a) outcome – what they achieved from the session and (b) service provision – what the client's experience was of the agency that provided SST. In this project, clients were contacted and asked to provide a 500-word reflection piece on their experiences of the session, what they took from it and the difference it made to them. They submitted this piece about three to four months after the session.

3

Helping the Client to Understand and Deal with Procrastination in Single-Session Therapy

I have found the following points helpful to remember while working with the client in SST to deal with their procrastination.

Agree on What Is Meant by Procrastination

It is important that my client and I agree with one another concerning what we mean by procrastination. I thus ask the person what they mean by procrastination. I also ask them if they are interested in my definition. This is 'putting off a task that is in your interest to do and putting it off beyond the time when it's in your interest to do it' (Dryden, 2012: 267). We can adopt my definition, use the client's or combine the two.

Is Procrastination a Problem for the Client?

Once my client and I have agreed on what procrastination is, we need to be clear if procrastination is a problem for the client. If so, I help the client to set a goal with respect to the problem (i.e., their problem-related goal) and to be clear with themself why they would like to see this change in their life. On this point, it may be worth spending some time doing a cost-benefit analysis on procrastination and whatever change the person nominates in its place, i.e., their problem-related goal). I am particularly interested in helping the client to articulate and question (1) the benefits they think they derive from procrastination and (2) the costs they think they will experience if they strive to reach their goal (i.e., what they consider to be the healthy alternative to procrastination).

What Can Realistically Be Achieved by the End of the Session

In my mind, there is a significant difference to be made in SST between two types of client goals: (1) the problem-related goal, which, as we have seen above, is what the client would like to achieve with respect to their procrastination problem and (2) the session goal which is what the client would like to achieve by the end of the session. In my experience, if I can help the client come up with a solution to their problem with procrastination by the end of the session, together with an action plan to implement this solution going forwards and ways to deal with obstacles to solution implementation[13] then in my view, I have done all that can be expected of me as an SST therapist. What I can't do for the client is implement their selected solution on their behalf.

The Role of Values

As part of my discussion with the client on their procrastination problem, I have found it helpful to help the client to articulate what values they have as a person that they could bring to their problem-related goal and to see clearly how procrastination goes against these values. In this sense, the person's values are useful leverage for change.

Ego-Based and Discomfort-Based Procrastination

Procrastination is avoidance behaviour, so it is vital for my client and me to determine what the client is avoiding. To help me to do this, I am guided by an important distinction between two types of procrastination: ego-based procrastination and discomfort-based procrastination. My client may have one or other of these types of procrastination or, of course, both. When a client has both types of procrastination, we may only have time to deal with their primary type, although my goal is to help them with both.

---

[13] Here I will be helping my client not to procrastinate on dealing with their procrastination problem!

Ego-Based Procrastination

Ego-based procrastination occurs when the person approaches a task that is in their interests to do or thinks of doing so. Then, as they approach it, physically or mentally, they experience a threat to their self-esteem. They then eliminate this threat by avoiding doing the task (i.e., procrastinating). In this type of procrastination, the client holds a self-devaluation attitude should the threat materialise. Here, I discuss with them the importance of developing an attitude of unconditional self-acceptance to solve their procrastination problem. This involves them recognising the following:

- They would prefer to do the task well, for example, but they don't have to do it well.
- It is bad if they don't do the task well.
- Their performance does not define their worth as a person.
- Rather, they are a complex, unrateable, and fallible, human being and this fact does not change whether they do the task well or badly.
- By doing the task, they can learn from their performance and improve, which cannot happen if they don't do the task.

Discomfort-Based Procrastination

Discomfort-based procrastination occurs when the person approaches a task that is in their interests to do or thinks of doing so. Then, as they approach it, physically or mentally, they experience a threat to their sense of comfort, broadly defined. As with ego-based discomfort, they get rid of this threat by procrastinating. In this type of procrastination, the client holds an attitude of unbearability towards experiencing discomfort. Here, I discuss with them the importance of developing an attitude of bearability as a solution to their procrastination problem. This involves them recognising the following:

- They would like to be comfortable, but they don't need to be.
- It is a struggle to bear the discomfort.
- They can bear it.
- It is in their interests to bear it.
- They are worth bearing it for.
- They are willing to bear it.
- They are committed to bearing it.
- They take action consistent with the points mentioned above.

An Attitude-Based View of Procrastination and How to Deal with It Effectively

When necessary, I offer the client a view of procrastination that is informed by Rational Emotive Behaviour Therapy (REBT).

An Attitude-Based View of Procrastination

This view points out that when the client procrastinates, they do so because certain conditions that they demand or insist be present are, in fact, absent. Until these demanded conditions are present, the person will refrain from doing the task. This is the case even though the client realises it is in their interests to do the task at that time. Table 1 makes this clear.

Table 1: An attitude-based view of procrastination

Condition	Demand (Rigid Attitude)	Outcome
Comfort	'I must be comfortable before I start work'	Procrastinate until I am comfortable
Mood	'I must be in the mood before I start work'	Procrastinate until I am in the mood
Competence	'I must feel competent before I start work'	Procrastinate until I feel competent
Motivation	'I must be motivated before I start work'	Procrastinate until I am motivated
Immediate Understanding	'I must understand what I have to do before I start to do it'	Procrastinate until I have such understanding
Pressure	'I must be under pressure before I start work'	Procrastinate until I am under pressure
Immediate Gratification	'Faced with the choice of doing something that I enjoy or starting work I must do what I want to do'	Procrastinate until I have done what I want to do

An Attitude-Based View of Doing Tasks and Not Procrastinating

This view points out that for the client to begin tasks they have been procrastinating on, they need to change their rigid attitude to a flexible attitude. Table 2 makes this clear.

Table 2: An attitude-based view of doing tasks and not procrastinating

Condition	Flexible Attitude	Outcome
Comfort	'I would like to be comfortable before I start work, but this condition isn't necessary'	Start work even though uncomfortable
Mood	'I would like to be in the mood before I start work, but this condition isn't necessary'	Start work even though not in the mood
Competence	'I would like to feel competent before I start work, but this condition isn't necessary'	Start work even though not feeling competent
Motivation	'I would like to be motivated before I start work, but this condition isn't necessary'	Start work even though not motivated
Immediate Understanding	'I would like to understand what I have to do before I start to do it, but this condition isn't necessary'	Start work even though I do not understand what I have to do
Pressure	'I would like to be under pressure before I start work, but this condition isn't necessary'	Start work even though I am not under pressure
Immediate Gratification	'Faced with the choice of doing something that I enjoy or starting work I would like to do what I want, but this condition isn't necessary'	Start work foregoing immediate gratification

Here is how I help the person make this change in SST. Once I have helped my client identify the condition(s) they think need to be in place before they commence the task, I encourage them to ask themself whether they can begin the task without the presence of their 'needed' condition(s).

Once I have helped the client see that their specified conditions are desirable but not necessary, I say the following: Imagine yourself doing the task without the (now) desired condition while reminding yourself of the reasons why you are doing the task now and the values that underpin your choice to do it. Can you imagine yourself doing it? How does it feel to see yourself do it? If they find this a helpful task, it forms part of the solution they seek.

If the person is interested, I will help them change their rigid/extreme attitudes to their flexible/non-extreme counterparts and help them think and act in ways that will support the development of these latter attitudes. The focus here will be on encouraging the client to see that their rigid attitude is false, illogical and unhelpful to them. In contrast, the flexible alternative to this attitude is factual, logical and more helpful to them. In particular, I will remind the client that their rigid attitude leads to procrastination, while their flexible attitude will help them get to work.

Dealing with 'Rationalisations'

When a client holds that a particular condition needs to exist before they start work (rigid attitude), they may well come up with several so-called 'reasons' to justify their procrastination. I encourage my client to be honest with themselves. They will see that such 'reasons' are rationalisations and self-deceptions if they are. They can respond constructively to their rationalisations and self-deceptions and even begin the task while these come into their mind.

Getting Specific

I have found it important to work with a specific example of my client's procrastination and encourage them to do the same after the session. Once the client has grasped these points and has practised responding constructively to your rigid attitudes and rationalisations in the SST session, they can use the following schema to implement this attitude-based solution after the session.

1. I encourage the client to set a specific time to begin the task
2. If they do not start at the appointed time, I suggest that they identify the condition they are insisting has to exist before they start and remind themself that this condition is desirable but not necessary.
3. I suggest they start work in the absence of the condition, even though it may feel strange and uncomfortable to do so and see what happens after a specified time.
4. I urge the client to identify and respond to any rationalisations they have given themself not to start work and then start work. They should do this even though the rationalisations may be somewhat in their mind.

Repeatedly acting in ways that are consistent with the client's flexible attitudes towards their work and not being seduced by their rationalisations are the defining characteristics of this approach to dealing with procrastination.

Procrastination and Meta-Disturbance

When people procrastinate, they may disturb themselves about this problem. If they have one, I may need to help my client deal with their meta-disturbance problem before focusing on their procrastination. However, I want to avoid focusing on the client's meta-disturbance problem when they want to work on their procrastination problem.

PART 2

THE SESSIONS

4

Getting Down to Work by Removing
Additional Conditions

Date: 17/04/23
Time: 26 minutes 14 secs

Windy: OK, Sofia, from your perspective what is the purpose of
our conversation this evening?

*[This is my typical beginning which I use in all sessions
in this book.]*

Sofia: I think what I want to do is I might have answered some
of the questions I had by listening to you earlier because
I was reflecting a lot on what I was planning to talk as
well because it was in relation to procrastinating. I
wanted to choose this topic because I thought other
people would find it useful as well. So, what I'm
procrastinating on is writing my accreditation, so I
thought that will be quite useful for other practitioners as
well, as I wonder if they're in the same space.
    I just want to get an idea, I suppose, of where I'm
stuck, but I think I've kind of got a bit of an idea now.

*[I did this session as a demonstration as part of an
evening workshop for Onlinevents entitled 'SST and
Procrastination'. All other sessions in this book were
conducted in private over Zoom with volunteers who
signed up for a complimentary session with me to help
them with a genuine, current issue with procrastination.]*

Windy: OK. So maybe let's start with that idea that you've got.

[*Sofia indicates above that she has an idea of where she is stuck, so I encourage her to start with that. SST starts with and builds on what the client knows.*]

Sofia: I thought about there is no pressure for me to do it now. So, when you were talking about ingredients, there is no pressure for me to do it. I'm OK where I am. There isn't that need. What it was initially, that I wanted to do it for myself so that I could have that peace for myself to write it all in one place and look at it and think, 'This is who I am, this is what I'm doing.' And then I realised at some point where I'm stuck is that I still wanted to do it but, once people started telling me, 'I've done it, I've got it,' I stopped, and that's when I've started procrastinating.

Windy: So, you're saying that you had created a space for yourself where you were going to do it – you had some time to do it and you were doing it – but then you heard that other people had mentioned that – when you said they had done it, you mean they'd finished their accreditation application or they'd got their accreditation through?

[*Here, I am endeavouring to understand the client's internal frame of reference.*]

Sofia: Both. So I think it was the doing it all, seeing other people, that created this wall now for me. Now, thinking of the ingredients, I'm questioning my confidence. I'm thinking, 'Come on, why am I not doing it this fast?'

Windy: If you hadn't heard of these people, what would be different about it if you hadn't heard what they were doing?

Sofia: ... [*Pause*] I think at the moment there is that fear of not being as good ... as good enough. There is that fear.

Windy: But did you have that fear before you heard that they had finished or they'd handed in their application or they got their accreditation? Did you have that fear?

Sofia: … I think I did but it wasn't as big.

Windy: Meaning what?

Sofia: As in, like you were saying, it was still something I could work with; it was there.

Windy: So you have had the experience of doing your accreditation application even though you experienced some doubt about your competence. Is that what you're saying?

[I am commenting on Sofia's successful experience of working on the task even though she had a doubt about her competence.]

Sofia: Yeah. I think what's actually underneath that is that I didn't think about it until you mentioned the idea of comfort as well, and I think comfort for me, what I'm avoiding is, because English is not my first language, that idea that I have to… get all these words: 'Where am I going to find them?' It's going to be that space of looking for that, I think.

Windy: Sorry, I missed that. Because English is not your first language, what are you saying there? You're looking for what?

Sofia: There's that discomfort now, I think, that I'm avoiding actually having to sit with it and not know from the beginning. I didn't actually think if I was a perfectionist or not before I heard Jen speaking earlier, and then I thought, 'Maybe I am.' I wouldn't say I am, but maybe I am now that I'm hearing myself out loud.

Windy: Putting all these factors together, if you could design your own ingredients for you to do the task, what would those ingredients be?

[*Here, I am referring to my view of procrastination that I outlined in the Powerpoint presentation that I gave in the first part of the online workshop.*]

Sofia: I think at the moment it's definitely comfort ... [*long pause*] there is a motivation. I don't have the pressure anymore, so I suppose that's something that I want. ... I'm curious about my own experiences because I didn't realise until today; I was thinking, 'Maybe that's how I worked in the past,' because I did write and I loved writing, and I did do it, but there was that external pressure because I was in academia – I had to do it. That's taken away now and I'm thinking, oh, just do it whenever I want. That's not working, so I'm thinking there is that element that I might need to find for myself, in one way or another.

Windy: So the element of some internal, not exactly pressure, but a sense of, 'When's it in my interest to do this?' because it sounds like that's a bit absent from your thinking: 'When's it in my interest to do this?'

[*I am referring here again to my view of dealing with procrastination where one of the points the person needs to keep in mind is the reasons for doing the task.*]

Sofia: ... [*Pause*] Yeah, it's true, because I also realised, when you were describing the difference between being on task and procrastinating, I thought, 'Am I really procrastinating, because I want to do it but I don't need to?'

Windy: Well, I'm talking about something different. Not exactly, 'Do I want to do it?' or, 'Do I need to do it?' but, 'Is it in my interest to do it?' So let's be quite clear about that, shall we? When is it in your interest? I assume that it is in your interest to do the accreditation application. Is that right or is that wrong?

Sofia: Yeah.

Windy: Why? Let's get that on the table. Why is it in your interest to do the application for accreditation?

[Here, I am inviting Sofia to be explicit about the reasons why it is her interests to do the task.]

Sofia: ... I think internally I don't have— When you say 'interest', all I think about is time, and I'm thinking I don't have a specific time.

Windy: No, by 'in your interest', I mean in a sense of what is healthy for you.

Sofia: ... *[Long pause]* Me personally ... it would help me ... put in words what I'm doing.

Windy: Do the application you mean?

Sofia: Yeah.

Windy: Let me be clear, is being accredited important to you?

Sofia: ... *[Pause]* I don't know.

Windy: Well, let's start there, because you seem to be treading a path and then you stop and you say, 'Well, wait a minute, is this the path I want to be on?'

[As the exploration of what is in her interests unfolds, Sofia begins to question the importance of being accredited as a counsellor for her.]

Sofia: ... Yeah, that's right. I didn't think about... *[pause]* whether I'm interested or not.

Windy: So let's take it a step back. You did counsellor training, is that right?

[What I have in mind is to take Sofia back to discover the reason why she wanted to become a counsellor.]

Sofia: Mmm [yes].

Windy: And why did you do counsellor training?

Sofia: Because I wanted to work with people and to be counsellor.

Windy: You wanted to be a counsellor. How important is that for you?

Sofia: Very important.

Windy: Are you now a counsellor?

Sofia: Yeah.

Windy: How important is it to be an accredited counsellor to you?

Sofia: Somewhat.

Windy: So why are you doing it?

[*Being a counsellor is important to Sofia. She is questioning how important it is for her to be an accredited counsellor.*]

Sofia: I don't know. It's interesting. I think at some point it became this thing that I need to do, when in fact I wanted to do it at the beginning. I said, 'If I want I will do it, but if I don't I won't.' And, at some point, I told myself, 'You have to do it or else go and do something else.' But yes, you're right.

Windy: So you may want to do a bit of the thinking: what are the advantages and the disadvantages of becoming accredited as opposed to, I presume, a non-accredited counsellor?

Sofia: I think the advantages would be that it would open more opportunities. It will give me that chance to do that exercise of actually writing … the whole piece.

Windy: What kinds of opportunities do you think will open up for you?

Sofia: I think in terms of job opportunities.

Windy: As you hear yourself talk about them, how important are those reasons to you?

Sofia: ... I would say up until now I felt they were 100% important: I need to do it. And I think going through, unpacking the whole idea of procrastination, now I feel like I'm at 30–40% importance to me with these things.

Windy: So maybe for something that's 30–40% important to you maybe you're giving 30–40% effort.

   [*Here, I am speculating that Sofia's approach to doing the work for her accreditation reflects how important it is for her.*]

Sofia: Yeah, makes sense.... Yeah, I didn't think of it that way, but yeah.

Windy: So it's not clear to you, I think, or to me whether you are procrastinating.

Sofia: Yeah, it's true.

Windy: Because it's not clear whether this is clearly enough in your interest to put the kind of effort that maybe you think you should've done. I don't know. It sounds like, if we go back a little bit, that you were going along fairly steadily until you heard people say, 'I've finished the accreditation.' So what impact did that have on you, finding out?

Sofia: ... [*Pause*] I think ... [*pause*] what I realised probably on a ten-minute break we had.[14] I didn't actually think I

---

[14] Sofia is referring to the ten-minute break in the online workshop I am giving before she volunteered for a single session.

wanted to do it for myself, for my own sense of, 'Oh, I've done it. It's my second language. I've done this massive piece of work.' And, potentially, when I heard other people doing that, I thought, 'I can't compete with that,' and then, instead of me ... [*pause*] continuing, I just said, 'No.'

Windy: What does compete mean here?

Sofia: ... [*Pause*] I don't know if compete is the right word. I suppose I can't ... [*long pause*] do the same work in the same amount of time, when it comes to it.

Windy: And how important is it to you, if you hear some of your peers doing it, for you to do it in the same amount of time as them, as opposed to you doing it according to your own drummer?

Sofia: ... [*Pause*] I think it is important, and I'm amazed that it is. I'm just thinking I didn't think it was, but it is. I'm still finding out.

Windy: What does it prove, then, that, if you could do it at the same speed as them, what would that do for you?

Sofia: Maybe that my English would be near native: that it would just come out in my head, potentially.

Windy: And how important is it for your English to be near native?

Sofia: Potentially, that is quite important.

Windy: And when do you want this state of near native English to occur?

Sofia: I think it has.

Windy: You think it has?

Sofia: And maybe it will.

Windy: So, you're in some kind of doubt, aren't you, about, 'Is my English native enough? Maybe if I do it as quickly as these people I'll prove to myself that it is native. But, on the other hand, maybe not.' So, it sounds like you're in two minds about that.

[I am still clarifying some of the different strands mentioned by Sofia to see how important they are in determining if she is procrastinating and if she is, how important the factor is.]

Sofia: ... *[Pause]* I'm still amazed by the fact that I didn't realise when I sat here; I thought I was procrastinating and I'm realising as I'm talking to you maybe I'm not, because I don't necessarily want to. It's not in my interest to do it.

Windy: But, if you're not procrastinating as you sit down here and you hear yourself talking, how would you describe what you are doing?

Sofia: ... *[Pause]* Taking one day at a time ... with what feels comfortably, really, when I feel ready.

Windy: Now, if you were to adopt that – 'I'll go a step at a time and I'll do it when I'm comfortable and ready' – can you see yourself doing this accreditation according to those guiding principles?

Sofia: Yes and no. I can see myself doing it but potentially in ten years, but even if it is, I suppose.

Windy: Yeah. It depends upon if being in a process for ten years doing an accreditation is in your interest.

Sofia: ... *[Long pause]* Yeah, it's true.... *[Pause]* So maybe I can't see myself doing ... *[long pause]*, I suppose continuing with that message.

Windy: You can't see yourself continuing with what message?

Sofia: I think maybe that in itself is just prolonging the feeling for me, because, if I tell myself, 'I'll do it when I want, when I can't,' and then that never happens.

Windy: Exactly. So you have a suspicion if you do that then it's not going to work and you'll be involved in a ten-year process of accreditation. Of course, in ten years who knows where accreditation will be. So, if that's not going to work for you, what will work for you?

Sofia: ... [*Pause*] In setting ... breaking it down, because that's something I haven't actually tried to do: to break it down and actually set a particular date, a particular day in the week when I do that work and sit with my work.

Windy: So you can see a situation whereby you would choose a day where you would sit down with yourself and work on your accreditation. And, if you did that and you did that steadily, how long do you think that would take you to do?

Sofia: A couple of months.

Windy: OK. And, so, if you had that idea in mind – 'Look, I'm gonna sit down every one day to be chosen and I'm going to work on my accreditation on that day, and I think it's going to take me a couple of months. So that's what I'm going to be doing because the reason I'm doing it is because I think it may open up more doors than not,' and other reasons that you would have to be clear with yourself about the reasons for having accreditation – is that vision a realistic one?

               [*Drawing on the points Sofia is making during the exploration, a potential solution emerges to what may be Sofia's procrastination problem. I say may here because this is not clear, and maybe with Sofia, it does not need to be clear.*]

Sofia: Yeah.

Windy: It strips it of all the native-speakery. The nativeness of your speaking is not brought into this space.

Sofia: My additional ingredients.

Windy: Your additional ingredients. You've taken it out and, 'Well, I may well be there now. I may not. I don't know, but I don't have to put it into this space where I might introduce it as a way to procrastinate.'

Sofia: Yeah, that's a very different ship.

Windy: Yeah. So, if you were able to imagine yourself doing that, can you see that you might stop yourself from putting that kind of process into action?

Sofia: ... [*Long pause*] Potentially, if I don't start soon.... Soon after this conversation I need to set a calendar.

Windy: So you're saying that, if you don't start by a particular time, what?

Sofia: I might forget this, I suppose.

Windy: Well, I don't think you will forget it because you will get a copy of the recording and you also get a copy of the transcript later.[15] So you ain't gonna forget it.

Sofia: It'll be there. OK.

Windy: You may not want to look at it but that's a different manner. So when would be a good starting time for you? Let's be really concrete?

Sofia: Potentially next Monday.

---

[15] When people volunteer for a demonstration with me, I always offer to send them an audio recording and a transcript of the session for later review. This is also the case with all the people who volunteered for help with their procrastination issue in this project.

Windy: So what time?

Sofia: 9am.

Windy: OK. And is this going to be your regular accreditation day schedule or is it going to vary?

Sofia: No, it will be because it's my day when I can actually look at CPD.

Windy: So, Monday, 24th.

Sofia: Yes.

Windy: At 9am. So what would you have to remind yourself of in order to get yourself into this space?

Sofia: ... [*Pause*] That I don't need the additional ingredient.

Windy: Additional ingredient of what?

Sofia: Of ... [*pause*], I suppose going in that space where I start comparing myself with other people.

Windy: Yeah. You can celebrate your uniqueness instead. Have you ever done that?

Sofia: Yeah.

                 [*Note that I introduce the idea that Sofia can celebrate her uniqueness as an antidote to comparing herself with others. I discover that she has done this in another part of her life, and I briefly make the point that she can transfer this factor to the current situation so that it is part of her solution. However, this is too condensed, and I wished that I had made more of this point.*]

Windy: Well, you could transfer it to this particular thing: 'I'm unique and therefore I'm going to bring to this task my uniqueness and I'm going to do it every Monday until

I've done it.' What about if you're not feeling comfortable at nine o'clock?

Sofia: ... [*Long pause*] What does comfortable mean?

Windy: I don't know. You mentioned it earlier. What does comfort mean to you or uncomfortable mean to you at this point?

Sofia: I kept telling myself I think because I will have read somewhere that the idea of having an accountability buddy helps you. I think what would help me is not actually telling anyone that I'm doing it; doing it with myself for myself.

Windy: We won't say anything.

[*This is a humorous intervention because we are, in fact, having the session in front of a large online audience.*]

Sofia: Nobody ask anything. Ten years from now don't ask anything.

[*Sofia responds well to my humour.*]

Windy: So you're gonna come to an agreement with yourself, you're not going to have an accountability buddy. So the agreement is with yourself and you're going to be accountable to yourself. So could you imagine bringing all these things together? That the reason you're doing it is this – you need to spell that out for yourself, have that somewhere in your mind that: 'This is not an activity that I'm doing for no purpose. It is something that is important to me. This is my unique reason for doing it and I am going to be doing it in my own unique way and I don't have to bring the nativeness of my English into this space.'

Sofia: ... [*Long pause*] I've written this down. I need to have this without looking at the recording.

Windy: Could you imagine yourself next Monday sitting down and working on this process?

Sofia: Yeah, I think so.

Windy: As you look at it, are there any obvious obstacles that might come up?

Sofia: No, not really.

Windy: So is there anything else you want to say about this that we haven't said or you want to ask about this that you haven't asked?

Sofia: No, this has been very helpful. Thank you very much.

Windy: So why don't you summarise the work we did and what the major takeaways are going to be for you?

               [*As mentioned in Chapter 2, this signifies that we are approaching the end of the session.*]

Sofia: I think I came here not knowing actually where I'm stuck, and by talking to you I realised where I was stuck is because I was adding those additional conditions for myself: that I have to do it only if my tick boxing goes native English tick, and, by removing that, I can my life easier and actually my work enjoyable and actually enjoy writing it because I'm doing it in my own way for myself. I think that's been very helpful. Thank you.

Windy: So shall we stop there and get the group's questions?

Sofia: Yeah, absolutely. Thank you.

Sofia's Reflections (29/08/23)

Attending the single session of therapy session at the time, I am aware my expectations were realistic, in that I didn't expect this to 'be a quick fix' at all, but to delve deeper into what was going on for me at the time.

I am noticing that the conversation around procrastination stayed with me and helped me clarify what I was procrastinating on and the underlying reasons for this.

The counsellor's questions and reflections helped me narrow down my concerns and I can still hear him asking me the question 'is it of interest to you?'. I do channel this at times in my internal dialogue, and it's been tremendously helpful to filter out my needs. I found it really helpful to systematically explore why completing my work was of interest to me, as I hadn't even contemplated on this before. I can now also see how at the time it felt strange to even attend the session by that point, as I quickly became aware of the fact that I wasn't even sure I was procrastinating at all; and that played on my mind for a while. I found it useful to leave a gap of a couple of weeks between the session and completing the task itself, due to these feelings arising.

Talking about this now, several months afterwards, I realise I gained a new sense of hope to accomplish my task, and a newfound awareness of the underlying feelings of fear of 'not being good enough'. I found it insightful and safe to reframe that the elements I feared, such as speaking a second language, could actually showcase my uniqueness in my work, and I am truly grateful for this.

Reflecting back on the session itself, I'm unsure setting myself a time aside to complete the task was helpful for me at the time. I might have slightly sabotaged myself in setting those parameters as I then started feeling guilty for not completing my task as I was 'supposed to'. Yet, I am wondering if this helped me subconsciously, perhaps, because I was able to identify that I do have the physical and emotional space to complete my task. Regardless, I certainly felt empowered leaving the session. And although I did not actually complete the task as 'agreed' in our session, I am proud of myself for having attempted this. I now think, this feeling in itself, allowed me to set other worries aside and at least try, if not complete my task, which was a great stepping stone in my growth.

Looking back, I am grateful for the opportunity to have experienced the single session of therapy. It has certainly inspired me to continue to sit with my own feelings, especially as to why any tasks are important for me in the future. I hope to be able to inspire the same sense of hope to others, that I gained from this session and I am also chuffed to say that I am also almost there, in actually completing my task!

5

Dealing with a Sense of Incompetence without Dee-termination

Date: 24/04/23
Time: 39 minutes 59 secs

Windy: So, Dee, what, from your perspective, is the understanding of the purpose of our conversation this morning?

Dee: I understand it's a single session just to zone in on procrastination, maybe the reasons behind it, whether I can get an understanding of why I do it and maybe find a way of addressing it.

Windy: And by 'addressing it', what do you mean by 'addressing it'?

Dee: Addressing it positively in a way that I will stop procrastinating. Find a way of dealing with it that might not be within this session, but it will set or open up another pathway or doorway for me to address it.

Windy: So you're looking to find a pathway forward, but, if we can do more than that, you wouldn't object?

Dee: No, definitely not.

Windy: So are you currently procrastinating on something?

Dee: To be honest, everything. That's the story of my life, to be honest.

Windy: Well, you didn't procrastinate on coming to see me today. You were there dead on ten o'clock. There was no procrastination there, was there?

[It is useful to help the client see that there are tasks that they do not procrastinate on.]

Dee: I almost did. I did my usual trick of 'Yeah, I'll be ready, sitting down.' Went downstairs to make myself a coffee on the coffee machine. Got involved in something else. Then I started coming here, finding the emails. That's why it was bang on ten . Yeah, it was a close shave.

Windy: So let's zone in on one thing you are procrastinating on that you would like to address positively, as you call it. Then we can generalise from there.

[Here I am creating a focus for our conversation.]

Dee: OK. One thing that is very integral to me is, as a student, my academic work, that is a central thing. If I had to choose one thing, it's the same pattern anyway for my studies. I'm always leaving it until the last moment. I always build myself up to, 'I will do it. I've got a week. I've got two days,' until sometimes it now reaches the day and I'm like, 'I'm just going to say it's going to be late.'

Windy: And you say that, do you? You say to your university, 'It's going to be late'?

Dee: Yeah.

Windy: And what's their response?

Dee: They're quite supportive, but deep down I find every excuse in the book.

Windy: When you say supportive, what do you mean by supportive?

Dee: They allow me the time. I always give a reason which is justifiable but which deep down I know is not.

Windy: I think one of the things I'm going to be asking you to do today is to be radically honest with yourself and with me, because I think what you're touching on is that it's easy to come up with a 'reason' which sounds plausible to yourself and to other people, and you say that your university is supportive, it sounds to me that they are supporting you to procrastinate.

                [People who procrastinate use self-deception as a defence or as avoidance, hence my invitation to Dee to be radically honest with himself and with me.
                    Parenthetically, institutions think that they are helping students like Dee. Unfortunately, in my view, they are not. Giving people with a procrastination issue more time to do a task when they have had plenty of time to do only serves as a problem maintenance factor.]

Dee: It would seem that way but, because they don't know that I am procrastinating, it would seem that I'm abusing the system for want of a better phrase. It's making excuses which I know deep down inside, they're not really stopping me.

Windy: No, they're not giving you a boundary. The point is procrastination is a genuine and real problem. So let's have a look at something current that you would like to start getting down to that you're currently procrastinating on? Is there one thing that we can really zone in on, because being specific is really quite important here.

                [Here, I emphasise the value of being specific which is so important in a single session with people with a procrastination problem.]

Dee: Yeah. I've got an essay which is overdue which I still haven't done.

Windy: When was the essay due?

Dee: End of last term. We're now in the first term now.

Windy: So what's your goal with respect to this particular piece of work?

Dee: I would like to say I will do it, but ... [*pause*] to be honest I'm actually now thinking, because it's powered up and I feel overwhelmed by it, one of the things that's obviously been passed through my mind is should I just defer the course for a while. It's got that dire with me ... in a sense.

Windy: Defer meaning what? That you'll stop your studies and then come back later?

Dee: Correct.

Windy: And what type of Dee will you be bringing back later to your studies? A new, radically transformed Dee who's not going to be procrastinating?

Dee: ... I would like to think so, but because this is a longstanding pattern of mine, I'm not sure. It's almost as if I'm pushing it further down the road.

Windy: That's right, and incidentally that's happening here with you and me, because I'm trying to get a specific example and you're pushing it down the road a little bit. Do you see what I'm saying? So let's take something. How do you define procrastination, Dee?

[It is not often that I comment on a parallel process with the client doing with what he does with others or with work, but I thought it important to do so here with Dee.]

Dee: ... Putting off something that I should be doing now, now being relative. Doing what I could do today and pushing it or planning to do it tomorrow.

Windy: Yeah, I've got a slightly different definition, if you're interested?

Dee: OK.

Windy: That is that you put off 'til later what is in your best
              interest to do today, and you do it at a time when it is in
              your best interest to do it. So I think the difference
              between my definition and your definition is my
              definition includes the term 'best interest' and your
              definition includes the term 'should' as if this is in the
              hands of somebody else.

              [*I was not as clear as I would like to have been. For me,
              procrastinating is putting off doing a task that is one
              interest to do and not doing it at a time when it is one's
              interest to do it.*]

Dee: … Yeah, and I suppose I'm wary of that word 'should',
              but it slips into my language every time. It's almost as if
              I beat myself and I get overwhelmed by it where I just
              mentally shut down.

Windy: Yeah. The point is, when people procrastinate, then they
              do disturb themselves about procrastinating. That's a
              common feature. But I'm still quite keen to see if we can
              get to grips with what happens, because at the moment I
              don't understand what happens with your
              procrastinating. The only way I'm going to do that is if
              you can come up with a specific example of something,
              Dee, that is in your interest to do at a time when it is in
              your interest to do it. So can you think of something?

Dee: It's something similar, but even at work when I apply for
              a job – I'm supposed to read up and I know I've got an
              interview coming up and I've got all the material.

Windy: Is that current now? Is that happening now?

Dee: It is, yeah.

Windy: So tell me about the task. Let's be as specific as we can
              get.

Dee: OK. I've got a promotional interview coming up and it's going to be some tests and I've got some practice material that I – I was about to say 'should'.

Windy: You use your own language.

Dee: Yeah. I've got promotional material to read up on it. It's in a week's time. I haven't done it yet.

Windy: So is it in your interest to read up on that promotional material?

Dee: It is.

Windy: Why?

Dee: ... [*Pause*] Because I want the promotion, I suppose.

Windy: You want the promotion 'I suppose'.

Dee: ... [*Pause*] I know that at the end, to me listening to it, it sounds ambiguous or incongruent, but I am in a place at work where I'm comfortable and it allows me to do other things. And I am aware that, if I get this promotion, it could skew the time I've got off, my pattern.

Windy: It will skew what? I don't understand. Help me to understand that.

Dee: My pattern. At the moment, where I work, it's supposed to be a 24-hour shift. I manage to work in the evenings only. I manage to get time off to attend my course. And during the day I manage to go to my placements. So I've got a fairly good routine going on. If I get this promotion, for the training it's going to be maybe Monday to Friday which will mean I can't attend my placements. It could affect my ability to attend the course.

Windy: So I think what you're saying is that on the one hand it's in your interest to go for this promotion and to read up on the material, but on the other hand you're comfortable at

the moment; you've worked things out that you're able
to attend your course and you think that, if you went for
this promotion and you got it, then you wouldn't have the
time to go to your placement. So, in other words,
although there's a clear benefit for you to go for the
promotion, there's also a clear cost in doing so.

Dee: There is a cost. Yes, definitely.

Windy: The anti-procrastination is basically saying, 'Even
though there's a cost, it's still, on balance, worth it for me
to do so.' Otherwise, if you say, 'Actually, on balance,
it's not worth it for me to do so,' then you haven't got a
good enough reason to do the task, and therefore, even
though part of you thinks that you should, on balance it's
not going to be something that's in your best interest
because you'd be giving up your placement and
presumably that would affect your training. Do you see
what I'm getting at?

Dee: I do understand. So it's almost as if, if I understand
correctly, subconsciously I don't think it's worth my
while seeking the promotion because of how that could
disturb my pattern – this cycle I've got going at the
moment.

Windy: Particularly with regard to (a) your comfort level but also
(b) your professional development in terms of doing your
placement, because, if you didn't do your placement,
how could you get your qualification?

Dee: … Yeah. Yeah, I know that, but it doesn't help… the
feeling of … constantly waking up saying, 'Why am I not
doing this? Why am I not studying?'

Windy: Well, I know, because it's as if you wake up with half the
picture. You're focused on the bit where it's in your
interest to do it, and you don't, and then you say, 'Why
don't I do it? Why don't I do it?' But the whole picture
is, on this particular point anyway, if I've understood you
correctly, there are benefits and there are costs. And the

costs you edit out. I don't know why you edit them out but you edit them out and you just focus on what you're not doing and then you beat yourself up for not doing it. Do you see what I'm saying about not having the whole picture?

Dee: Yeah, I do understand, but it still leaves me with that feeling of ... as you said, I constantly beat myself up even though there's an awareness of why I'm doing it, and it's almost sometimes I think to myself, 'Well, do it and have that choice of, if you're offered the job, then you're in a position to say, 'Am I or am I not?''

Windy: Right, OK, so that would be a good way forward, wouldn't it? It would be actually saying, 'Well, let's go forward with the job. Let's have a look at the promotional material. If I'm procrastinating on that, then I need to address that. Then I can always get the job and then make a decision at that point. If I don't apply for the job, I'm not going to get the job and that's going to leave me where I am.' So does it make sense for us then to assume that it is in your interest to do the reading for the promotional material for the interview, and that you are not doing it, and that not doing it comes under the heading of procrastination? Is that a useful working assumption?

Dee: That's what it feels like to me.

[*It is not uncommon with people who procrastinate that it takes a while to get clarity on whether the person is procrastinating or not. On balance, it seems as if Dee is procrastinating.*]

Windy: So let's have a look at that. One of the things about addressing procrastination, Dee, is that it's important that you specify with yourself clearly a time when you are going to start the task so that then you know if you don't start it at that time, you're procrastinating. Does that make sense?

Dee: Yes.

Windy: So, can you specify a time when it's in your interest to sit down and start reading that promotional material?

Dee: Yeah. I'm usually free in the mornings, because, as I said, I work in the evenings. Nine o'clock.

Windy: Nine o'clock. So would it be a useful agreement, then, with you with yourself and also with me for the purposes of understanding what's going on, that you are going to sit down tomorrow at your desk at nine o'clock tomorrow and start work on this promotional material?

Dee: … Yes.

Windy: OK. Now I hear the hesitation in your voice. Don't worry about that. That's alright. I would expect that.

Dee: Yeah.

Windy: So what ingredient would you need, Dee, that you could say, 'If I had this in place I would sit down tomorrow at nine o'clock and do the work'? What would that ingredient be?

Dee: … Weirdly enough it's determination.

Windy: Determination.

Dee: This thing is stopping me. Yes.

Windy: So, in your mind, you need determination in order to sit down and do this task. Now, what do you mean, Dee, by determination? Interestingly enough, determination begins with D, which is good. So what do you mean by determination in this context, Dee?

                [For the purposes of clarity, I want to understand what Dee means by determination. I use this opportunity to

inject a bit of humour into the conversation to lighten it a bit.]

Dee: … It's … [*pause*] almost like going through all the crap that comes to mind, I would always think about, 'Tomorrow something will come to mind.' It's not urgent, but in my mind just anything but what I'm supposed to do specifically. And I don't want to wish it on myself, but because I know this pattern.

Windy: So, determination would, as you say, cut through the crap. You'd come up with some stuff in your mind, which you are calling crap, and determination would be cutting through it, yeah?

Dee: Yeah.

Windy: That's important to know. Since procrastination is basically about avoidance, I don't understand at that point tomorrow, for example, at nine o'clock, what you would be avoiding. So imagine sitting down at that task and coming up with the crap and then going along with the crap, what would you be avoiding at that time?

Dee: … [*Pause*] I'd just be avoiding starting what I should be doing in its most basic form. I know what I've sat down to do.

Windy: But what is it about doing what you 'should' be doing that is aversive to you, to the point in which you will avoid doing it?

Dee: … I struggle to answer that because I'm just going on my past experience: I will make the utmost effort to do it tomorrow, but sometimes I probably will – 'I feel all fired up now. Yes, I am going to,' and I hope not.

Windy: It's interesting. We get to the point which happens in a lot of therapy on procrastination and it boils down to, 'I don't know what I'm avoiding because I've spent so much time avoiding it I don't know what I'm avoiding.'

So, if you bear with me, I'd like to put certain things to you and see if they resonate. One is that you might avoid the sense that, if you sat down, that you might get in touch with a sense of not being confident about doing something. So, rather than face up to that, you will avoid. Or it might be a sense of incompetence or it might be a sense of rebellion: 'I'm not going to do it. Somebody wants me to do it, I'm not going to do it because I'll be giving in to them.' It might be a sense of, 'I might not do it well enough and then I might get disapproval.' Or it just might be a sense of, 'I just don't want to struggle. I think, if I sat down, it would be a struggle, and I just don't want to struggle.' So I'm wondering if any of those might resonate with you or, if not, it might give you a sense of what you might be avoiding.

[*Dee's procrastination issue has been present for a long time, and since, as I say, procrastination is about avoidance and Dee is good at avoidance, he genuinely does not know what he is avoiding. As such, I decided to help Dee out by giving him some possibilities.*]

Dee: One of them I could resonate with. It's second to the last one. I think it was about, if I sit down, I might discover that maybe a sense of incompetence in it, the fear of that. So, when I'm not doing it, that doesn't come to the fore.

Windy: Well, let's have a look at that a little bit more closely. Let's suppose you sit down and you don't avoid but, in not avoiding up comes this sense of incompetence, which means what for you? What does that mean, in your own words?

Dee: That means I'd be doing these examples and making research for such examples and I would be struggling with it.

Windy: Struggling in what sense?

Dee: In doing them. Funnily enough, I know it sounds like counselling, but competencies – where I've done my straight exam competencies which I've got to talk about or even some psychometric tests as well that go with it. I'm struggling to find, especially with the psychometric tests how it works.

Windy: So you might get in touch with some sense of not knowing how to do things. That's what we're talking about. Is that what you're saying in terms of incompetence?

Dee: Yes.

Windy: So, if we gave you the ingredient – because I think determination is somewhat a separate issue, you want to blast through this: determination, blast through – let's suppose that you knew at that point when you sat down tomorrow you'd be competent. You knew for sure that you'd be competent in doing this preparation for this promotional interview or whatever it is. Now, would that make a difference to you for having that ingredient in place?

Dee: Definitely ... there was an uplift in my mind, if I could sit down and I didn't have any problems doing it, yes. I'd probably look forward to.

[*By giving Dee options, we have finally hit upon what Dee is avoiding – a sense of incompetence.*]

Windy: Now, have you ever in any other part of your life – I'm just going to take you away from what we're talking about just for a moment – have you ever had the experience, Dee, of doing something that you really wanted to do and at the beginning you struggled because you didn't quite know what to do; there was a sense of incompetence, but you stuck with it and, in sticking with it, you learnt more about the subject and after a while you learnt an increasing sense of competence? Have you ever had that experience?

Dee: ... None come to mind at the moment.

Windy: Do you have a family, Dee?

Dee: Yes.

Windy: Who's in your family?

Dee: Myself and my children.

Windy: How old are your children and what gender are they?

Dee: I've got five. So I've got a daughter who's 27, a daughter who's 25, a son 22 and 15-year-old twins.

Windy: Well, let's take one. Who's more likely to come to you and talk about their problems with you?

Dee: My daughter, 25.

Windy: So let's suppose your daughter comes to you – what does she call you? Dad? Father?

Dee: Dad.

Windy: 'Look Dad, I'm struggling here. I've got this task to do and I don't feel competent in doing it.' And you listen to her and you say to her, 'Well, my daughter, I love you. Don't do it until you feel competent.' Would you say that to her?

Dee: … No.

Windy: Why not?

Dee: I would try to explore why she's struggling, and it has happened in the past. It's one of those: healers heal thyself in a supportive atmosphere, and actually go through why, even make a research for her as to how she can…. Yeah, I would.

Windy: So, in other words you wouldn't tell her to stop just because she felt incompetent?

Dee: No.

Windy: So now let's bring it back to you. What if you had a way of dealing with not being competent in starting off a task that allowed you to stay with it and grapple with it and then develop competence as you go? Would you be interested in that?

Dee: Yeah, definitely, because that would be the natural order of things anyway. If you don't sit down you can't get competent. If you sit down with it then your competency grows.

Windy: Yeah. So then the question I'm going to ask you, Dee, is that, not why it would be nice to start off a task feeling competent, because it would – it would be nice – but is that a necessary condition or is that a desirable condition but not necessary in order to start the task?

          [*Here, I am bringing an REBT perspective to the work I am doing with Dee. It would have been better to ask him if he was interested in hearing my 'take' on his issue.*]

Dee: It's desirable but definitely not necessary.

Windy: Right. You are acting as if it's necessary at the moment.

Dee: … Yeah, I can see that now…. Yeah, that's very true, actually. But competence can only grow. It'll diminish.

Windy: So can you imagine tomorrow sitting down with this task and getting in touch with that sense of incompetence and recognising it and saying, 'Look, Dee, you're not feeling competent about doing that. You could leave it right now or you could stay. And, if you stay, you need to remind yourself that you don't need to be competent right now. You can become competent by sticking with it'? Could you imagine doing that?

Dee: I can imagine. It will be a welcome course of events.

Windy: Yeah, and you could practise that.

Dee: Definitely.

Windy: Determination is not necessarily the ingredient that's going to help you because it's like blasting through rather than dealing with. So it's a bit like the difference between finding the right key to open the door and blasting the door off of its hinges. You can do that.

Dee: Not successfully.

Windy: In a way, you waiting for determination which never comes is also part of the problem, not part of the solution.

Dee: ... That's interesting, that it's part of the problem, not the solution. But it is true.... Yeah.... That's correct, actually, when I think about it.

Windy: Now, is this sense of incompetence that you feel, is it related to self-esteem, Dee, or not?

Dee: It's definitely related to self-esteem. I know that.

                [Having encouraged Dee to take a flexible attitude to not feeling competent at the task and that he can begin the task without this ingredient, I ask him whether this relates to self-esteem. He recognises that it is.]

Windy: So what do you call somebody who starts off a task that they don't feel competent, they stick with it and they grow in competence as they stick with it? What do you call such a person?

Dee: ... *[Pause]* A grinder comes to mind because you grind away at it and don't give up. I'm not sure what the phrase I would use, escapes me at the moment, but I know that's what I'd like to do eventually.

Windy: Well, what I would call it, if you're interested in terms of what I would call such a person is an ordinary human being whose worth is not defined by whether they can do anything at any particular point in time.

Dee: ... [*Long pause*] Yeah, maybe. Yeah.... [*Pause*] Yeah, that should be a normal course of events.

Windy: Right. The point is tomorrow when you sit down you'll still have a tendency to want to put off because this is a habit. So don't worry about that. But the thing is if you practise in imagery the whole picture – let's try it now. So just close your eyes a minute if it helps. You can keep your eyes open if it helps. Let's see how this works for you. So tomorrow you sit down at nine o'clock and you start looking at the task and you feel a sense of incompetence coming up because you don't quite know what it is you're going to do and there's a part of you that really wants to avoid, and you acknowledge that but you then remind yourself, 'Look, I don't have to be competent at this at the start. It's not necessary. I'm an ordinary human being just doing things in the normal course of events. So let me stay here and let me tolerate the struggle because it's in my interest to do that.' Now, can you imagine doing that?

[*Here, I am encouraging Dee to rehearse the solution by using imagery as I outline the process.*]

Dee: ... Yeah, I can because I have done in the past when my back is against the wall, and the feelings that come up then are, 'Why did I leave it so long? Why did I push it away?'

Windy: Yeah. Part of your procrastination and parts of many, many millions of people's procrastination is that we don't want you to be motivated by your back against the wall.

Dee: Yeah, definitely.

Windy: We want you to be motivated so that you're ahead of the game, not trying to avoid the firing shot.

Dee: Yeah.

Windy: So it's good that you're able to do that. Now you can transfer that. Why don't you take me through the imagery in the same way but this time using your words, because I want you to own that experience? I've gone through it with my words, now let's see if you can go through it with your words.

[*This is important, I am encouraging Dee to be actively involved in rehearsing the solution.*]

Dee: I can see myself getting up early enough in order to make myself my double espresso, because I usually can't move without that, and sitting down at the table getting the initial material in front of me and trying that out and timing myself, seeing how I do with that... and practising with it 'til I get better speed-wise. And then trying to find other examples, research online to complement that. I can see myself doing that and breaking my work down, so not dealing with the competencies, not flitting from one to another; just breaking it down and starting out with that. And then maybe the day after going through the competencies and having a cycle, a timely cycle of doing and practising this without trepidation or anything.

Windy: Yeah. And I would just add the bit reminding yourself that you don't have to be competent right at the start.

Dee: Yeah. I know that would grow.

Windy: 'My competency would grow.'

Dee: Yeah, definitely.

Windy: Now, is this process generalisable? Can you take that as a prototype and generalise it to other areas?

[*As mentioned in Chapter 2, helping a client to generalise a solution is an important feature of SST.*]

Dee: Yeah. It's definitely a plan I could lay onto other aspects because of that general trend of starting, that fear of starting and making the task seem bigger than it is, rather than breaking it down. In my mind, I clump things up. It might be a simple task that I'll clump up or I would lump it up with anything, many things. So I've got to do this at nine o'clock tomorrow but I've also got to do that and I've also got to do that, and then I'll question my competence.

Windy: Yeah. It sounds like it might be useful for you to have some kind of schedule so that you know at nine o'clock that you should be doing x?

Dee: X rather than x plus, yeah.

Windy: Plus y plus z, right. Can you see any obstacles that might stop you from implementing this tomorrow?

Dee: At the moment, no, funnily enough. I don't want to build them up. I'm trying not to let the thought patterns come to mind as to why I can't do it, because then I'll succumb to that.

Windy: Well, actually, I would put it to you that just because you might start thinking why you can't do it, you can still do it while thinking that you can't do it. In other words, we can have thoughts in our mind and choose to be guided by them or choose not to be guided by them.

Dee: I think I was talking more in terms of actual thoughts that would affect my actually starting the task: the feelings that, 'Oh, tomorrow I need to do some laundry before nine o'clock,' so I'll push it to 9:30.

Windy: What would you call that? What language would you have for that type of thinking?

Dee: I'd say it's just avoidance.

Windy: OK. So maybe you can label it as, 'Oh, that's avoidance thinking. I don't have to be guided by that.'

Dee: Yeah, definitely.

Windy: 'Just because I think it, I don't have to go along with it.'

Dee: Yeah.

Windy: Dee, sometimes I say that there's only one thing I want you to avoid in this and that is avoidance. I want you to avoid avoidance.

Dee: Yeah. If only it were so simple, but yeah.

Windy: Well, the point is on this one you may have some, 'Oh, I've got to do some laundry,' you could say, 'No, that's avoidance thinking. I'm going to choose not to be guided by that. I'm going to choose to sit down and practise a new way forward for me.'

               [*Here, I have been helping Dee to identify and deal with obstacles to him implementing the solution.*]

Dee: Yes.

Windy: So we're coming to the end in a moment. Why don't you summarise the work we've done today and particularly what you're going to take away from it?

               [*A typical intervention at the end of SST.*]

Dee: What we've done today is going to the specifics and actually nailed, rather generalising what procrastination, trying to find something relative and timely that I can address. We've talked about ... when I would start addressing it. That's why I said nine o'clock. We've talked about the feelings or thoughts that would stop me from achieving my goals and recognising these mental barriers that I have normally, almost as my default setting in terms of not doing it because I'm incompetent, rather than recognising that my competency will grow the more I sit down with it.

Windy: That's right. In terms of default settings, when I go on my computer it defaults to a certain font and a certain size. For some reason, I can only change it after it's defaulted to that. So the default position is just the starting off position. It's not the ending up position.

Dee: Yeah.

Windy: OK, good. So is there anything else you want to say on this issue that you haven't said or want to ask me something you want to ask?

[Another typical ending intervention in SST.]

Dee: No, thank you. I've got some good takeaways to reflect upon. So thank you very much for that.

Windy: I'm going to send you a little later on this week the recording of the session and then after it's transcribed I'll send you the transcript so you've got a record of that. Then we'll write to you in three or four months' time and see how you get on, OK?

Dee: OK. Thank you very much for that, Windy.

Windy: Thank you very much, Dee. It's been a pleasure meeting you.

Dee's Reflections (31-08-23)

The session was a single session which I had with the knowledge that it might not result in an immediate change in my behaviour but might enable me to start exploring the underlying reasons behind my actions and eventually lead to my ability to deal with it.

The session was helpful in that it made me focus on the issue and address it head on. I was made to focus on one incident in particular rather that take the problem as a whole and by 'seeing' this problem through to a conclusion enabled me to take the tools learned during the session and then eventually try to layer this into the other areas of my life which had been affected by my deferring habit. I felt I could have benefitted from having more sessions just to reinforce what I learnt but it was still very useful.

Amongst the things I learnt from the session was looking at the term procrastinate in another way. Rather than just looking at it as 'putting the things I should be doing now off till later', I was encouraged to view the issue as whether I regarded the 'thing' put off to be *in my best interest* which might impact on how important I really thought it was. I also looked at why I used the term *should* which seem to indicate things were in the hands of someone else. I am now able to look at the whole picture which includes not only why I am procrastinating but also why I am not doing the task or why I feel I don't really want to do it. Putting boundaries in the mix such as time also focused me on setting clear cut objectives which in turn helped me to identify when I was procrastinating and therefore examine why I was doing it at that point. Rather than procrastinate because I feel that I might not be competent enough or achieve the objectives I set out to do, I focus on getting thing started.

The session made a difference in how I was dealing with times in the past as opposed to when I started using the new tools discussed during the session. The change has not been immediate, but it has been gradual but steady. Rather than wallowing in the discomfort of why I am not doing things, I am examining why subconsciously I do not regard it important enough to deal with in a timely manner. I compare this to other times or things I have felt are important enough and therefore dealt with appropriately.

6

Prioritising Self and Creating Boundaries and a Structure

Date: 24/04/23
Time: 45 minutes 2 secs

Windy: So, Jane, what's your understanding of the purpose of our conversation today?

Jane: ... To hopefully ... I wanted to say hopefully get more insight onto what I say is my procrastination problem, but, as I'm saying that, I don't actually think it's insight I need. I think what would be helpful is to have some actual actionable behavioural changes to move the needle on it, because I don't think I need to think and reflect on it. I think I need to do something differently.

Windy: And do you think the behaviour needs to be based on an understanding of why you procrastinate or you think that's not important?

Jane: ... I'm open to it being important.... Yeah, I'm open to it being unimportant. I guess my reticence is because over the years, and it's been many years, I feel like I've done a lot of reading about procrastination, I understand it. For me, from my understanding right now, is that it's me just trying to soothe myself and avoid uncertainty, etc. So I'm definitely open to more insight in a helpful way. Just where I'm at in my journey I sometimes think that thinking and understanding's a bit of a hiding place and I'm not actually doing anything differently.

Windy: Yeah, so you might be looking for a thinking and understanding that will lead to action rather than thinking and understanding that would lead to more hiding.

[Here, I am clarifying my understanding of what Jane is saying.]

Jane: That's it.

Windy: You have the advantage of me because you understand your procrastination better than I do. So let me see if I can understand it as well. Are you currently procrastinating on anything that you want to be doing?

Jane: Yes.

Windy: Tell me what that is, please?

Jane: I would like to be … I'll just spit it all out – I'd like to be doing more decluttering in the house. There's a lot of things that I want to tidy up and get rid of that I find myself procrastinating on. Also, I can quite often procrastinate on work, meaning like writing. I'm quite good at writing notes up, but, if I have a consult with someone, maybe getting back to them in a timely manner. And also, we were speaking about accreditation, etc., the other day, I'd like to crack on and do my accreditation but I'm procrastinating on that as well.

Windy: So there are three issues. So which one has the greatest primacy for you at the moment?

Jane: … *[Long pause]* I think I'd like to look at the accreditation one.

Windy: OK. Where are you in the accreditation process?

Jane: Actually, do I want to look at this, Windy? I'm procrastinating on making a decision…. Forgive me to take a backstep. I don't know if this is what I want to target as opposed to, one of the things I'm procrastinating on is I haven't got a routine in my week, meaning I have an employed job and I'm always there and I do that, but in the days that I'm not in work I don't have a routine. I suppose what I'd really like is to sit down and create myself a routine and a structure, which might look like working on accreditation in there. And I feel like I'm procrastinating on actually committing to making that routine. Does that make sense?

Windy: Yes, and you would like to commit to making that routine?

Jane: Yes.

Windy: So that would be the focus for our discussion today.

Jane: Yeah. That feels better, yeah.

[*We agree a focus.*]

Windy: That's fine. Have you ever had the experience of creating a routine for yourself before?

Jane: No, not really. I'd say often times my routine's been dictated by another thing. So, when I was full-time employed, that created my structure. But now, in the last few years, now that I work part time, I've procrastinated on doing that. Actually, no. When I was a teenager doing my GCSEs and A Levels, I was really good at creating a timetable for my study and executing on it. I was really good at that back then. I didn't procrastinate back then.

Windy: What enabled you to do that?

Jane: ... [*Pause*] I was very clear on the syllabus of what I had to get through and the various bits. So I sort of reverse engineered it – so for each subject I'd know what I needed to know when I needed to know it by and then I'd reverse engineer what time I had available. So it was what allowed me to do it, I suppose, was a level of structure in the syllabus and my own will and determination to do well.

Windy: So there are two elements there. One is the structure that was outside you – you didn't have a hand in the syllabus; the syllabus was given to you, so that had clarity. And, because that had clarity, you made the decision to reverse engineer it, as you say, and to work out how much time you needed to devote to which particular task. Is that right?

Jane: Yeah.

Windy: It sounds to me different now because there's no external structure that you've been given, and you're the author of that structure, in a way.

Jane: Possibly.

Windy: And how good are you at actually developing your own structure for things?

Jane: That appears to be the sticking point. I don't think I am very good.

Windy: So it's not as if you want to sit down and actually have a schedule because before you do that do you need to be clear with yourself the things that you want to have in your schedule?

Jane: Yeah.

Windy: And at that moment that's difficult for you? Is that what you're saying?

Jane: As I'm talking to you, I think I have got more clarity than maybe I'm giving myself awareness. Like this is what comes to my mind now: in my ideal structure I would like to put time for physical exercise, time for admin. So time for exercise, time for admin and then time for house chores.

Windy: Exercise, admin, house chores.

Jane: Yeah.

Windy: Does that include the decluttering or is the decluttering a separate issue for you?

Jane: That's a good question. If I had a block of time committed to housework, I'd be happy for that time to either go towards a decluttering project or tidying up. I'm happy to be flexible.

Windy: So it sounds like the three issues are exercise, admin and house chores – general/decluttering.

Jane: Yeah.

Windy: So, if that's your structure, can you reverse engineer it in terms of how much time you are willing to give within a schedule, when you create a schedule? Do you have in mind how much time you need to devote to each?

   [I am using her term, 'reverse engineering' here. Using the client's own language is important in SST.]

Jane: … I think when it comes to exercise I'd like that to be happening five days out of seven.

Windy: What exercise are we talking about?

Jane: Anything really that moves my body. So, if I had an exercise slot, I'd be happy if it was a 20-minute DVD or 20 minutes on my cross trainer or going out for a walk for half an hour. I'm happy to be flexible around that. What's important for me is that I'm doing some form of physical activity.

Windy: And when would that happen?

Jane: I think this is why I'm here because I've been procrastinating.

Windy: Well, morning, afternoon or evening? Which is better for you?

Jane: It depends on the day because of my employed job. But on a Monday, say, I think a.m. would be preferable.

Windy: And we're talking between 20 minutes and half an hour, are we?

Jane: Yeah. I think... a Tuesday it would have to be here in the afternoon or evening. On a Wednesday a.m. On a Thursday a.m. or p.m., really, it doesn't matter because I have a free day there. I think Friday I'd quite like to be off.... [*Pause*] I'm going into thinking again.... [*Long pause*] Yeah, I think Friday afternoon and Saturday morning.

Windy: It sounds like you've got 20 to 30 minutes in mind in doing that.

Jane: Yeah.

Windy: And can you allocate specific times to that, like nine o'clock or half past nine? Is that something that you could do?

Jane: Yeah, I can do it. I think the problem is that I'm not.

Windy: What stops you from actually assigning specific times to those activities?

Jane: There's two blocks at the moment. Number 1, in addition to doing some employed work, I do private client work as well, and I find what I often do is ... on the times I'm not in work, it's almost like I just go, 'Right, Client, you can have whatever time you want,' and I just fill my diary that way. So sometimes the block is I'm actually seeing clients.

Windy: Yeah, but you've created that.

Jane: I've created that, yeah.

Windy: You could actually give yourself some specific times to do your private work and, if a client wants to see you in exercise time, then you could say, 'Sorry, I'm not free at that time.'

Jane: Yeah.

Windy: That kind of involves you prioritising yourself over your clients.

Jane: There's a bit of emotion there so I know that that's something I do struggle with.

Windy: How do you feel about prioritising you? I mean, it's not as if you're not prioritising your clients, but you're not giving them exactly the time that they want.

Jane: … I think the word that comes is fear. Fear of if I don't give people a preference or what they want, and it isn't just clients. It's even if a friend wanted to see me because they're in dire straits or something, and I've got exercise time, I think what I've done in the past is I say, 'That doesn't matter. I'll make myself available.'

Windy: That doesn't matter or you don't matter?

Jane: … I think it might be me.

Windy: So it's a question of how do you matter to yourself so that you can actually, in a sense, make sure that you do the things that you want to do and also have clients and friends to be seen but not precisely when they want to be seen.

Jane: Yeah.

Windy: So do you matter to yourself in other areas of your life?

Jane: … [*Long pause*] I'm doing a qualification at the moment and I noticed when it comes to that external structure again I'm very good at saying no, like I'm not available for that. So I seem to matter to me when I'm learning or I'm doing some training.

Windy: So when you're doing training and when you're learning, then you matter to yourself.

Jane: Yeah.

Windy: What would you call the activities when you're exercising and doing admin and chores, then? What word would you describe those?

Jane: Really honestly?

Windy: Yeah.

Jane: I think I've got the word boring. I feel a bit embarrassed saying that, but I think whereas with learning I love it, there's an energy, when I think about exercise or admin or decluttering/housework, I kind of go, 'Oh, that's boring.' So maybe a part of me doesn't mind, in some ways, letting those slip.

Windy: So, it sounds like you matter to yourself when you're engaging in tasks that are intrinsically positive.

Jane: Yes.

Windy: But when it's intrinsically negative like exercise or admin or house chores, then it sounds like you're pushing it away for two reasons: one is because it's boring and also because, in a way, you don't really matter; you can put it off.

               [*Through patient questioning, I am helping Jane to get to the heart of her problem with procrastination.*]

Jane: Yeah, that's the emotion so I know there's something in it. There is the part that it's boring but I do think there's something about me not…, yeah, valuing myself to show up to myself to do those things that might be boring but I know I would actually feel proud and I'd build something from that within me, I think.

Windy: Yeah. You mean proud of who you are or proud of what you've done?

Jane: I think both. I think because I've had this habit, I feel, for a long time of letting those things go by the wayside, I think I would be proud of myself actually doing them and be like, 'Oh, you did that thing you didn't want to do, Jane,' because I do often say I don't feel very good at adulting. So I think I'd feel like my inner adult as more fortified by doing this. But I also just feel inherently proud of, 'The kitchen looks really nice and clean.' So I think it would be both.

Windy: Yeah, but also you need to take some stance towards the boringness of the activity.

Jane: Yeah.

Windy: Have you ever had to do things that are boring?

Jane: Yeah…. Well, that's a really good question, Windy…. That's a very good question. If I'm really honest, I think I've got to a point in my life where I've got really good at being able to avoid doing boring things as much as possible.

Windy: Yeah, and that makes sense if there's a reason not to do it. But it sounds like for these things there's a reason to do it.

Jane: Yeah. So, in answer to your question, again there's something about learning here. When I've been doing qualifications, there's some really boring things sometimes like putting a portfolio together which I don't go, 'Yay,' but when it's nourishing my value of learning, I can really bring my disciplined self to the table but I think there's something about maybe not valuing those other tasks the same.

Windy: But what you could bring to the table is the process of, 'What can I learn to do boring things so that I can end up being proud of what I've done and proud of myself for doing them?'

Jane: I love that. How can I learn ... to do boring things? Yeah.

[Jane has mentioned 'learning' a number of times so, I use this word myself in the service of the client finding a solution to her procrastination issue.]

Windy: So, in this way of looking at things, you need the boredom in order to learn.

Jane: ... *[Long pause]* Immediately, that feels like, even just the energy in my body, rather than it being a deflation of like, 'Oh, I've got to do those adulting things,' when you bring in the, 'How could I learn how to do boring things and be proud of it?' that now feels like an opportunity.

[What I am doing is helping Jane to put doing boring tasks into a new frame, using doing it as a learning opportunity.]

Windy: Right.

Jane: Ooh, that feels different.

Windy: Does it? OK.

Jane: Yeah.

Windy: So let's see how that insight could play out in terms of what we're talking about: you developing a structure that will enable you to do exercise, admin and house chores, but in a way that is going to capitalise on what we've just talked about.

Jane: Yeah.

Windy: Do you want to take the lead on that?

Jane: What was the question again? Could you say that?

Windy: How can you take that learning and apply it to the generation of the structure that we've been talking about, with the admin, the exercise and the house chores?

Jane: ... [*Long pause*]

Windy: One narrative is: 'Look, this is boring, and I'm not going to do it, and I'm not very good at doing things that are boring for myself. So, therefore I'm not going to do it.' That's one narrative. The other narrative is: 'This is an opportunity to learn something more about myself by learning how to deal with boredom.' So, in other words, you can construct two different types of narratives.

[*I often use the concept of 'narrative' to indicate that the client has a choice of different ways forward.*]

Jane: Yeah, I like that.... Let me see if I can translate because that immediately feels energising to me: the idea of getting to learn. And what's coming to me is... [pause] let me see here – I'm really mindful that I can have a sort of inner perfectionist and that can be a block sometimes. So I can get myself in a muddle in terms of trying to maybe create a structure because I want to do it perfectly, but actually, if I'm going to do this in the spirit of learning, I think I need to give myself permission to just start off with something that might be good enough and to reiterate.

... [*Pause*] So what's coming to me now is..., if I'm here saying today, on 24th April, that what I want to do is to create a routine and a structure where I serve my clients, do my employed work, but I also have an opportunity to learn about boredom and doing things, and that involves admin, house chores and exercise. I think the next logical step is writing out a diary, if you will, from Monday to Sunday, starting off with putting in what my obligations actually are that are set and then just, in a good enough stance, putting in a window for exercise, a window for admin and a window for house chores, and starting off with that external structure and... maybe being like a scientist and being like, 'Right, this is the model that I'm going to use. This is my curriculum that I'm going to use to try and learn about tolerating boredom.' That's what comes to me.

Windy: OK, right. And there needs to be a bit where a client rings you up and says, 'I can't do that, but can I have this time?' and it's a time that you've allocated to exercise. So how are you going to deal with that?

Jane: I'm grateful you've asked that question because, if I'm really honest, I think ... I'd like to do both, really.

Windy: You mean see the client while doing the exercise?

Jane: Or swapping it, saying, 'OK, well, my exercise schedule said it was going to be ten o'clock on a Monday, but Client A, you want ten o'clock on a Monday, so I'll see you then and then I'll do my exercises.'

Windy: OK. I'll be a bit devil's advocate-y, if I may?

[If I want to challenge a client in SST, I will put in the form put by a third person. I do this to minimise push back.]

Jane: Go on.

Windy: Would you swap it the other way around?

Jane: Which is what?

Windy: Client's wanting to be seen but you want to do the exercise. So you ring up the client and say, 'I'm sorry, I can't make it.' I think the hidden trap there is that you're very willing to let yourself go second in favour of the client. And maybe you need to get the practice, the learning of putting yourself first even if it means putting off a client. The point is, is a client going to suffer that much if they can't be seen exactly when they want to be seen?

Jane: I think you raise a very good point that, if I was to do what I've always done which is to prioritise other first, which is often what I do, I'm actually not giving myself the learning to actually see what that feels like. So I think actually, yeah, the invitation would be a, 'I'm sorry I'm not available then. These are the other times I've got.'

Windy: Yeah, exactly. They're not going to say to you, 'Why, what are you doing at that time?'

Jane: Yeah.

Windy: In the same way as you wouldn't say to a client, 'You can't see me at three o'clock? Why not?' You wouldn't do that. So I think, if you can actually get used to sticking to something, because that's what we're talking about: about how to learn how to stick to something even though it might not be as interesting as client work, but it's something that is important to you otherwise you wouldn't be putting it in. And maybe you need to prioritise yourself over other people occasionally.

Jane: Yeah. I think I didn't realise until this conversation that I think, until this conversation I didn't really see the piece that... I've just sort of being beating myself up saying, 'I'm rubbish at doing boring things and I'm not very good at adulting and I'm just lazy.' And, actually, I didn't fully see the piece of there's also that emotional piece of actually prioritising myself, and I didn't really quite see that as clearly as I do with you now.

[Here, the client is putting the issue into a new frame for herself.]

Windy: So it's about prioritising yourself, it's about giving yourself opportunities to learn in areas where you dismiss that as an opportunity. It's like you can only learn in these areas of your life and not in these other areas where there's housework. And maybe also you could actually apply that to later on when you think about the decluttering.

Jane: Yeah. Forgive me if I'm going ahead here, what's coming up for me now, I suppose, as another block is… so here's me creating this structure, which I'm feeling more motivated in this moment because it's like, 'Ah, yeah, I could actually use this as an opportunity to learn how I do boring things, how I can prioritise myself, show myself how I can stick to something,' and I'm really curious about that. I think the next bit I'm worried about is, OK, so I have this structure, my worry then is actually showing up for myself in the moment and doing the things.

Windy: OK. So give me an example of you showing yourself up in the moment and give me an example of you not showing up about the same task?

[Rather than ask Jane to give me an example of her not showing up, I ask her for two examples, one where she shows up and one where she doesn't, so that she can see the difference between the two.]

Jane: The key one that comes is, OK, so I put in the exercise and then it comes to it and I have the thought, 'I don't feel like it. I'm too tired.' That's a big block for me: I often at times feel too tired.

Windy: So what do you do on those as alternative activities?

Jane: I think I end up giving in to the tiredness.

Windy: And doing what?

Jane: ... What that tends to look like is ... a lot of sitting down, maybe scrolling on social media or listening to a You Tube thing about trying to get yourself motivated to do a thing. It often ends up being learning in some way, like intellectual learning.

Windy: Yeah, which is what you wanted to break away from, if I recall, at the beginning.

Jane: Yes.

Windy: It sounds like to me you have an idea of what state you have to be in, in the moment, in order to do exercise.

Jane: That's right.

Windy: What is that state?

Jane: I was going to say energised is ideal, but often these days I don't feel particularly energised. But at least some energy.

Windy: In terms of the exercise, give me an example of an exercise? What would it be? Going out for a walk?

Jane: Cross trainer.

Windy: So what do you need to be able to go onto the cross trainer?

Jane: ... The story I keep telling myself is ... I need to feel energised and to feel motivated.

Windy: Are they desirable qualities or are they absolutely necessary? Absolutely necessary means that it would be absolutely impossible for you to do it without those things. Desirable means that, 'It would be nice but I could do it without that and maybe get into the energy later.'

[*Here I am bringing to the conversation insights from REBT (see Chapter 3).*]

Jane: Desirable.

Windy: So you see how you've converted something which is desirable into something that is necessary, and then you stop yourself because you haven't got the necessary condition.

Jane: That's it.

Windy: So you say, 'Yeah, it would be nice if I was more energised but I don't need to be. Let's see if I can get energised while being on the cross trainer.' Have you ever had that experience, Jane, of actually getting energised through an activity?

Jane: Absolutely, yeah.

Windy: So that's what we're talking about. It's like you're waiting for the energy to come first, which is very interesting because the whole point of doing the cross trainer is to get the energy.

Jane: Right, yeah.

Windy: You don't say to yourself, 'Oh, I'm very energised, I don't need to go on the cross trainer.'

Jane: Yeah, exactly.

Windy: So I think, at times when you think you're not showing up for yourself, you could ask yourself the question: 'What conditions do I think I need in order to do this and do I actually need them or are they desirable?'

Jane: OK.... [*Pause*] Yeah.... Yeah. Just what's coming to me in this moment, I think there are times actually that, if I'm super, super tired, like properly tired, I do think there is a time sometimes where it moves from being a desirable to a necessity.

Windy: I often say to people who procrastinate, you need to be super honest with yourself because we want you to distinguish between the tiredness that you are using as an excuse and the tiredness that was really out of good reason. So you need to ask yourself the question, 'Is this a good reason or is this a rationalisation?' a rationalisation being something that appears to be a good reason but isn't; that involves self-deception. Whereas a good reason is really a good reason; there's no self-deception involved.

[*I encourage Jane to be 'super honest' with herself so that she can distinguish between a good reason and a rationalisation.*]

Jane: I like that and I know myself well enough to just inside know the difference now.

Windy: Yeah. OK. So why don't you summarise where we are at the moment?

[*As we are approaching the end. I encourage Jane to summarise.*]

Jane: Well.... [*pause*] so far I'm seeing that... [pause] I have been doing some procrastination because I have had some conditions around I tell myself I need this, this, this and that in order to x, y, z, and actually they're not necessities, they're desirables. And, actually, if I could remind myself that in the moment, that could be really good to get me into action. And I'm also seeing that, if I create structure where I put in admin, house chores/decluttering and exercise, and have that as a non-negotiable, if you will, that it's giving me the opportunity to learn about sticking to something and about prioritising myself. And it gives me a framework to learn, and I enjoy that.

Windy: OK. Can you create something that would either be a vivid example of the desirable versus necessary bit or something that might symbolise that, that, if you brought it to mind or see it, then it would actually help you to remind yourself of that particular point?

               [*Having a vivid example of a point can be helpful to bring it to mind at the appropriate time.*]

Jane: Could you give me an example just so I can sense into what you're pointing to?

Windy: Well, like sometimes people put things on their phones, some sort of image or they can create some phrase that they can load up as their phone screenshot. So they might have: desirable or necessary? So you'd be actually able to have a look at that quickly and actually have a reminder.

Jane: Yeah, I think that is what you've said in itself. … I think what would be helpful is to, yeah, ask myself two things… or maybe just, 'Is this a good reason or is it a rationalisation?' I like that one.

Windy: Yeah, reason or rationalisation.

Jane: Yeah.

Windy: OK.

Jane: I don't know why but I have a picture of a sunflower in my head when I think about that,

Windy: If that works for you, that works for you. It's your image, your unique experience that we're looking for here.

Jane: Yeah.

Windy: So do you think you've got enough to sit down and create your structure and then to start rolling that out?

Jane: … [*Long pause*] Yeah, I think so.

Windy: You hesitated, so there may be something else that we need to consider.

[*This is a good example of me picking up a sign that there may be something else that we need to attend to.*]

Jane: Yeah, and I'm not sure what it is. I think … the last bit, actually, the block is … thank you for helping me with this – I find myself in a bit of a circular position at the moment, meaning – I'll just put my employed work to the side for a minute because that's like a set routine, and I have to be there at a certain time and finish, but then I have private work which some people see me weekly, some people are biweekly and some people are on a monthly drop-in, if you will, and some people even less than that. And recently I've noticed that I'm struggling with some burnout and feeling tired. And I feel myself in a bit of a circular argument. When I'm thinking about this structure and routine, I think the, 'Yeah, but,' comes in of… that I do feel I have a commitment to my clients. And, so my worry is – how can articulate this? Yeah, if I'm really honest, my worry is that the admin, house chores and exercise bits will go out the window if I have clients that want to be/need to be seen that week and I'm struggling with windows to put them in, because sometimes the only way I'm able to manage making sure that I serve all of those clients is just to work very long hours.

Windy: So you never go on holiday, I take it?

Jane: … In the last couple of years I've been notoriously quite bad at going on holiday.

Windy: Does that mean you haven't been or you've been notoriously bad at going but you go anyway?

Jane: I generally have ended up booking a week off work because I'm burnt out and then that week I don't end up

doing anything particularly restorative because I feel
burnt out. So I suppose actually, yeah, I have had
experience of going on holiday.

Windy: What happened to your clients then?

Jane: They have a break.

Windy: You mean your clients have a break when you have a
break?

Jane: Yeah, both.

Windy: Do they have a break because they say what? 'Jane's
away, therefore,' what?

Jane: … [*Pause*] I suppose the difference with those planned
breaks is I try and give people notice that it's happening.
… [*Pause*] Yeah.

Windy: What you could do is you could give your clients notice
of when you're working and when you're not working.

Jane: OK, yeah.

Windy: You could say, 'These are my new times for working.'
And then, when you do that, then you give some thought
to the bit of you that needs to do the exercise, the admin
and the house chores, and building in rest time so that
there's that bit for you, because it sounds like you've
edited that out.

Jane: I was just becoming aware of that as I was talking to you.
Rest is something that I feel I need more of but don't
create the space to do it in a restorative way.

Windy: What would you do if you rested?

Jane: … How would I rest?

Windy: What would you find restful, let's put it that way?

Jane: I find restful not seeing clients and being able to read a book.

Windy: OK, read a book. What else?

Jane: ... Going for a walk, meeting someone for coffee, having a nap.

Windy: So maybe we have to add that to the exercise, admin, chores bit. There's a bit which says rest, which you've edited out, which you may need to edit in. Do you want a long career in counselling or do you want a short career in counselling?

Jane: Long.

Windy: Well, how are you going to do that if you don't prioritise looking after yourself?

Jane: I know, yeah.

Windy: Meaning resting. If a client rings me up and I can't see them and I say, 'I can see you in a couple of days,' you know what, they're perfectly OK with it.

Jane: Yeah. It's me, actually.

Windy: Maybe you're not as crucial to them as you would like to be.

Jane: Do you know what's just coming up? It's more my anxiety, actually. I've been framing it as like, 'Ooh, they might have to go a couple of days,' but actually it's my anxiety about sitting with that. It's my anxiety about putting me first.

Windy: Yeah. And, if you put yourself first, I would say you're only being a good model for your clients.

Jane: Yeah. I've just noticed that's part of the fear that comes up. If I put me first and I don't please everyone, then fear is ... I'll lose that client or that person won't want to be my friend, which I know really does not make sense, but there is that fear.

Windy: But you've got to then experience it. It's a bit like any kind of fear, if you think there's a ghost under the bed, you've got to look under the bed.

[*Here I am making the point that facing what you fear is the best antidote to fear.*]

Jane: Yeah.

Windy: In other words, the only way you're going to answer your question is to actually test it out: to say to a client, 'Sorry, I can't see you that day.' I'm sure the coroner would understand. But I think you need to find out. This reminds me of an old joke that was attributed. I'm sure he never said this, but Albert Ellis was my mentor and he used to work incredibly long hours, and the board of trustees said, 'Albert, you've been working for long hours and we're going to give you a long sabbatical. We're going to give you a month off fully paid. Go where you like and do something like that.' So he thought about it for a minute and he said, 'Well, that's very kind of you, but there are two reasons why I'm going to respectively say no.' And they said, 'What are those two reasons?' He said, 'Well, (1) If I go away for the month the institute might collapse and, (2) it may not.'

Jane: Ah.... [*Pause*] Yeah.

Windy: What do you think the point of that story is to you?

Jane: ... [*Pause*] Something about ... I can't quite articulate it, but something about seeing that you're maybe not as important as you think you are.

Windy: Yeah. You've structured it so that you are crucial in your mind to your clients.

Jane: Yeah.

Windy: But maybe you're not as crucial and maybe that's OK.

Jane: Yeah.

Windy: Maybe by seeing yourself as crucial and treating them as somebody who needs to be attended to and changed immediately, maybe you're not helping them to develop themselves.

Jane: Yeah. Yes. Yep. Again, there's learning, so I like that. Yeah, that's helpful.

Windy: So maybe you could add that to the structure and say, 'Well, look, I am going to prioritise my rest because I need the rest. I do need to take care of myself. And, yes, it's important for me to take care of my clients, but not the 'drop everything and forget about what I'm doing' type of help.'

Jane: Yeah.

Windy: And maybe you could do that with your friends as well.

Jane: Yeah. I liked what you said about the only way that I'm going to test out that fear that something bad is going to happen if I don't please people is actually create the opportunity to actually see if the catastrophe happens.

Windy: Yeah, because you're so busy avoiding the possibility of it happening that you're maintaining the fear.

Jane: Yeah, that's a download. That's really helpful. I'm so busy avoiding and maintaining it. Yeah, I didn't see that. That's really helpful. Thank you. That's really helpful.

Windy: So is there any final thing that you want to say or ask that would bring this to a close or you're good?

[A typical closing question in SST.]

Jane: No. I feel like you've really helped me both ... create an energy – it was the bit about learning has created a motivation, like I actually want to do this now as opposed to I should. I'll get to learn something, but also it's been really helpful to look at what practical blocks are and navigate in those, again with the spirt of learning again. Even the testing out is a learning thing, and that's been really helpful.

Windy: And, if I've helped you to have a long career in our profession, then that's good enough for me.

Jane: That's really helpful, thank you. I'm so grateful for this time together. I appreciate it and I appreciate you.

Windy: My pleasure. And I'll send you the recording a little bit later and the transcript in two or three weeks' time when it's done, OK?

Jane: That's fantastic. Thank you so much, Windy, have a lovely day.

Windy: Take care. Bye.

Jane's Reflections (31-08-23)

I very much enjoyed my meeting with Windy about the procrastination I'd experienced in creating and committing to a weekly routine that balanced work with house chores and rest; something I'd previously found difficult for reasons I wasn't fully aware of until the session. In particular, I valued Windy's simple, focused and effective style of questioning. For me, this felt like cutting through the busy 'snow globe' of thoughts and feelings within me regarding the procrastination I was experiencing and quickly got 'underneath the issue' to gain clarity on (a) what I wanted to achieve as an outcome from the session, (b) understanding the blocks that had previously been in place to making a weekly structure happen and (c) creating a clear plan that felt both achievable and addressed potential issues that might get in the way.

Windy's grounded and practical style of enquiry felt like peeling layers off the 'onion' of my procrastination habit, helping me gain clarity on the 'layers' of thought, emotion and practical issues that together were keeping procrastination in place. The session felt both structured (which imparted a grounding and 'containing' quality to the confusion I felt), but also had a fluidity that allowed for a personalised exploration of my experience leading to meaningful personal insights that had otherwise been out of my awareness. However, rather than just finishing the session with more self-understanding that led to no real change post-session, by being guided in the meeting to link those insights to practical actionable changes, I left the session hopeful, and it has since led to real-life changes.

The session had a great impact for me and I took away a number of things. Via guided exploration of past experiences, Windy helped me identify that learning is a value I find inherently motivating and helps me culture discipline. By framing my 'sticking to a routine' as a means for me to learn about overcoming the factors we identified as underpinning my 'procrastination habit' (including learning to tolerate boredom, tiredness, fear *and* acting anyway) I've managed to not only far more successfully stick to a weekly routine, but have also since applied the question of 'how do I get to learn here?' to other avoided tasks.

I appreciated Windy's 'devil's advocate' questions as it not only addressed how I might realistically deal with potential blocks post-session, but highlighted deeper emotional factors I didn't recognise were playing a part in maintaining my procrastination. For instance, until the session, I hadn't fully recognised that I'd been prioritising other people's needs for help above my own needs for rest and to commit to things important to me, which were contributing to burnout, frustration at myself and lowering self-esteem. Since the session, I've been leaning into prioritising my own needs to test what actually happens (versus believing fear-based thoughts of rejection and disappointment) and lo and behold, the world didn't fall apart. I still have friends and clients *and* I am more rested! This has been immensely freeing.

During the session, an image of a sunflower emerged as we explored the idea of 'reason vs rationalisation' when recognising I am avoiding planned tasks. This feels a very apt metaphor for my appointment with Windy and the meaningful impact it had. Indeed, in addition to shedding a (sun) light of understanding on the procrastination I'd experienced, by leaving the session with a practical plan of action that including ways to deal with challenges, I left feeling rooted and grounded and this has led to real growth and change post session.

7

Going Easier on Myself and Going Against the Avoidance Habit

Date: 24/04/23
Time: 26 minutes 25 secs

Windy: OK, Moon, what's your understanding of the purpose of our conversation today?

Moon: To look at why I avoid coursework and anything that stems around learning.

Windy: And what's your hope about what you might achieve by the end of our session today?

Moon: To be able to get on with things and not avoid.

Windy: Is there any particular task that you're avoiding at the moment that we could look at, and then we could maybe generalise the learnings from that situation to other areas?

Moon: Yes, my accreditation. I've been trying to do it for five years but I've managed to avoid it.

Windy: And why is it in your interest to have accreditation?

Moon: To be able to open a few doors for me working with some of the professionals. So like working with veterans in the army and also work with hospital staff.

Windy: And why's that important to you?

Moon: Because I work a lot with trauma and I'd like to be able to help the staff so they've got extra options and the waiting list doesn't have to be so extreme.

Windy: So the purpose of getting accreditation is that you would be able to then have more doors open for you to work with the people that you value working with and to help them more promptly.

Moon: Yes.

Windy: And that's important to you?

Moon: Yeah, it is.

Windy: I mention that because it's important when we're dealing with procrastination for you to keep in mind the longer-term purpose of any particular task that you are currently putting off.

              [*This is a good example, I think, of me helping the person be clear that it is in their long-term interests to do the work for accreditation.*]

Moon: Yeah.

Windy: So, in terms of the accreditation process, where are you in that process?

Moon: … So I'd say I've probably worked my way through it to about three-quarters of the way to completing it…. But, yeah, it's every time I've gone to pick it up, I find something else to do…. The washing up seems more interesting and putting things in the dishwasher.

Windy: I think one of the things that I'd invite you to do is make a specific time to restart your accreditation work. So imminently when would be a good time that you would be able to do that?

[I emphasise the importance of working with a specific example.]

Moon: I'd like to get on with it today.

Windy: What time today, Moon?

Moon: After we've finished the session.

Windy: Directly afterwards or you would have a break for a cup of coffee or a cup of tea?

Moon: Probably have a bite of lunch and then I'll get on with it this afternoon, yeah.

Windy: Starting what time?

Moon: 12:30.

Windy: So at 12:30 where would you be sitting down?

Moon: At the table to be able to get comfy and be able to just work my way through the rest of what I need to get done.

Windy: And are you on your own in that space?

Moon: Yes.

Windy: So there's no external interruption?

Moon: No.

Windy: So, as you see it now, how would you stop yourself from doing that?

Moon: … I guess it would be picking up a book and reading something completely different or making a telephone call or going for a walk.

Windy: So you'd be avoiding sitting down and doing it.

Moon: Yeah.

Windy: Now, do you have a sense what you are avoiding?

Moon: I guess it's sending it in and it coming back that it's not good enough.

Windy: OK. And, so, if we gave you a guarantee that you would send it in and it would come back good enough, would you then do it?

Moon: Yeah.

Windy: What do you think that says about your procrastination?

Moon: Seeking approval, I suppose.

Windy: Well, it's about two things: one is having the certainty and then having the sense that your work has been judged as good enough.

[In my experience, when uncertainty is a feature of procrastination, it is largely connected to some other variable. In Moon's case, this is her work being judged as not good enough.]

Moon: Yeah.

Windy: What if it came back and they said, 'It wasn't good enough. You've got to change this, that and the other'? How would you take that?

Moon: I'd be disappointed that I didn't get it right the first time.

Windy: And what would that lead to?

Moon: Avoiding getting on and sending it back off.

Windy: Why would you avoid because they've given you some feedback, they've given you a tip? I imagine they would do that, wouldn't they? They wouldn't just say, 'Not good enough,' and that's it. So why would you necessarily avoid doing that?

Moon: ... Because I like to get things done where when I get things back it's been spot on what it needed to cover.

Windy: Yeah, that would be nice. It would be nice to want to have things spot on, but do you see the difference between holding an attitude which says, 'Yeah, that would be nice but I don't need it,' or, 'Yeah, that would be nice and I need it'?

[Here I am drawing from REBT the distinction between a rigid attitude and a flexible attitude.]

Moon: Yeah.

Windy: What's the difference?

Moon: ... *[Pause]* One were right, one were wrong.

Windy: In what way?

Moon: ... *[Long pause]*

Windy: In other words, is there a need for you to get things spot on or is that something that you've created?

Moon: I suppose I've created it.

Windy: Right. And can you uncreate it?

Moon: ... *[Pause]* Yeah, I think I could do.

Windy: What would you uncreate it to? What would be the new position that you would be creating?

Moon: ... *[Pause]* That getting some feedback would help in areas if I didn't get it right first time?

Windy: Right. And are we talking about this being a self-esteem issue, Moon?

Moon: Yeah.

                [While procrastination does not always involve a person's self-esteem, it often does.]

Windy: So it sounds to me that what you're avoiding is, in a way, your own judgement of yourself, because all they'd be judging is your piece of work. They're not saying, 'Oh, and by the way, Moon, you are worthless. Go away.' They'd just be saying, 'This bit of work on these criteria needs attention here, there and other ways.' And you're viewing that and saying, 'No, it had to be spot on, and the fact that it wasn't spot on means what about me?' Now, in your mind, Moon, what does it mean about you?

Moon: That I'm a failure.

Windy: That's right. Do you have a lot of clinical experience?

Moon: Yes.

Windy: With clients?

Moon: Yeah.

Windy: Somebody comes to you, then, and tells you a similar story and said, 'Look, I have been avoiding doing something because I need to have things just right the first time.' And you listen to this, and you say, 'Actually, you're right. You've got to do it exactly right the first time; otherwise, you'll be a failure. You're quite correct.' Would you say that to a client?

                [This is a feature of my SST work, I look for instances where I am reasonably sure that the client would not hold the same rigid and devaluation attitudes towards others. This gives me a 'foot in the door' in encouraging attitude change.]

Moon: No.

Windy: Would you think that about a client and not say it?

Moon: No.

Windy: Why not?

Moon: … [*Long pause*] Because I don't judge…. I don't hold high expectations of them.

Windy: Well, you can have high expectations of them, but it sounds like the kinds of expectations you've got for yourself are rigid: 'It's got to be spot on the first time or I'm a failure.' You've got two things here: you've got the rigid expectations of yourself and the judgement of you being a failure. Now, do you have high expectations of your clients or would you encourage them to have high expectations of themselves?

Moon: No.

Windy: Well, I would because high expectations means, 'I hope and I will strive to do as best as I can do. I don't have to, but I'm going to try to get the most out of myself.' Do you see the difference between those two kinds of statements?

[*Here, I make what I consider the important distinction between holding a high expectation and the attitude that brings to this situation (rigid vs flexible).*]

Moon: Yeah.

Windy: What's the difference from your perspective?

Moon: … [*Long pause*] Having high expectations … so they've got to try their best at everything they do.

Windy: Whereas to be rigid about it?

Moon: … [*Pause*] High expectations.

Windy: Plus rigidity. You can have high expectations with rigidity or without rigidity. But otherwise to have low expectations, is that a good way to encourage yourself and your clients: 'Don't expect that much from yourself'?

Moon: No, because then … they don't have to try.

Windy: That's right. So, if we put all these things together and say something like this: 'When it comes to my accreditation, what I'm going to do is I'm going to do it and hope I can get it spot on first time, and that's what I'm going to strive for, but I don't have to succeed and, if I don't, I'm not a failure.' By the way, what are you if you don't get it right, spot on the first time? What kind of person are you really in your own mind?

                  [*I realise that I am doing much of the work here, verbally. However, while Moon does not say much, she is listening attentively to what I am saying.*]

Moon: Human.

Windy: That's right, yeah. So, what I'm asking you to do is to bring the same conditions to yourself as you would with your clients; to be your own client, in a way.

Moon: I'm useless at giving myself advice, though. I never listen.

Windy: You don't listen to yourself?

Moon: Mmm [yes].

Windy: Why's that?

Moon: … [*Long pause*] I'm good at helping other people out, just not taking my own advice.

> [*I am thinking at this point that there are two issues here, (i) Moon's rigid and self-devaluation attitudes and (ii) she is unused to helping herself.*]

Windy: Because?

Moon: … I suppose I've got high expectations. I've just followed on from what everybody else had of me.

Windy: And what do they have of you?

Moon: They had really high expectations. My brothers all did OK, all went to university and they all got good qualifications, where I didn't.

Windy: And what attitude did you take towards yourself as a result?

Moon: … I took that it didn't matter. It was the taking part that counted, trying my hardest.

Windy: Right. What about the significant people, what was their attitude towards you?

Moon: That I didn't try hard enough. That I was messing about.

Windy: Which wasn't true? Is that what you're saying?

Moon: Yeah, it wasn't true. I've since found out I'm majorly dyslexic. So trying to retain information and different things it's a lot harder.

Windy: Sure, yeah. And, therefore, one could say, if it's a lot harder, you need to be a little it more flexible with yourself.

Moon: Yeah.

Windy: Whereas you seem to be rigid with yourself whether or not you're dyslexic, and that's the reason why you keep on putting things off because you don't get it right the first time, which you believe would prove what about you? Let's suppose you did your accreditation and they wrote back and they said, 'This is spot on,' how would you view you?

Moon: … That I achieved what I set out to do.

Windy: And what would that prove about you?

Moon: That I know what I'm talking about.

Windy: I see. So anybody who actually fails the accreditation the first time and then passes doesn't know what they're talking about, right?

Moon: No, just me in general.

[*It is not uncommon for a client to have one rule for others and one rule for themself. In SST, I deal with this as a habitual response which can be changed.*]

Windy: So what we're talking about is really the idea that, in a way, you've got two obstacles: one is what you tell yourself, and what you tell yourself you could apply the same thing to yourself as your clients, but the other obstacle that you said is, 'I'm useless at listening to myself.' So I'm wondering what ingredient would you have to have in place for you to start listening to yourself and taking your own good advice?

Moon: … I guess more patience with me-self.

Windy: Would you say you're impatient?

Moon: Yeah.

Windy: And, if you had more patience with yourself and you brought that to the task of accreditation and preparing the accreditation, so we brought the ingredients of, 'Look, I don't have to get this spot on the first time. If I don't, I'm not a failure and I can listen to myself even though it's going to take a bit more time than I would like,' if you brought those ingredients to the task, what difference would that make to you?

Moon: A lot.

Windy: But can you imagine doing that? Could you imagine saying, 'OK, before I sit down to do my accreditation I need to be patient with myself, recognise that I am worth listening to' – do you believe that statement, by the way, that you're worth listening to?

Moon: Yeah.

Windy: 'I'm worth listening to, and therefore I could, if I chose to, take the same healthy attitude towards myself in this task that I would encourage my clients to take. I've still got high standards but I don't have to get it spot on the first time, and I may be disappointed if I don't, but I can learn from that and move on because these are the things I really want. I really want to help people, I really want to open up doors for people who are struggling with all kinds of trauma. That's important to me.'

Moon: Yeah.

Windy: Can you imagine bringing all those ingredients together?

Moon: … Yeah, I think I could.

[*I wish I had asked Moon to put this into her own words at this point. I am definitely doing too much of the work here.*]

Windy: Because at the moment what you're doing is you've got this idea in your mind, 'I'm the kind of person who never finishes things and I'm the kind of person' – once we unpack it – 'who's got to do it spot on the first time otherwise she's a failure.' Now, with that narrative, is it any wonder that you're going to procrastinate?

Moon: No, it makes sense why, yeah.

Windy: Whereas, if we brought a different type of narrative which says, 'Yeah, I want to do it spot on the first time but I don't have to. I can learn from the feedback. I can listen to myself and be patient with myself, and I'm doing this because I really want to help people who's doors are not open, and I want to open those doors for myself so I can open some doors for them.'

Moon: Yeah.

Windy: Now, you've got a choice of those two narratives.

Moon: … [*Pause*] Definitely the second one.

Windy: Although bear in mind that it's not going to be as familiar and as natural to you as the first one.

Moon: Yeah, I know. It sounds good. It just feels a little bit uncomfortable.

Windy: Yeah, but the question is are you going to see that discomfort through or are you going to back away from it and go for the familiar?

Moon: No, I'm gonna definitely give it a go.

Windy: So why don't you summarise, in your own words, where we've got to at the moment?

               [*A little late, but better late than never!*]

Moon: … Just going easier on myself and taking my own advice. Being able to self-care myself as I do when I'm talking to my clients.

Windy: And to recognise that you still may want to avoid, because that's the habit, but you have a choice to go along with the habit or go uncomfortably against the habit initially until you develop a new habit.

Moon: ... Yeah, because I'm good at helping others. It's just ... I don't really know why I'm so hard on myself. I guess ... [*pause*] it comes more natural than just being gentler with myself.

Windy: Have you had personal therapy as part of your training?

Moon: Yeah.

Windy: So you may want to reflect on that and ask yourself the question, 'What is it in my past that might account for me being hard on myself now?' But, in a way, from my perspective, it doesn't really matter that much where it came from. It's where you want to take it in the future.

[*This is an important point, in conventional therapy, we may have gone back at this point, but in SST, we go forward.*]

Moon: Yeah, definitely.

Windy: And, so you could say, 'Yeah, I got this somewhere in my past,' and you can go into it, but I often say, in going into the past with procrastination, you're procrastinating on dealing with the procrastination in the present.

Moon: Yeah.

Windy: So you could say, 'Yeah, I have been hard on myself. I can continue to do that or I could actually learn to be more gentle with myself. That's going to be uncomfortable but it's worth doing for me because I want to develop a new attitude towards myself and it's worth doing it for my clients.' Now, can you see this new narrative that we're talking about here you can generalise to other areas of your life?

[*Asking for generalisation at this point is a little early, and my use of time is not the best, but I would raise the issue of generalisation at the wrong time than not raise it at all.*]

Moon: Yeah, definitely.

Windy: In what areas do you think you might be able to generalise it to?

Moon: ... Anything that I'm giving myself a hard time about.

Windy: What kinds of things are they?

Moon: ... [*Pause*] Me reading – if I've got a book, if I get some of the words wrong, I tend to be hard on myself instead of just acknowledging that it's OK the fact that I got it wrong and just try again.

Windy: Then, if you find yourself getting hard on yourself, you can notice that and recognise that you don't have to continue with that. In other words, just because you've started off being hard on yourself, does that mean you have to continue?

Moon: No, it doesn't.

Windy: It's what I call the opposite of Magnus Magnusson, the compere on *Mastermind*. 'I've started but I don't have to finish.'

Moon: Yeah, definitely.

Windy: Is there anything that we haven't touched on that's important to touch on to help you with your accreditation at 12:30 today?

Moon: No, I don't think so. I think it's just reminding myself to not be so hard on myself and to enjoy the process.

Windy: When you talk to yourself, Moon, do you talk to yourself as 'you' or 'I'?

Moon: ... [*Pause*] I haven't really thought about that.... [*Long pause*] 'I', I guess.

Windy: So let's compare two different versions. Let's take the idea that you're reading and you come across some words that are difficult for you. Let's first of all hear the self-critical, hard-on-yourself version out loud. What would that sound like?

Moon: … 'You know that word wasn't right. … [*Pause*] Do you have to be so stupid? … [*Pause*] No wonder it doesn't make sense because that didn't make sense. No wonder you don't get it right every time.'

Windy: Incidentally, when you talk to yourself, it is as 'you', isn't it?

Moon: OK, yeah.

Windy: Now, let's hear you talk to yourself from a more easy-on-yourself position, not hard on yourself, more self-accepting and self-compassionate? What does that sound like?

Moon: … [*Long pause*] 'You can try it again and just go slower as you're reading it.… [*Pause*] It's OK that you made a mistake. Just try again.'

Windy: Do you see the differences in feeling between those two?

Moon: Yeah.

Windy: Which comes more natural to you?

Moon: Yeah, the first one, a lot harsher.

Windy: Yeah, but more natural because you've been practising it. That's what I'm saying. It's important to recognise realistically that the harsher will come up first, but just because it comes up first, you can say, 'No, I'm not going to go along with that narrative, actually, because it's not true. I don't have to. I wouldn't treat my clients like that and I'm not going to treat myself like that. So I'm going to treat myself differently. I'm going to be more patient with myself and I'm worth doing it for.'

[Here I am outlining that Moon can expect her more habitual self-response to come up first, but that she can respond to this in a productive way]

Moon: Yeah.

Windy: I think that's an important maybe step forward for you, to give you something that actually puts you in the table. How long do you think accreditation will take you from this point to actually handing it in?

Moon: ... *[Pause]* I'd probably send it to my supervisor first just have a quick read through it. So within the month.

Windy: And can you take that, 'I'll do it at specific times,' because I think that would be helpful to you?

Moon: Yeah.

Windy: So it would be interesting to see what happens when you get that. I would just add the ingredient that you don't have to know now that it's going to be spot on later, because, unless you have one of these, Moon – you see that?

Moon: Yeah.

Windy: What is it?

Moon: A crystal ball.

Windy: Unfortunately, this one doesn't work.

Moon: Yeah, my magic wand broke.

[With online work, I sometimes use visual representations of points. In this case, I showed Moon a crystal ball. She got the humour and responded in kind.]

Windy: I've got mine here, all intact just in case. So have you got what you've come for today?

Moon: Yeah, I think I have. It's just reminding myself to go easier on myself instead of giving myself such a hard time.

Windy: Right, and that that's a habit that's going to be uncomfortable to implement because you're not used to it.

Moon: Yeah, definitely.

Windy: OK, well, it was nice to meet you and I'll send you this material through in due course, OK?

Moon: OK, lovely. Thank you very much.

Moon's Reflections (29/08/23)

I found the single session thought-provoking, to think that in one session it helped me from the questions asked, the tone of voice and the calm demeanour of Windy, helped me look at my thought process.

I have always been a procrastinator, but after I had the single session, I have found I am getting on with things, it feels uplifting to know that the block I had always come up against has now disappeared. It's great to get things done and not find any excuse to get things completed. Thank you, Windy Dryden

8

For Every Problem, There Is a Solution

Date: 28/04/23
Time: 34 minutes 53 secs

Windy: So, Margo, what's your understanding of the purpose of our conversation today?

Margo: To discuss a little bit about my procrastination, hopefully get a better understanding for myself about what I need to do to take some steps forward. I understand that it will be transcribed and that it will be in a book, which is fine. And you'll be sharing the recording with me as well.

Windy: Yes, that's right. And, if I helped you with that understanding that you're looking for, what do you hope that understanding would lead to?

[In SST, when clients mention that they are looking for 'understanding', I suggest asking them want they hope such understanding would lead to, as I did with Margo.]

Margo: Lead to action on my part.

Windy: And are you clear about what action you'd like to take?

Margo: Yes.

Windy: We can talk about that a little bit later. So why don't you tell me what particular issue you have with procrastination currently?

Margo:	I think the biggest one currently is probably procrastinating about my paperwork for work, actually. So session notes, just the general gist and then also the assessments.
Windy:	So you have to write assessments?
Margo:	Yes.
Windy:	And you have to write session notes?
Margo:	Yes. It's not that I don't know how to do it. I'm very good at it. I'm... pretty lazy about it.
Windy:	What do you mean by lazy?
	[*In SST, clarity is an important principle, so I tend to ask clients to be clear about what they mean by words such as 'lazy', which are general and pejorative.*]
Margo:	I just don't really want to do it.
Windy:	OK, yeah. I guess there are two versions of that, because you could say, 'I don't really wanna do it so I won't do it,' or, 'I don't really wanna do it but I will do it.'
Margo:	Yes.
Windy:	So which route do you take?
Margo:	I know that I will eventually do it. I just put it off and put it off and put it off.
Windy:	When will you do it?
Margo:	Usually the end of the month I get anxious about it and I end up doing as much as I can within a short timeframe.
Windy:	And will get into trouble if you didn't do it in your job?
Margo:	No.

Windy: So you could not write session notes, you could not do assessments and you could still do your job and you wouldn't get into trouble about it?

Margo: I could charge everything and my supervisor doesn't really pay attention very much to the paperwork. The only thing that could happen is if ... insurance actually pulls the records and wants to see it and then they could ask for money back.

Windy: And you'd have to pay it out of your own pocket or what?

Margo: Yeah.

Windy: Does that happen a lot?

Margo: No. Very rarely.

Windy: From an external point of view there doesn't seem to be too many costs. There's this vague idea that you might have to pay some money back but that's unlikely. But, other than that, there's nobody checking on you. Your line manager doesn't seem to be involved at all in that. So I guess it's you and you, isn't it? It's your relationship with you on this one.

Margo: Yeah.

Windy: So the question is do you have any values as a person or a professional that it's important for us to bring into the space and talk about on this issue?

Margo: I guess so.... [*Pause*] As a professional, I know I'm doing what I need to do.... If anyone's having very serious issues, like if they're suicidal, I'm making sure to document right away, I'm making sure to do all of the safety planning, I'm making sure to assist them with that, if I see anyone who has any psychotic features, I'm making sure to address those.

Windy: And you're writing them up as well, are you, or are you putting those off as well?

Margo: I'm not putting those off. Those usually get done right away.

Windy: Why aren't you putting those off?

Margo: Because I feel like ... [*pause*], if the person ends up going to the hospital or they need immediate care or something terrible happens, then I wanna make sure that I'm covered and that my notes can provide some assistance if they need to go to the hospital.

Windy: So there's a defensive aspect of it: 'I wanna make sure that I'm covered.'

Margo: Yes.

Windy: But there's also an altruistic aspect of it, isn't there: 'I wanna make sure that their care is covered because I've actually provided that cover.'

Margo: Yes.

Windy: How would you put that in terms of percentages? How much altruism – I'm calling it altruism, I don't know whether that's the right word, but certainly defensiveness – how much of each would you say is there?

Margo: The defensive is probably more like 90% and 10%... to assist my patients, because ... usually, if they're going to seek more immediate care, then their presentation is already so apparent.

Windy: Yeah, your notes may not add much to it because it's in their face, so to speak.

Margo: Yes, exactly.

Windy: It's interesting, the picture you paint of yourself in certain areas of your life, Margo – I'll use one of your words, one of my words – that you're somewhat lazy and concerned about covering your own back.

Margo: Yes.

Windy: Is that how you like to see yourself as a professional?

Margo: No.

Windy: How would you like to see yourself as a professional?

Margo: … Responsive and responsible.

Windy: But we know you've got these other two in the locker, don't we?

Margo: Yeah.

Windy: So, it's a question about what are you gonna do with those in the locker? Are you gonna keep them in the locker? Are you gonna bring them out and put them on the desk and say, 'Well, this is me, lazy and defensive,' or, 'responsible and responsive.' So it sounds like you've got two Margos in there, and I think you'll always have two Margos in there. I think we've all got two Margos in us, in a way. The question is, which one do you want to hold sway in your professional life?

          [*This is a common feature of my work with people who procrastinate, helping them see that they have a procrastinating part and a responsive part.*]

Margo: Yeah, definitely. I feel like with the interactions with my clients I definitely show them the responsiveness and responsible.

Windy: And I'm sure you do. We're not talking about that. We're not talking about you in the room. We're talking about you doing the other stuff.

Margo: Yes.

Windy: Do you wanna be lazy and defensive there or do you wanna be responsible and responsive there as well?

Margo: Responsible and responsive.

Windy: OK. So, in a way, if you want to do that, you gonna have to have some way of actually responding to you, yourself, when you say, quite accurately, 'I don't want to do this now.'

Margo: Yeah.

Windy: Which is fine because I guess there's a lot of things that you and I don't want to do but we do 'em.

Margo: Yes.

Windy: So the question is how are you gonna respond to that part of yourself? What's your image of how you'd like to be with the assessments and notetaking before we get into that? What would you like to achieve as a result of our discussion in this part of your life?

Margo: I'd like to have more of a plan, an action plan. So I've already talked to myself and said, 'I'm gonna make sure I do them every night before leaving the office,' but that doesn't work, because sometimes I work until nine at night and that's just not possible and sometimes I have ten sessions, and I am not at all in the headspace to do those after ten sessions.

Windy: That's right, yeah. The question is, 'When am I going to do this that maximises my chances of doing it and that gives me a sense that I'm not putting it off and leaving it until the last minute?'

Margo: I think every week I do supervision with my supervisor and it's on one of my days off, and I think right after that maybe eat something but then do that. I think that would be the perfect time because the cases are fresh in my head, I'm already more in work mode.

Windy:　So you have supervision with your supervisor. That lasts for how long?

Margo:　An hour.

Windy:　So you have an hour. Then straight after that how long have you got?

Margo:　I'm off for the day so however long I want.

Windy:　So how long do you think that will take you to write your notes and your assessments up?

Margo:　If I do it regularly for a week, like just for a week, it will take me maybe two to three hours.

Windy:　You mean if you did it as a habit a week, it will take you two to three hours directly after the supervision.

Margo:　Yes, because that will be like 20 to 30 notes and any assessments that I have.

Windy:　And these will be fresh in your mind because you would have covered some of them in your supervision.

Margo:　Yeah.

Windy:　What do you do now in those two to three hours that follow your supervision?

Margo:　It depends how I feel. Lately, I've been just going and taking a nap.

Windy:　Because you're tired?

Margo:　Yeah.

Windy:　Right, OK.

Margo: But other times I just go in and I'll have some food and I'll hang out a bit with my husband and my dog and just not do a lot.

Windy: Is that not doing a lot recuperative, because it sounds like you are tired? What do you attribute your tiredness to?

Margo: Unfortunately, I have severe sleep apnoea, and I use a machine and everything, but I feel like it's also stress too.

Windy: Stress?

Margo: Yeah, I think that contributes to my being tired.

Windy: What kind of stress?

Margo: Well, sometimes there's client situations that come up, but also I'm the only breadwinner for my family. My husband's not employed, he hasn't been employed for nearly four years now. So I'm the one who's bringing in all the income.

Windy: Right. That would be the case whether you did the notes or not, wouldn't it?

Margo: Yes.

Windy: My thinking is that I wanna help you to create the environment that works for you rather than against you.

Margo: Yes.

Windy: So what you've tried to do before is really to pick a time which was really a bad time – it was like after nine hours of this. I'm just wondering if the time that we've got, that you've chosen, the two or three hours after the supervision which might mean at times you would do that even though you're tired, whether that would be a good thing for you or not, health-wise.

Margo: I think it would be OK.

Windy: So can you imagine then a scenario where you've just had the supervision and you sit down and you say, 'OK, I'm now gonna write up these notes. I don't want to do them,' because you don't, 'but I'm going to do them. Why? Because I want to be as responsive and responsible as I can be outside the clinical room as I am inside the clinical room. That's important to me because those values are important to me. I have it in my locker to be defensive and lazy, but I'm not gonna choose to bring those aspects out on this occasion.' Could you imagine doing that?

[While it may seem that I am doing a lot of the work, I do get the sense that Margo is actively involved in the conversation.]

Margo: Yes. Yes.... I could very well imagine doing that.

Windy: And, as you imagine doing that, does any obstacle form in your mind? You could say, 'OK, yeah, that's gonna solve the problem. I've now seen that I've chosen the right time. I'm accessing the parts of me that I wanna access. I'm recognising that I don't wanna do it but I can do it. I don't have to always want to do things. So I'm pretty confident there's nothing gonna stop me to do that.' Or you might say, 'Yeah, but there might be a little obstacle coming up which I will have to deal with.' So what's your view on the obstacles or the no obstacles, Margo?

Margo: I'm sure there will be obstacles.... I'm ... thinking ... if my dog wants to play, because at this point in time it will have been an hour after my husband's been taking care of her because she recently had surgery, so we have to stop her from doing things.

Windy: OK. So your supervision, is it online?

Margo: Yes.

Windy: So you're at home?

Margo: Yes.

Windy: And where are you doing the supervision?

Margo: Here, in a spare bedroom right here where I am now.

Windy: So where's the dog?

Margo: She's outside the bedroom. She's with my husband.

Windy: So how are we gonna deal with that obstacle? The dog may want to play with Margo.

Margo: Yeah.

Windy: What potential ways could we find of responding to that so it's not obstacle?

Margo: Well, treats or just having her lay down or ... confining her a bit, so putting her somewhere where she's less likely to be so needy.

Windy: And what's your husband's role here?

Margo: He'll be doing housework or he'll be going to stretch his back because he has back problems.

Windy: Can you recruit him to help you? The reason I say that is, as part of single-session therapy, only you can do this but you don't have to do it alone. Your husband can be on your team.

Margo: Yes.

Windy: The dog's gonna be the dog.

Margo: Yeah.

Windy: But can you recruit your husband to help you with this?

Margo: Yeah, I think so.

Windy: How would you do that vis-à-vis the dog?

Margo: Just letting him know that, if she becomes too much, I might need his help. Like if I can't do what I need to do, then I will need to ask for his help.

Windy: And, if you explained to him why you're doing that, what do you think his likely response is gonna be?

Margo: … It depends. I think most of the time he'll be like, 'Yep, that's fine.' Other times he'll say something along the lines of, 'Well, I need to do all these different things and I've been dealing with her all this time. You need to take care of her too.'

Windy: Right, OK. What I'm saying is, if you can get an agreement with him to say, 'There are these two to three hours afterwards that I've really set aside because I really wanna get the problem, because it's gonna help me to be less stressed at work. If I'm less stressed at work, there's gonna be a hold load of benefits. Can you help me out here?'

[*Here, I am encouraging Margo to utilise the external resources available to her.*]

Margo: I think he would be very happy to help me out there.

Windy: I think it's the way you frame it. If you put it in a frame which really helps him to see that he could be helpful to you.

Margo: Yes.

Windy: So we've dealt with the dog. Let me put the obvious – what about if Margo wants to play with the dog?

Margo: Yeah, that's the thing.

Windy: We know about how to deal with the dog, but how are we gonna deal with Margo and the dog?

Margo: Yeah. I think for me I can use it more as a reward. I can get her to calm down and I can get her to just hang out.

Windy: So your reward is actually rewarding the doing of the notes and the assessment, isn't it? 'After the assessments and the notes I get to play with the dog.'

Margo: Yes.

Windy: So you might do a bit of behavioural contracting: 'No playing with the dog until I've done this work, and then I can play with the dog as much as I'd like.'

Margo: Yeah.

Windy: Do you think that would actually be a good way of dealing with that obstacle of you and the dog?

[*Having helped Margo to identify a way of dealing with the named obstacle, I ask her for opinion of it.*]

Margo: Yeah, I think that would be helpful.

Windy: Any other obstacles that would come up?

Margo: Just being tired. So caffeinated myself.

Windy: OK.

Margo: … Which is not really a bad thing, but distractions are another.

Windy: OK. So the caffeinating yourself you're willing to do.

Margo: Oh yes.

Windy: And what kind of distractions? I can't see the room. Is this the room you do your notes in as well?

Margo: No. I go into the living room and I'll sit down with my dog and then I'll do notes there.

Windy: OK.

Margo: A lot of the time I'll try to in between sessions. Like, if I have a cancellation, I'll try to do notes then or, if I have breaks, I'll do notes then, and that seems to work out pretty well too.

Windy: Yeah, you could do both. You could actually reserve this time and do the notes under those conditions. It sounds like, if you do the notes under the other conditions, you may not need to spend as much time with the notes after the supervision as you plan to do.

Margo: Yes.

Windy: You mentioned distractions, Margo. What distractions?

Margo: Literally anything. I allow myself to get distracted by anything: a text message ... somebody's watching TV and, oh, I want to watch that.

Windy: Sorry, who's watching TV?

Margo: Anyone. My husband.

Windy: Or the dog?

Margo: Or my mum.

Windy: So, I'm wondering if the living room is the best environment for you to do those notes.

Margo: Fair point. But the only other places are bedrooms and they have a bed, which is not good for me.

Windy: No, I agree. Where are you sitting at the moment?

Margo: In the spare bedroom and there's a bed right there.

Windy: And you're sitting on it?

Margo: No, I'm sitting in a chair and I have a curtain backdrop.

Windy: Is it a real curtain?

Margo: No, it's a sheet.

Windy: It's a real sheet, not one of those virtual sheets that you find.

Margo: No, it's an actual bedsheet.

Windy: And, when you do your notes, do you do them on the computer?

Margo: Yes.

Windy: Have you got a computer in front of you?

Margo: Yes.

Windy: So I'm curious, let me play devil's advocate for a minute and then you can shoot me down. The devil would say, a nice devil, 'Well, look, if distractions are gonna be a problem for you and you've got this environment that seems to be walled away from those distractions, why not maximise the chances of you being responsible and responsive and do it there?'

Margo: … It's a very uncomfortable chair.

Windy: Right. Do you have any comfortable chairs in the place?

Margo: Yes, but it's an odd setup.

Windy: Do you understand where I'm coming from?

Margo: Yes.

Windy: Where do you think I'm coming from?

Margo: Well, if there's distractions in that area that you would most likely work in, then why not find an area where there are less distractions?

Windy: Yeah.

Margo: And it's not like I can't go to the library: it's right down the street. Or even a coffee house. I probably wouldn't go to a coffee house just because my screen could be seen.

Windy: Yeah.

Margo: The library would be fine, though, because there's not many people. I can find a corner where no one can see anything.

Windy: And the library will be open in the two to three hours that you've nominated to this task?

Margo: Yeah.

Windy: Well, what do you think of that idea, Margo?

Margo: I like it.

Windy: Also, the dog is not going to be distractive.

Margo: Yeah, and I can grab a coffee on my way if I want to.

Windy: Yeah, to get caffeinated, and the thing is to bring your husband on board.

Margo: Yes.

          [Here, I am encouraging Margo to make her environment work for her and ask her husband to support her.]

Windy: Let me paint a picture for you. You've got these different aspects of yourself: you've got the lazy and watch-your-back type Margo, you've got the responsive, responsible Margo. The responsive, responsible Margo comes out to the fore in the counselling room. At the moment, the 'I don't wanna do this' Margo has actually come to the fore with the notes, because you've said, 'Well, I don't wanna do, therefore I ain't gonna do it. End of.' What I'm saying is that you can still not want to do it and still do it.

Margo: Yes.

Windy: Are you OK with that idea? It's possible to do something you don't wanna do?

Margo: Yes. I do it all the time. Yes.

Windy: So just bring your strengths from those experiences to this area, because it's in your interest to do it because you wanna do it, you want to be on top of it, you want to be responsible and responsive. Is it true to say as well that, if you are on top of things more, it relieves some aspect of stress for you?

[Note that I am encouraging Margo to bring her strengths in one area to the one we are discussing.]

Margo: Yeah, absolutely.

Windy: And that's important to you.

Margo: Yeah.

Windy: So it's a stress reduction way, it gives you an opportunity to bring the parts of you that you wanna bring to the table more, we can deal with some of the contextual aspects of it and just play to those particular, both personal, interpersonal and environmental strengths.

Margo: Yeah.

Windy: Now, when I put it like that, what do you think of the chances of you actually following through on what you wanna do?

Margo: Pretty good.

Windy: Now, in England 'pretty' means 'not very'. So I have to be clear here. What are we talking about? Very good?

Margo: 75–80% yes.

Windy: So what's the 20% that we need to deal with to really get it up into the 90s?

Margo: … The… [*pause*], I think just… the bottom line is it doesn't matter, I'm going to do it. Like whatever else is going on, it's like, 'OK … it could be bad weather. OK, well, that's fine, I can still drive there. It's not a big deal. I could not be feeling well, but then it's like I should still make sure to do as much as I can.'

Windy: You see what you're saying here, Margo, is so impressive, because what you're saying is that you're bringing a 'for every problem there is a solution' mindset to this issue.

                [*Here, I compliment the client. This practice comes from narrative therapy, and I am happy to draw upon this work.*]

Margo: Yes.

Windy: Is that something that is one of your strengths in life?

Margo: Yeah, I think I'm a fairly positive person. I think I'm more positive for everyone else.

Windy: Well, this might also give you an opportunity to really be positive for yourself, doesn't it? To really prioritise this whole thing because it is important for you to do it.

Margo: Yes.

Windy: You don't wanna do it, but it's important for you to do it because it's gonna be stress-relieving, it's gonna access parts of you that you want to show up more in the workplace.

Margo: Yes.

Windy: So why don't you just summarise what we've talked about and particularly what you're gonna take away from our conversation today?

Margo: So we've talked about the aspects of procrastination that I've been struggling with, specifically with documentation for work. And what characteristics do I want to show and be present in my work even if it's not with the clients? So making sure that I'm holding myself accountable as well, because practising what you preach too. And bringing aspects of a very positive mindset of, 'I can do this. Whatever obstacle there is, I can definitely manage it.' I need to just get in my head that there is no action otherwise. Like this is it. It's not like it's a voluntary thing. This is part of the work. I don't get to have the fun in sessions and the good aspect that all clinicians like and not do the aspect that we don't like.

Windy: Yeah. Well, there's always the option to procrastinate, because you've been exercising that option.

Margo: Yes.

Windy: But the question is do you want to exercise that option? That's the question.

Margo: Right.

Windy: There is an option, but do you wanna access it? And it sounds like you don't want to.

Margo: No, I don't, and I wanna actually start doing the things that I tell my clients to do.

Windy: Even though it's true that you don't want to do them at that time.

Margo: Yes.

Windy: Is that one of the things that you help the clients to realise: that you may not want to do something but it may be in your interest to do it, so don't let not wanting to do it stop you from doing it.

Margo: Yes.

Windy: So, then you can bring yourself into that frame as well. Is there anything you wanna mention about this issue or ask me about it, Margo, before we finish?

Margo: … [*Long pause*] I don't think so, no. But thank you, I do appreciate your time.

Windy: Have you got what you've come for?

Margo: Yes.

Windy: Which is what?

Margo: I have an action plan.

Windy: Right. This is what you wanted right from the start.

Margo: Yes.

Windy: You've got the understanding and the action plan.

               [*Here I am tying things up, helping Margo to see that she has got what she wanted from the session.*]

Margo: Yes.

Windy: Great. Lovely to meet you, Margo.

Margo: Nice to meet you too.

Margo's Reflections (07/08/23)

When I think back to my session with Windy, two things stand out to me. The first thing is that I have a lot more to work on than just my procrastination. I think this was highlighted to me when I started mentioning everything else in my session, i.e., my relationship with my husband. In my opinion, this means that I could not stay focused because I am not processing what I am going through. I have started seeing a therapist for this reason and will try to continue to see a therapist consistently throughout my career so that I can have some additional accountability and oversight of my thinking process. Windy did a great job of redirecting me and coaching me in a non-judgemental way.

The second thing that stood out to me is that I was very focused on Windy mispronouncing my name. He did not pronounce my name correctly after pronouncing it correctly at first. This stuck in my mind during most of the session. I recognize that this is inconsequential and I saw that I might be using this as something for me to focus on rather than myself. Therefore, I continued to try to focus myself back to what Windy was saying.

When Windy reflected back to me about how I want to see myself outside of the clinical work, that was very impactful. For the next month, I would reflect back on wanting to be responsible and have integrity in my work when I thought about my notes. I have also received additional coaching on my procrastination, as I am practicing with other helping professions who are learning how to coach. By allowing this additional coaching to influence my work ethic, I feel that I have stopped focusing on the sinking feeling of being behind and have started to make it a goal of completing paperwork during missed/cancelled session times to avoid doing work outside of work. The ability to keep 'work' at work is the benefit that I need to see for myself, which seems to be a helpful motivator. Soon, I might start scheduling paperwork sessions in my work week to help me stay current.

The outcome of this session has fluctuated. I fluctuate between being on time and being behind with my notes. At the moment, when I am writing this, I am about two weeks behind on my paperwork. However, 1 week after my session with Windy, I was caught up on my paperwork. I never took the actions that Windy and I talked about, i.e. going to the library to complete my paperwork on Fridays. Unfortunately, health issues arose that became more of the central focus of my life over the last few months. And as I continue to deal with those health issues, and they become less central, I expect that I will be better at holding myself accountable for my paperwork.

9

Towards an Energised Self and Dealing with Discomfort and Uncertainty

Date: 28/04/23
Time: 42 minutes 7 secs

Windy: So, Belle, what's your understanding of the purpose of our conversation today?

Belle: To talk about something ... that I find I procrastinate on, perhaps to reflect on procrastination itself and then for it to be used as a transcript in a future book.... And, yeah, I think that's a short summary.

Windy: So what are you procrastinating on at the moment?

Belle: Ooh, which one to pick? I'm gonna go for the big one, because there's the daily little things and then there's the big one. I think the big one is probably moving jobs. Yeah, so it's a big decision, but I've gone for that one because I think that's what I struggle with more: those sort of big decisions, even when I've got all the information to make those decisions, usually.

Windy: So let me be as clear as I can. So, at the moment you are in a job?

Belle: Yeah, two jobs.

Windy: You're in two jobs?

Belle: Hmm-mmm [yes].

Windy: What, two half jobs?

Belle: Yeah, pretty much. It's a sort of 80% / 20% split.

Windy: So that's the current situation. And the one that is on the horizon and a possibility for you to move to is what?

Belle: So it's the job that I'm moving from is in the same field that I'm moving to. So the idea would be to move from just one counselling position to another. But, because I currently have two jobs, the idea would be to also do something different. So to move from two jobs to a different two jobs, and those ones on the horizon would be in counselling and also in teaching and training.

Windy: So the two on the horizon, have they been offered to you? What's the status?

Belle: No, but it's sort of moving into that career and I'm quite confident that the work I can find is there. So it's not like I'm accepting a job offer to move tomorrow, but it is to say I am gonna quit this job and move to something different.

Windy: So let me be clear again. At the moment you are being employed?

Belle: Yeah.

Windy: By two different organisations?

Belle: Yeah.

Windy: And the positions that you will be moving to, are they also employed positions or self-employed positions?

Belle: That's what it is. So the teacher element would be a training position and the counselling would be moving into private practice.

Windy: So the counselling would be moving into private practice. The training position – would you be setting up your own training business?

Belle: No, it would be teaching, sorry. It would be moving into a teaching post.

Windy: Yeah, but what I'm trying to understand is who's gonna be employing you in that teaching post?

Belle: So that would be a school. So there's a lot of work in schools that I can get quite easily because of my background.

Windy: So, even though there isn't one that's been offered to you, you're pretty confident that you could get that job should you indicate that you were interested in a position like that.

Belle: Yeah, there's a lot of work available.

[I have found it very important in helping someone deal with a procrastination issue that I have a full understanding of the relevant context]

Windy: I understand you. Now, tell me about how you're stopping yourself from going from the current two to the planned two?

Belle: So the jobs that are on the horizon, like I say they're not an offered position but it's something where I know I can get work. Private practice is obviously something a little bit more risky, but the job itself in teaching is something where I know I can get work easily. The sort of thing that's stopping me is … I think it's my worry that I'm looking at that as the grass is greener and saying, 'This is the answer to my problems and this is a better field,' and I've just got this massive doubt that it's all gonna go wrong; that it's not gonna be a good experience.

Windy: Which is not going to be a good experience?

Belle: Any move. And I think that's why it's quite vague at the moment and why I haven't actually gone, 'Right, there's a position and I'm gonna take it.' It's because just the idea of that move is ... really ... scary, and I think it's just the risk factor of what if it goes wrong. I could give you a lot of those, a lot of 'what ifs'.

Windy: Can you give me a lot of answers to the 'what ifs'?

Belle: Oh gosh.... So, 'What if it goes wrong?' would be multiple things: what if financially it goes wrong? ... I think I've got savings, so I don't think that actually is that big a risk. I'm financially comfortable. I don't feel like I would be ... homeless or anything. I've got a lot of support behind me as well. I've got a lot of family, my partner, people who would support me financially. Again, that would be really, really catastrophic to waste all of my money and not get any job at all, to use all my savings and then have to be ringing people. I can't even imagine that happening. So, yeah, I don't think financially – I answered that one quite quickly – it's probably as much of a risk as I think it is, but it's the one I tell myself a lot.

Windy: Yeah, but you don't then move to the next stage. You're just saying, 'What if it doesn't work out financially?' and then you stop, presumably because you're regarding that as catastrophic, so you stop thinking about it. And, when I asked you to think about it, you said, 'Well, I've got savings, I've got people to support me,' and then you surprised yourself by saying, 'I answered that pretty quickly.'

Belle: Yeah.

Windy: So I'm wondering whether that's a prototype of what happens to you: that you come up with a 'what if', you don't answer it and therefore you don't use your problem-solving faculties to say, 'OK, if this happens, this is a problem. These are my possible solutions.' I wonder if you don't do that.

Belle: Yeah, I think, if anything, if I do do that, it is the catastrophic thinking, so I will answer it with that automatic answer of..., 'What if it's a financial risk?' and then my answer will be, 'Well, yeah, it could be and you could waste all your savings.' So I'll go to that answer instead of going to the other answer.

Windy: OK, but then, having wasted all your savings, then what?

Belle: ... Then, yeah, I'm ringing round. Well, I'm not homeless because I know I've got family that would put me up. ... And I know from myself, my own resilience and that, I would work anywhere. So, if the job didn't work, I'd just go and get a normal job not in my field.

Windy: That's right. So what would it feel like to think it through like that, to work it through like that, to actually look at the catastrophe straight in the eye and say, 'Yeah, I wouldn't like that,' but there's life after the catastrophe. It's almost like you think there's no life after the catastrophe; you stop thinking.

Belle: Yeah. I think what happens is I don't even go into a memory because I can't think of a time when I've been completely financially unstable or panicked. In fact, the times in my life when I've had the least money I've felt the most secure. So, yeah, to look it straight in the eye, you're going, 'Where's this come from? Where's that habit come from?'

Windy: Well, yes, you can ask yourself where it's come from or you could say, 'Where am I going to?'

Belle: Yeah. That's harder.

Windy: In other words, you could have a look at all the 'what ifs' before we look at me helping you to see how you create the 'what ifs' in the first place. You could actually come up with a 'what if' and say, 'Well, what if this happens? So what if? I will do this.'

Belle: Yeah.

Windy: Just give me another 'what if' example and then we can see how you get on with that one?

Belle: Yeah, what if I lose all my money? ... [*Pause*] This is gonna sound a strange one: what if the environment is awful in a new job? So within that 'what if' what if they people are horrible? What if I don't like something as simple as the office that I'm in and it's a horrible environment to work in? What if the environment is horrible?

Windy: OK. Then what are the options?

Belle: So my mind immediately goes, 'Well, I'd leave if it was that bad.'

Windy: Yeah, and go where?

Belle: Somewhere else.

Windy: Right.

Belle: Yeah.... It sounds so simple.... And I have done that before as well.

Windy: Yeah. We're only saying if this happens. We have no idea whether or not it's gonna happen. But I think you've got a problem-solving brain which you don't use because you're so busy saying, 'Wouldn't it be catastrophic if this happened? Full stop, close the book, not making a decision, thank you very much, because I don't wanna go down that route.'

Belle: Yeah.

Windy: As opposed to open the book, 'This is what I'm gonna do with the finances, this is what I'm gonna do if the working environment is not to my taste, and I'll rely on my problem-solving.

[Here, I am using my 'book analogy' strategy where instead of responding to a 'catastrophic' situation in their mind with 'closing the book after Chapter 1, the person is encouraged to go on to further chapters with a problem-solving mindset.]

Belle: Yeah.

Windy: Do you understand how you create the 'what ifs'?

Belle: Yeah.

Windy: How do you create them?

Belle: Well, I think I do. I feel like I create them from memories that aren't real. So I take a situation where I perhaps didn't quite like the environment where I worked, maybe I've worked somewhere before that was a little bit noisy or a little bit too hot or a bit too cold or maybe one person wasn't very nice, and I take that and I make it into a massive ball of, 'What if it's all worse?'

Windy: It sounds like to me, and you correct me if I'm wrong on that one, that you start off with a sense of what's important to you, and what's important to you is, 'I like a working environment where everything is to my taste.'

Belle: Yeah.

Windy: 'The people are to my taste, the office is to my taste, the wallpaper's to my taste, the colour of the carpet's to my taste, etc.' Now, listen, from my perspective don't change that because it's what's important to you and that's not the problem. Are you interested in my perspective on this, by the way?

Belle: Yeah, absolutely. I was thinking you were gonna say the opposite then.

[I wish I had clarified what Belle meant by this.]

Windy: So you tell me which route you take that leads you to get stuck? They both start the same way, which is: 'It's important for me that all the major aspects of the work environment are to my taste and that's how it must be. Wouldn't it be terrible if there's any one that didn't work out for me?' So that's what we call the rigid mindset. The flexible mindset again starts off the same way: 'It's really important to me that all the elements of my working environment are to my taste, but, sadly and regretfully, it doesn't have to be that way. That's not great, but my job is to say it hasn't got to be perfect but I need to think about is it good enough at this point in my life?'

                 [*I am bringing to my conversation with Belle insights from REBT – see Chapter 3.*]

Belle: Yeah.

Windy: Now, which attitude do you think you bring to the table that leads to your putting things off, Belle?

Belle: Yeah, absolutely the first one.

Windy: Yeah.

Belle: I've never looked at it like that.

Windy: What would life be like, Belle, if you brought the second mindset to the table?

Belle: … I think it would be different. I definitely think it would be different. I don't think I've ever seen how rigid it is until you've just said there about everything being perfect.

Windy: Yeah.

Belle: I really think, yeah, I can't imagine tolerating stuff even though I know I have in a lot of environments. No environment is perfect, but I just don't think in that way.

Windy: Well, no, but I think that's why you need to get some practice of thinking that way because any shift from a rigid mindset to a flexible mindset involves doing what you have to do with any habit and that is practise thinking the new way and reminding yourself, look, the old habit's gonna come up first because it's well practised, but the new one is to say, wait a minute, does it have to be that way? Or does it not have to be that way? Is there a law of the universe that says Belle has to have a perfect working environment or has she just created that and is creating procrastination that goes along with it?

Belle: Yeah.

Windy: I'm quite happy to accept any evidence that you have that there is a law of the universe that says that Belle has to have exactly the perfect working environment. Have you got any?

Belle: … No, I don't think so. Actually, when you say that, I think most of my memories of my happiest jobs have been in chaos, surprisingly.

Windy: Yeah. So I think you haven't connected the different parts of your brain together, and that's what I think you need to do. Actually, I think, probably, once you start to look at things from a more flexible mindset, it does open your mind up to the reality that you were probably happier when things were more chaotic and things like that.

Belle: Yeah.

Windy: So, if we bring these things together, Belle, which is the flexible mindset, which says, 'Yeah, of course things are important to me to be exactly as I want them to be, but they don't have to be. If they're not, I can use the problem-solving part of my brain to take the horror out of it first of all,' because it's probably unfortunate that, if you don't like somebody at work, that is unfortunate, but it happens, and to say, 'Well, look, OK, what are the conditions when I would leave?' So you would actually bring that problem-solving part of your brain, because at the moment what you're doing is you're bringing the rigid part of your brain and the horror part of the brain and then you stop.

Belle: Yeah.

Windy: And I'm saying, if you bring the flexible part of your brain and your problem-solving part of your brain and you then apply it to this problem, which is, 'Do I stay or do I move on?' what do you think would happen?

Belle: … What were the two words you used, sorry? You said the flexible part of my brain and the?

Windy: And the horror part of your brain, the catastrophising that you create.

Belle: Well, from experience, I'm just thinking that… the reason that I want to move jobs is because … I'm not completely happy with other stuff and, when I worry about moving, it's because I go, 'Well, my environment's perfect. There's a lot of flexibility and all this.' So I think, if I could bring those together, I'd perhaps start to see the things that aren't actually perfect in my current job and that are actually stopping me from moving on.

Windy: Yeah.

Belle: I've got this perfect view of my job, but I also desperately want to move on and do something different.

Windy: Yeah. It's almost like you create the perfect view of your job when you're thinking of moving and say, 'Oh, I'm not doing that,' but then, when you stay, you think, 'Oh, actually, it's not that great.'

Belle: Yeah, and I think other people support that as well. So, when you hear other people's horror stories and they say, 'My boss is awful,' and I think, 'Well, my boss is nice.' And they say, 'Oh, my office is horrible. I have to share with ten people or 100 people,' and I go, 'Oh, I get my own office.' So their horror stories sort of become my own fears and that traps me further.

Windy: The other thing is if you could recognise that there is, presumably, or is there a point for you, an image that you would like to see yourself in the future, some sort of future self that you would say, 'Actually, here is how I would like my professional life to unfold.' Do you have that kind of picture?

Belle: Yeah.

Windy: What is that picture like?

Belle: I know what it isn't because I've sat in my current job and thought, 'I don't want to be doing this in ... I don't know, even ten years' time,' and that becomes a fear in itself. And what I'd say it is, is quite an active role. I work with children now, but I used to teach with children, and get back to that. And I see myself back in that ... lively role, which I think a lot of my current job in counselling is very subdued almost and very calm. And I'm seeking that activity again.

Windy: And that's the school-based work, is it?

Belle: Yeah. Currently, I work in a school but it's one-to-one counselling.

Windy: What are you looking for?

Belle: I'm looking more for teaching. So to continue counselling but adult counselling in private practice and then to go back into teaching.

Windy: So what's the balance, the 80/20? Is the 80 the teaching and the 20 the private practice or the other way round?

Belle: More 50/50, I think. So it would actually be a case of leaving both and doing 50/50. Currently, I'm 80% counselling and I think I'd just like to reduce that.

Windy: I just want you to focus on – not the working environment, not the people or the colour of the carpets or anything like that – you as somebody who's doing a professional job and I want you to compare what you're doing now, in the proportion that you're doing it, and I want you to compare it to a future self working 50/50, half in private practice, half in an active role teaching. And you see those two on screens in front of you, like there are two screens here, you could imagine that one's on one and one's on the other.

Belle: Yeah.

Windy: What's your viewpoint? What's your feelings about what you see?

Belle: So I'm in my 30s now and it sort of feels like I've gone back to in my 20s when I felt quite … inspired by work. And it feels like what I'm seeing, regardless of the environment, is just someone who is quite energised.

Windy: Right. And what's more important to you, Belle? To be inspired and energised at work or the environmental conditions in which you work?

Belle: That's a great way of putting it. Well, yeah, I know the answer. So definitely I feel like it's more than a lot of people as well; that mine is above the other one – my inspired, energised, motivated. I'm at my best performance, I think, when I'm like that, and I don't think feeling subdued in that job, a job that I enjoy in counselling, but for a long time it's just very reserved and very … calm, and I'm not used to that. So I feel like to do it 50/50 just gives me that time to be that energised person as well, as well as having that counselling.

Windy: Yeah, exactly. It sounds like what you are missing out on is that part of you that is energised, and you miss that part. And you see a way, once we just look on the screens, and say, 'The 50/50 of the adult counselling and the teaching, I can see myself having a balance of the energy and the calm,' and you compare it to what you've got now.

So it sounds like being energised and being really engaged in work, whatever you do, it sounds like it's quite important to you?

Belle: Yeah. I think being active, not in a physical sense, just being active. I used to work in research and just have your mind ticking over is what I miss. Not that it doesn't happen in counselling, but it's just to have that variety, I think.

Windy: OK. So let me ask you the question: I know it doesn't exist but just bear with me, let's suppose I guaranteed you that if you moved to the share that you want – the 50% in private practice and the 50% teaching – let's suppose that I guaranteed you that it would work out as you would like it to be.

Belle: Yeah.

Windy: Would you still put off and procrastinate on making the move knowing that it would work out for you?

Belle: … In all honesty, knowing myself, I probably would because I've thought of, if you could absolutely guarantee it—

Windy: Yeah, that's what I'm saying, and you believed the guarantee.

Belle: OK. If you were completely guaranteeing that it was all gonna be amazing and that was gonna be something that got me energised.

Windy: I didn't say it was all gonna be amazing.

Belle: OK. Yeah, that's well observed.

Windy: I said that the thing that you see on the screen, the energy and the balance, it will work out for you.

Belle: I'd say I'd be sort of 70% there.

Windy: What extra 30% would you need to make the decision?

Belle: Ooh, that's a good question.... [*Pause*] What 30%? ... I think the feeling maybe of security, of feeling like that will be the same. I think my worry is that it will lapse.

Windy: I think that you start off with some other things that are important to you and it goes something like this, and you correct me if I'm wrong: 'What's really important to me is that before I make a move from one to the other, (1) I want to know for sure it's gonna work out, and (2) I'll be secure right from the start.'

Belle: Yep.

Windy: Now, again, let's bring the rigid and the flexible mindset to it. The rigid mindset says, 'Yeah, those things are important to me and I have to have 'em. I've gotta know it's gonna work out and I've gotta be secure before I move.' And the flexible part of you is saying, no, wait a minute, these things are important to you but you don't have to have those things. First of all, certainty doesn't exist. You can only go along with probability. You said you were a researcher – in research we just have probability. And, second of all, yeah, it would be nice to be secure right from the start, but we can become secure even though we're not secure at the beginning.

                  [*Dealing with uncertainty about future conditions and one's future feelings of security (in Belle's case) is a frequent issue in helping people deal with their procrastination problems.*]

Belle: Yeah.

Windy: It doesn't have to be right from the start.

Belle: All or nothing. That feeling.

Windy: Yeah. So can you imagine adopting the flexible mindset towards those things: 'I don't have to know for sure it's gonna work out. It would be nice. And I don't have to be secure right from the start, although that would be nice.' Can you imagine adopting that?

Belle: I can, actually, yeah.

Windy: What difference would it make to you in terms of making your decision?

Belle: I think it would actually make me consider things that I think I've already considered. What you've evidenced to me is that I've never really considered them. So friends will say that I'm quite open-minded and I'll consider different points of view. Again, as a researcher you're quite critical, as a counsellor something I do every day. But then, I don't think I do that with my own decisions very well at all. So, I think it would make me consider things that I've gone, 'Oh yeah, I've considered that before,' but I haven't. I haven't actually thought about it. I haven't actually, like you say, been flexible. I've just considered it and ticked it off, like the finance thing: 'OK, well, forget it then.' So, yeah, I think it would help.

Windy: Alright. So let me put those two versions to you, bring it altogether. So first of all I'm gonna bring the rigid mindset to the picture which says: 'Environmental conditions and people that I work with are important to me and that's what I have to have. And I have to have to know that any change is gonna work out and it's gonna be amazing. And, secondly, I have to be secure from the start.' That's the rigid version.
          The flexible version is saying: 'All these things are important to me, but I don't need these things. If I don't have 'em, I can deal with them and, if they become so bad, then I can move. But, if not, I'll use my problem-

solving part of my brain. And, look, I don't need to know, for God's sake. All I've got is the probability and all I've got is the idea that these are the things that seem important to me. So that's gonna be good enough. And I don't have to be secure right from the start.'

Have you ever had the experience, for example, Belle, of doing something that you started off not being secure about and then becoming secure as a result of doing it?

Belle: Yeah.

Windy: What comes to mind?

Belle: Oh gosh, a lot of things. So, when I left school everything was planned at school and then I went to uni and within the first few months of doing psychology I was like, 'Oh, this isn't for me. I don't know what I'm doing.' And then by the end of it ... it was amazing. I was doing really well and I went on and carried on doing more study and a career in it. Then I went back to it and the same thing happened again, where I went into counselling training and went, 'Oh, this isn't for me and this is awful.'

Windy: Yeah. I think, if you look at yourself as part of a narrative that, whenever you start something new, you start with doubts: 'Not for me, I don't feel secure,' but then, when you stick with it, you actually learn to love it. And you've lost touch with that part of yourself.

[Here, I am doing two things, encouraging Belle to learn from experience and helping her to see that her experience is located in a process where she begins with doubts, stays with it and it generally turns out well.]

Belle: Massively.

Windy: And I'm saying you could get reacquainted with that part of yourself. Do you think you're more likely to be reacquainted with that experience if you've got a rigid mindset towards these things or a flexible mindset towards these things?

Belle: A flexible mindset, because I think a rigid mindset is just making me risk averse.

Windy: That's right, and it's becoming tunnel vision and you're forgetting parts of your experience that you can remember and access if you're flexible.

Belle: That is very true.

Windy: Why don't you summarise the work we've done so far?

Belle: So I feel like I've learnt that I'm a much more rigid thinker than I thought I was.

Windy: On certain things.

Belle: On certain things, yeah, and I think I apply that to myself a lot more than I do to other contexts. So I can see how rigid I am on things that now seem a bit silly, like environment. I know that tethers me to where I am right now, when actually experiences that I've had, thinking about that flexible mindset, where I've started off insecure in something but then you said 'learnt' to be secure in it or something, and that really resonated with me: this idea of learning to cope with something and then it becoming a habit. That flexible mindset really appealed to me there.

So, yeah, the idea of not rigid thinking, flexible mindset and ... yeah, not looking for security immediately.

Windy: Yeah. It's interesting that when you're rigid you edit out your strengths, which means that you don't say, 'Well, OK, if this gets really bad, this is how I'll cope with it. If I can't afford it, then I'll use my savings,' etc., etc.

Belle: Yeah.

Windy: So you don't do that when you're in a rigid mindset and you don't remember your strengths of starting off being insecure and actually learning to be secure. You've edited that out. But, when you bring the flexible mindset in, you can really see yourself as a good problem-solver in the future and you've actually learnt how to go from being insecure to secure in two instances.

Belle: Yeah.

Windy: And I think you just might be a person who may be a slow starter when it comes to that, but then you catch up and say, 'OK, I'm into it now and I love it,' as opposed to, 'Oh no, it's not for me.'

Belle: Yeah.

Windy: And my guess is that you end up by saying, 'It's not for me,' because you don't have the idea it's for you right from the start, and it's gotta be for you right from the start and, if it's not, 'It's not for me.'

Belle: Yeah.

Windy: So, again, that rigidity about starting off.

Belle: I think it's impatience as well.

Windy: Yes, I wasn't gonna mention that but I think you're right. That's the bit which says it's gotta be right, right from the start. Do you have experience of being patient in your life?

Belle: Ooh…

Windy: I mean, when you're with clients, are you impatient: 'Come on, come on, try and change, for God's sake.'

Belle: My head is. So I think training has taught me not to be obviously outwardly like that, but that's probably what I reflect on the most, is why is my head trying to get them to get there, and I'm having to hold that back. So evidence of me being patient, I suppose. I'm very patient with the children when it comes to the teaching. So, when they're struggling to learn, I'm not worried if it takes them five days or five months to learn something. But not for myself.

Windy: Well, but you could choose to practise that. There's no reason why you couldn't. You could say, 'I'm gonna choose to see myself as somebody in this instance like a child learning something new.'

[*Here, I am encouraging Belle to respond to herself as she would a child learning something new.*]

Belle: Yeah.

Windy: 'And, as a result, I'm gonna be patient and I'm gonna really be flexible and I'm gonna see that I have got the strengths to solve problems. I've done that in the past, I can do it in the future,' and so you could do that for yourself as well; you could create those conditions for yourself. It'll be a struggle because you're used to being impatient with yourself, but you could certainly do that.

Is there anything you wanna say about this that you haven't said or anything you wanna ask before we finish?

Belle: … No, not really. I suppose the only thing that comes to mind is that voice that ultimately always holds it back. So I'll leave here and I think I'll feel much more inspired over the weekend for the things that I was gonna do, the applications that I was thinking of. I'm going to make those and I am gonna make that move. And then it's just quietening that voice of, 'Oh yeah but,' that rigid thinker.… Are there any prompts, I suppose, that can prompt me to question that rigid thinker?

Windy: Well, you've got the evidence of it. You've got the two things which are: 'yes, but' and, 'what if' So 'yes, but' and 'what if' assigns that you're moving into a rigid frame of mind.

Belle: Yeah.

Windy: Now, at that point you can go to the source and say, 'OK, what am I being rigid about? What am I demanding right now?' and then say, 'Does it have to be that way?' No. It would be nice but it doesn't have to be. Then, 'How can I answer the 'yes, but'?' Don't try to answer the 'yes, but' and the 'what if' when you're rigid. That's what you've been doing.

Belle: Yeah, massively.

Windy: Yeah. The time to answer those is when you get yourself into a flexible frame of mind and then you can actually access those answers, OK?

Belle: Yeah. That makes sense.

Windy: Is there anything else you wanna ask or raise before we finish?

Belle: Nope.

Windy: Have you got what you came for?

Belle: Yeah. I think I've got, not to give you this label, but it almost feels like a cheerleader. When you were talking about noticing those strengths, it feels like, yeah, I've adopted with my friends of saying, 'I'm pessimistic,' and, when they say that, I say, 'No, I'm realistic. That's why I look at the negatives.' So for somebody to come across and say, 'But have you looked at the times when you've been successful and the times when you have problem-solved?' and I'm like, 'No, I haven't looked at those.'

Windy: Well, I think one of the things that you might want to consider as a result of doing that is an audit of your strengths and experiences where you've actually come through adversity and having a sort of positive aspect at the end. I think you need an audit of that.

Belle: Yeah.... Sorry, can I just ask one more question as well?

Windy: Of course.

Belle: One of the things that holds me back is just this idea of the status quo is easier.

Windy: It is.

Belle: Yeah.

Windy: It is. That's a fact, probably, unless you're in a really bad situation. Maybe it's more comfortable and maybe what is comfortable and continue there, there's a route to a county that no longer exists. Do you know what that county is?

Belle: No.

Windy: Rutland.[16]

Belle: Yeah, massively. I keep saying that because it just feels massive.

Windy: So, if you wanna be in a rut, stay comfortable and miss out on your dreams.

Belle: Yeah. I think that's the biggest thing. I know it's at the end, but that's quite a shocker when you put it like that.

Windy: What's a shocker?

Belle: Just that idea of Rutland, even as a term. I've heard of being stuck in a rut, of course.

Windy: Yeah. There was an old county called Rutland.

Belle: There was?

---

[16] Rutland is a small county in the UK Midlands.

Windy: That's what I'm saying. There was an old county called Rutland, and I'm just saying Rut-land – the land of the rut.

Belle: Yeah. I can envisage that cycle of the monotony of, 'Well, this is comfortable but it's not inspiring, it's not energetic.'

Windy: Yeah. When I asked you to look at those two things, I think that's what we were looking at. You were looking at comfort versus energy. In a way, what you're looking for is a guarantee to go from one to the other knowing it's gonna work out and knowing that you're gonna be secure as you make that transition.

Belle: Yeah.

Windy: That's the bit where flexibility comes in because you have to ask yourself, 'Does it have to be that way or not?'

Belle: Do you know what's the most interesting thing about that? When you talk about this Rutland or this monotony, this image I've got now, that is a bigger figure and being there than taking that leap. I'm more scared of being stuck there than I am, I think, of ending up in a really bad office.

Windy: Yeah. But you don't have to go there. That may be one of the possibilities how you might live your life, but you've always got ways of actually stopping that, even just before you get to, 'You're now here, the final rut.' You can still move away. So why not move away when it's easier, now, than do it when it's harder? It's almost like saying the easy thing is actually the hard thing, and the hard thing is the easy thing.

Belle: Yeah. I see that now.

Windy: It's been a pleasure speaking to you. What I'll do is I'll send you the recording straight afterwards and you'll get the transcript after. Just email me with your email address that you want us to use, OK?

Belle: Yeah, I have got your email. I can do that after, just because this is a work email.

Windy: That's fine. And you might not be there for much longer.

Belle: You never know. But thank you so much. This has been so useful. And it's lovely to meet you.

Windy: OK. Thanks a lot.

Belle's Reflections (07/08/23)

At the start of this process, I really wasn't sure what to expect. I had heard the opportunity for a single-session therapy appointment advertised and it felt like a good time to a pose a problem that I had been procrastinating over. Then the meeting day came around. Even as Windy asked me what my problem was, I wasn't entirely sure what direction to go in (perhaps I was procrastinating, wanting to make 'the right decision'!).

Then I realised that I had been procrastinating over taking up opportunities for work. I had gone for jobs, then turned down interviews because it didn't feel like 'the right time'. I thought I would put the problem out there, and wasn't expecting much more than some challenge and empathic listening.

As I talked initially with Windy, it felt like he posed many questions, one after the other. However, the process seemed to flow so effortlessly. Straight away he asked 'What's stopping you [from changing careers]?', and I found that I had to voice my biggest fears quite early into the session! I identified that I was worried that I could end up hating a new job, or feeling penniless. But unexpectedly, as Windy challenged these, it seemed to draw out some of my biggest strengths; for example, I was encouraged to identify how, in the past when I had changed jobs before, I had persevered, I had a tendency to 'give things a go' and I'd equally shown strength in handling money. The questions went on like this for a while but it seemed so quick, as I actually put voice to the fears and could conceptualise them almost as objects in front of me; objects that were there for me to 'get over'.

One part of the session that really reached me was when I realised that I was most concerned about moving to a new job and it not being 'just right'. Windy said 'Oh so it's got to be perfect right now, has it?'. It was at this point that I realised again one of my biggest achievements in my career history to that point: persevering. Moreover, I identified that it was in these jobs that I had found the most satisfaction!

Finally, the session closed with me asking a sort of 'What if?' question, and Windy delivered what felt like a harsh prospect: 'Well yeah, what if you get to retirement and the dreams are still a dream? It's your choice to make.' Whilst this seemed almost 'blunt', it felt like this was the point the session had been leading to. It felt like such a direct challenge that it really made me consider the point of procrastinating any further.

In summary, the session itself was ... well, quite simply 'refreshing'. Having previously had a very positive experience of longer-term counselling, I was expecting this session to be supportive, empathic, and potentially useful, but given its limitations on time, I was expecting nothing more in terms of exploring an issue, than remaining 'surface-level'. As we began, I thought the session would drive towards a solution that perhaps Windy had a predetermined idea of (i.e. 'Leave the job' versus 'stay put'). However, the questions instead felt completely self-made; my answers to one question led to the formation of the next and I felt facilitated through, what was, entirely my own process rather than steered in a particular direction. And finally, the close of the session, where I was asked if I had any more questions, allowed me to air my worries, challenge these, and then almost immediately answer them with a sort of 'Of course I don't want to get to retirement and regret not taking these opportunities!'. It felt almost a 'gut-instinct' level of revelation, but the session gave me an empathic 'sounding board' to allow me to consider listening to and trusting in that own intuition. And I really got the answer that I knew I wanted and perhaps needed to hear. This offered a huge amount of reassurance and most importantly, gave me the confidence to stop procrastinating ... and maybe even go for it.

10

Believe Before You Act vs
Act Before You Believe

Date: 05/05/23
Time: 42 minutes 21 secs

Windy: So, Niklas, what is your understanding of the purpose of our conversation today?

Niklas: Well, I'm quite curious and intrigued, I guess would be the right words, both because it's a single session and also in the field of psychology. I'm finishing my Master's thesis and this process is really highlighting how good I am at procrastinating and how difficult it is for me to motivate myself. So, yeah.

Windy: So are you procrastinating on something at the moment?

Niklas: Yeah, definitely. I'm procrastinating every day in smaller or larger scale.

Windy: Is there any particular task that you're keen to do that you're putting off?

Niklas: Yeah. Well, I don't know if I can be super specific, then it has to be writing my theory or result thing in my Master's thesis, but simply just sit down every day and start to work – that's a very, very difficult thing for me.

Windy: And that's your goal, to sit down every day and work?

Niklas: Yeah, for at least a couple of hours because I have a deadline on 1st June, so I need to put in some work to actually finish, to deliver a finished product.

Windy: What is the finished product you need to deliver?

Niklas: That's an 80-page, more or less, Master's thesis in psychology.

Windy: So shall we focus on that and help you with that?

Niklas: Yeah, that is the most prominent thing in my life right now.

Windy: So it's due June 1st.

Niklas: Mmm [yes].

Windy: So you've got about—

Niklas: 26, 27 days.

Windy: And how much of it have you written?

Niklas: It's difficult to say. I have a really messy introduction and theory.... There's a lot of text there and it needs to be streamlined, but it's there. I've done my data collection. I've done my interviews. I've transcribed my interviews. So I basically need to analyse, discuss and conclude, and streamline of course.

Windy: And, if you set aside two hours a day, you were saying?

Niklas: Well, yeah, preferably two hours, but I have a problem with both setting goals and also being content when I reach the set goals, because then it seems like it's never enough. So it's a little bit of a difficult conundrum, so to speak. But, yeah, it should be definitely two hours a day at least.

Windy: When you say 'never enough', never enough for whom?

Niklas: For me. I can make it feel—

Windy: In other words, if you finished your Master's, you would fail it because it was never enough?

Niklas: I would probably pass. If I actually deliver something, I would pass.

Windy: You mean you would pass it yourself?

Niklas: I probably wouldn't, no.

Windy: That's what I'm saying.

Niklas: I would always think, 'You could've done better.'

Windy: Yes, OK. And, because you could've done better, what?

Niklas: I could've been more motivated, I could've worked harder, I could've started sooner, I could've been better at studying, everything.

Windy: No, I meant, 'Because I could've done more, it could've been better, then I will fail it because it could've been better.' Is that what you're saying, if you were in charge of whether you passed or not?

Niklas: If I was in charge of that, ah, that's difficult.... [*Pause*] That's difficult for me to wrap my head around. I would probably always find ... another reason for it not to pass.

Windy: So you fail it?

Niklas: Well ... in my own sense, yeah, probably, but not in an academic way.

Windy: Well, no. I don't know which university you go to.

Niklas: It's in Denmark.

Windy: Let's suppose that they had this strange system in Denmark which means that you were in charge of passing or failing your own Master's thesis, and you got to the end of it by the time and you looked at this thing and you said, 'Ah, this could've been better. I could've done more,' what I'm asking you is would you fail it or would you pass it?

Niklas: Oh, so are you asking if I would turn it in or not?

Windy: No. You turn it in and you're the examiner.

Niklas: So, from an outside view, so to speak, right?

Windy: No, you're the examiner. Niklas is the submitter of the piece of work and Niklas is the examiner. What I'm saying is would you pass it or not?

Niklas: ... [*Long pause*] Thinking if it's gonna end up like I think it would, do I also know my progress? Do I know the work that I've put in when I'm the examiner?

Windy: You read it. You hand it in and then there's a period of time and then you come back and you're now the examiner and you read it and you conclude that this could've been better. What I'm saying at that point would you pass it or would you fail it?

Niklas: That's difficult to answer. ... [*Long pause*] When it's me I would probably fail it, but, if it was somebody else, I'd probably pass it.

Windy: No, I'm talking about you. So, if it's you, you'd probably fail it, but if the same piece of work, exactly the same piece of work was submitted and you were examining it, you would've passed it?

Niklas: Probably, yeah.

Windy: So what does that tell you?

Niklas: Well, one of the biggest challenges of my life: that there is a weird, absurd set of rules that, for some reason, apply to me and it's always pushing me down, and it doesn't apply to others. And I know the right thing and the most positive thing is to do what I would do to others, so to speak: I would look at it and say, 'It could've been better but I'll pass it.' But, for some reason, I can't get it into my head. I simply just can't get that way of looking at life into my head, it seems.

Windy: The reality is you're not the examiner. So what do you think would happen if the same piece of work that you would fail would be examined by examiners? Would they pass it or would they fail it?

Niklas: They would pass it.

Windy: So what is more important to you: handing in a piece of work that you are happy with, and it sounds like that would never be the case because you could always do more, or handing in a piece of work that your examiners would be happy with and giving you a pass mark and presumably get you your Master's?

Niklas: I would like the first but the second is obviously the most important.

Windy: So, even if you did nothing with that idea – that, 'It's never enough, it could've been more, therefore I'd fail it because I have a special rule that applies to me that doesn't apply to other people' – even though that is happening, even though that could be on the radio, so to speak, then you could say, 'Well, fine, that's that, but I can do it because I'm not marking and other people are marking it. And, so my goal is to satisfy them, not to satisfy myself, which is good because I'm never satisfied.'

[I am making the point that Niklas can do the task if his focus was on the actual examiners not on him as the examiner.]

Niklas: Yeah. And this is something that my brain keeps on doing: then there is a little twist because they will only pass it because they're either not intelligent enough to see behind it that it's actually a piece of crap or I'm lucky. There's always an explanation why they're not failing it.

Windy: Sure, but does it matter?

Niklas: … Well, pragmatically, it doesn't, no.

Windy: Exactly. So the point is you can choose to go forward even though you've got this one narrative, the Niklas narrative, which is basically saying, 'This piece of work could always be better and I would fail it. If the examiners are gonna pass it, they're idiots,' or whatever it is,' and so fine, you can have that narrative going on, but you can have another narrative going on which says, 'Look, OK, all that is true psychologically, but there's another pathway I could follow which is the pragmatic pathway, which is I can do this thing and hand it in because I want to get the piece of work done because I want the Master's, and I want the Master's because,' why?

Niklas: Well, because I feel like being a counselling psychologist is maybe not what I was meant for. That's a little bit too deep. But it's something that I can actually make a fulfilling life out of. I can actually make sense.

Windy: It's important to you.

Niklas: And meaningful.

Windy: Right. It's important and meaningful. So that's the reason why you're doing the Master's and that's the reason why you're doing the piece of work that we're talking about. Could you imagine really saying, 'Look, I can follow two narratives here: I can follow the Niklas narrative which is, "I'm not gonna do this because there's no point in doing it because I wouldn't pass it, it's never gonna be enough and, if they pass it, they're idiots," or the pragmatic narrative which is, "This is important to me, this life is important to me. If I'm a counselling psychologist, that would really fulfil me, and I think they would pass it. I don't know them, so I don't know whether they're idiots or not. It doesn't really matter. They'll probably pass it, and that will help me."' Can you see those two narratives clearly?

Niklas: Yeah, I can.

Windy: Now, can you imagine choosing to work on the pragmatic narrative even though on the radio in the background, if you like, there is this other narrative going on?

Niklas: I completely understand the meaning of it. I completely understand, yeah, the building blocks of it. And for some reason, and I don't know why just yet, but it's so difficult for me to accept that it is like that, even though I believe that it is like that. There's a thousand different narratives, right? For some reason, I don't know if I'm waiting for a certain feeling to be feeling it's actually true before I can follow it.

Windy: Right. That's an interesting point. Are you saying that, 'I will choose to follow the narrative only when I really feel it's true'?

Niklas: That is a possibility because – and I don't even know if this makes sense – it feels like I have a key in one hand and there's a locked door in front of me, and I know how a key works, I know how a door lock works, I know how everything works here, but I just, for some reason, can't put it into the hole and turn it.

Windy: What conditions would have to exist for you to put it into the hole and turn it? That's what I'm asking you. What ingredient will you need to put it into the hole and turn it?

Niklas: … It's basically just down to wanting to do it. It's an action. It's a start of an action.

Windy: Sorry, wanting to do what, Niklas?

Niklas: Wanting to … maybe believe is the wrong word, but you probably know what I mean, but believe in the other narrative.

Windy: Yeah. I think what you're doing is, if we put aside that, there are two ways forward for you which are: 'I can get to believe this, I can see the advantages of it, I can see the sense of it, I can get to believing it if I act on it;' the other one is saying, 'No, no, no, no, I will only act on it if I really believe it.'

[*I have used my two narrative approach and in our subsequent discussion, Niklas reveals that he needs to believe it before he acts on it. The alternative is to act on it and believe it later.*]

Niklas: … [*Long pause*] Yeah. … [*Pause*] Yeah, that might be a precise point of my struggling, so to speak.

Windy: Yeah.

Niklas: … [*Long pause*] Well, again the next thought that pops into my mind is I find it rather difficult and then I start thinking, 'It shouldn't be difficult. It's pretty straightforward.'

Windy: What's pretty straightforward?

Niklas: Well, not waiting to feel like it should be like this and just simply act like it. It is pretty simple.

Windy: But it's not easy.

Niklas: No, it's fucking difficult.

Windy: Exactly. Because you're thinking, 'It's simple, therefore I should be able to do it because it's easy.' I'm saying it's simple but it's difficult. Now, then the question arises are you prepared to do the difficult thing, Niklas?

Niklas: … [*Long pause*] Yeah, so basically it all boils down to that. That is the difficult thing. It's to … start taking action.

Windy: Yeah, taking action. Have you ever seen the film *Field of Dreams*?

Niklas: … I don't think so, no.

Windy: It's about this guy who's got this dream about building a baseball pitch in a very remote farming, and the famous phrase that comes from that field is: 'If you build it, they will come.' So what I'm saying to you, if we take a field of dreams, if you act on it, belief will come.

Niklas: Yeah.… Again, it is pretty simple. It's the same thing if you believe that you have to sit and wait for motivation to come – you're gonna wait a long time, probably.

Windy: That's right. The point is, it would be great. I'm not knocking the fact that your desire is something like this: 'I really want to be in a situation to really believe these things and then I'll act on it. That's my ideal and that's what I wanna do.' And that's great. You tell me if you're holding that idea flexibly or rigidly. The flexible version would go: 'Look, it really is important to me to be able to believe in this before I act on it, but it doesn't have to be that way. I'm flexible enough to see that in certain areas fine, but in this area it ain't gonna be that way. So it doesn't have to be that way.' The rigid version says, 'It's important for me to believe it first before I act on it, and that's the way it has to be. I ain't shifting from that.'

Niklas: … It's so weird because I am definitely rigid about it. That's pretty obvious. But it happens so frustratingly automatically for some reason.

Windy: But the point is it's bound to happen automatically, but that's only the first chapter, Niklas. So, if I was to write a book on Niklas and his procrastination, it would be: Niklas automatically starts to believe in the idea that, 'I have to believe in something first before I do it' – end of Chapter 1.

[*This is what I call the 'book analogy'. See Dryden (2023b) for a discussion of this analogy.*]

Niklas: Yeah, and end of book.

Windy: And end of book. That's it. Now, the point is you could create a new ending, if you allow for your first response to be that way and then respond to it.

Niklas: … And that's definitely also a challenge, yeah. I'm very fast to, 'Oh, that's Chapter 1, now I can't continue.' I'm really trained in that.

Windy: OK, but just because you've been trained in it doesn't mean that you can't learn something new.

Niklas: No.

Windy: So, if you can recognise that you could learn something new, which is saying, 'Look, I can recognise that that's gonna come up. If I try to stop it from coming up, it's gonna be like one of those water leaks that, if I let go, everything's gonna spray around. So, yeah, it's gonna come up, so I'm anticipating that. But I can respond to it and say, 'No.' It would be nice if it was that way but it doesn't have to be that way. In this case it isn't that way so, since I wanna get this thing and practise the pragmatic narrative, I'm gonna have to do it in the way I prefer not to do it. But I can do that because I can be flexible.'

Niklas: That kind of conversation I can definitely have with myself when the sun is shining and the day is good. I can have that conversation with myself and say, 'Oh yeah, I actually know what the right thing to do is.' But the thing is it feels like I don't have the mental capacity thinking that when I'm starting to finish Chapter 1 on a bad day. Then I'm more easily hooked by this, 'Oh well, can't do it, fuck it. I'm done.'

Windy: But let me teach you my favourite phrase, and that is, 'Say fuck it to fuck it.' Do you see what I'm saying? Again, you're saying, 'Well, I can do it on a good day when the sun is shining, when the conditions are right, but I can't do it under more challenging conditions.' Well, is that true that you can't do it?

Niklas: No.

Windy: No, exactly. Again, that's the other thing to watch. That's part of the first chapter.

Niklas: ... Yeah. It's basically just another way of saying exactly the same. I can see that, yeah. It's the same mechanism.... It's actually quite a good thing. I think I need one of those pathways, highways or something. Maybe, 'Fuck it to fuck it,' is pretty good.

Windy: Yeah, because you can then start to build a connection between the attitude that you want and the behaviour that you want, and eventually that connection will strengthen while saying, 'Fuck it to fuck it,' along the way. Because otherwise you're just gonna be practising the old connection, and I don't think you need much practice at that. I think you're pretty good at it.

Niklas: I'm rather good, yeah.

Windy: So let's pause there and why don't you reflect on what we've been talking about today. Why don't you summarise what we've been talking about today so far.

Niklas: Well, we've been talking about this struggle I perceive having in this Master's thesis but basically in many life aspects. And, for some reason, it makes sense for me to see that other people are working, like they work, 'It doesn't matter, you don't have to feel it before you do it. You can just do it. You can follow your compass or whatever you wanna call it. You don't have to feel right.' And, for some reason, I fall into that myself and I forget that stuff is important to me or this is valuable to me.

And, for some reason, I have this pattern that I need to be really aware of because right now it's almost automatically that I can say, 'OK, I don't feel like it so I can't do it.' And it's basically not what I want to do, it's not who I want to be.

Windy: In a way, I think we all have that capacity to do that. You're not gonna kill off that bit. It's about living with that bit and are you going to be living and saying, 'Well, OK, I'm gonna move forward even though that bit's there or am I going to not move forward because that bit's there, and I can only move forward if it's not there.'

Niklas: Yeah. Luckily, that's one of the good things, though. Many years ago I learnt that things usually don't disappear, and I accepted that and I see that as a truth in our kind, basically. I don't usually believe things will disappear; you will just have to cope and live with them. So, yeah, I totally accept that.

Windy: You do have a number of ideas, or we could call them narratives or mindsets, that you could act on or you could actually recognise that they're there; they're like a channel in the background, and bring to the foreground the ones that aren't natural for you, and it would be nice if they were natural first and you believed in it first, but it doesn't work that way in psychology. Therefore, you could learn along the way, if you like, and strengthen the belief along the way.

[*I am stressing the importance of Niklas acknowledging that his first response will be habitual and unproductive but that he can respond to this first response and act on the second response even if he does not believe it and even if it is difficult.*]

Niklas: Yeah. That's basically a thing: accept this as being truth. Yeah, true.

Windy: So do you think that there's anything we've discussed today that's gonna make a difference to you as you approach this task?

Niklas: Well, growing up as a Dane, we're quite humble around it. So I would say maybe, probably or possibly.

Windy: We've now covered all the bases. But you haven't said definitely not or definitely yes. That shows how flexible you are.

Niklas: Yeah, maybe. I better not bet 100% for or against now. But there's definitely something about, I've had this running conversation in my head while talking to you, as we probably most do when we're having conversations, I've realised that I'm maybe not that ... specifically in this area, maybe not that strong to know because I haven't trained or worked out a lot in this area about to live through a pain – it's way too big a word, but discomfort when I have this self-monitoring shit going on. Do I feel like it? No.

Windy: Do you work out physically?

Niklas: Yeah.

Windy: There's a guy called Ed Garcia and he wrote a book called *Developing Emotional Muscle*. So, what that means is that, in order to develop your physical muscles, you've gotta work out, as you say. The same thing is true with emotional muscles. So, if you want to learn to tolerate discomfort better, which you can, you've got to work out and strengthen those emotional muscles in those areas. In order to do that, you've got to seek out discomfort, in the same way as you go to a gym and you seek out whatever apparatus you use. You could seek out discomfort. See discomfort as your friend rather than your enemy, in a way.

Niklas: Well, the positive thing is that that discomfort is gonna come easily, whereas going to the gym is a little bit difficult, the trip up to the gym.

Windy: Yeah, you've got to make more effort to get to the gym than you do have to make an effort to find discomfort. I agree.

Niklas: Yeah. So it is something to do with that. Actually, pause under the primary or the first side of discomfort and then maybe have this phrase, say, 'Fuck it to fuck it,' and then, with that being able to think, 'What's important to you right now? Oh yes, this. But I'm tired? Yeah, well, you have done things when you're tired before, so you can do it again.'

Windy: That's great because what you're doing is the healthy part of you is having the last word.

           [*Niklas is spontaneously rehearsing the solution.*]

Niklas: Yeah.

Windy: And I think what I've been hearing from you is the unhealthy part of you has been having the first and the last word.

Niklas: Well, basically the first is the last word.

Windy: The first is the last word, right.

Niklas: It just ends there, yeah.... And I also need to accept, and I think I'm able to do that, that it's gonna happen again, obviously: I am gonna not do something, like all of us do. But I definitely wanna approach this as a more ... [*pause*] I don't even know what to call it in Danish, but this phenomenon... the opposite of being intertwined: because, 'You don't feel well, you don't have to do this, you can't do this.' No. It's way less intertwined. I can't remember the other word for it, but it's just, 'You don't feel like it. OK. So?'

Windy: That's right. It's about recognising that it would be nice to have certain internal states before you act.

Niklas: Yeah, it would be nice.

Windy: Yeah, and you can make those internal states necessary or just desirable but not necessary. And I can't make that choice for you. You're not gonna make that choice perfectly because you're a human being. You could always do it better. But, in a way, that's always gonna be true, isn't it? Usain Bolt probably could've run 0.1 of a second faster. Is he gonna say, 'Oh shit, I could run 0.1 of a second faster, so therefore I ain't gonna enter that race.'

Niklas: That hits something because, it's funny, I always hated that sentence myself. I had a friend, she was studying medicine and she was like, 'Yeah, well, I can always do better,' and I was always thinking, 'That is such a painful way to look at it.' She was coping rather well, but I actually took that or even had that probably already back then. So, yeah, it is a possibility in another universe, in another dimension, you could've run faster, you could've jumped higher, you could've written better, you could've done something else. The difference is that I become discouraged by the fact, even though it's just a fact, it could also have been worse: you could also have been slower.

Windy: Yeah.

Niklas: So I'm putting some emotions into it.

Windy: Yeah. The point is, in a way, the idea that, 'I could've done it better,' could be a way of encouraging you to do better, rather than to then, what you did before, if you're grading it, you would've said, 'Right, it's failed, because it had to have been better,' and, if it wasn't, you wipe it out. Whereas the 'it could do better' as a form of encouragement would be somebody saying, 'You know, Dryden, the interview you did with Niklas was really great. It was fantastic. Can I make a few suggestions how it could've been better?' What could I do? Erase our recording because I could've done it better? I could do, but I could listen and say, 'Yeah, I think that's right.' Incidentally, that's what I do. I often go over these single sessions and I'm supervising myself, and I say, 'You know, Dryden, you could've done that. Oh yeah, that's right. Why do you say that?' I'm not wiping it out. I'm just saying I'm doing this to improve.

Niklas: There is a flicker of … [*pause*] perfectionism in my brain right now, because … in a little part of my brain, if I was in your shoes, and I don't know why, it sounds silly, but… the thought is a little bit appealing to erase it and then do it perfectly, because then it's in order; then it's like it should be. I know that's an ideal and I can never reach that, but I don't know why I'm so drawn.

Windy: That's a flicker. You could say, 'OK, that's a flicker and I could add to the flicker. I could pour oil on the flicker. I could turn it into a flame. I could engulf myself with the oil and destroy myself, or I could keep it as a flicker and say, "Well, I've got a tendency towards perfectionism. I'm not the first, I won't be the last."' So fine. Incidentally, have you heard of Torvill and Dean, the British ice skaters?

[*I am framing the flicker as something to respond to*]

Niklas: No.

Windy: So Torvill and Dean went to the Olympics and they danced an ice skating routine to Ravel's *Bolero*, and they got, uniformly from all the judges, 6.0 – unheard of. That was great. They did a perfect dance. Now, let's suppose that after five minutes the judges said, 'Now, wait a minute, there was a technical hitch here. I'm afraid you're gonna have to dance this routine again.' Do you think they would've got 6.0s again?

Niklas: No.

Windy: Why not?

Niklas: … [*Long pause*] Well, without taking into consideration how difficult it must be mentally to set you up again, then it's something that only happens, it depends on how you view it, but everything comes together in like one in a million times.

Windy: That's right. Perfect is possible, but to maintain it every time is probably impossible.

Niklas: Yeah. Not even improbable. It is. And it's a weird fight. Seeing it a little bit from a distance, it's a weird fight to think that you can win or maybe even just call it draw with it when you actually hit perfection and then you just start another battle all over again. You're probably gonna lose because perfectionist is the only win or draw condition there is.

Windy: Exactly. Therefore, I'm gonna have to accept myself that I'm probably never gonna do the perfect counselling interview, and that's OK. It's unfortunate. It would be nice if we showed something and everybody agreed, but there's always gonna be somebody else who's gonna say something like this, and I'll end with this little last story. Moses comes down from Mount Sinai and he then has to lead the children of Israel to another pathway. And they come to the Red Sea and there's no bridges, they can't swim across it. So Moses is in touch with God, and God raises it for Moses, and Moses parts the Red Sea, and he's feeling pretty pleased with himself. There's a little guy who said something, and Moses said to him, 'What do you mean it's a little muddy?'

[*Maybe I am using too many analogies with Niklas.*]

Niklas: … Yeah.

Windy: What do you take from that story?

Niklas: … I just need the words to be translated. Well, to part the Red Sea, to do something like that, to achieve a thing like that is pretty impossible. So achieving it is really… something that you admire. But you can always find the little faults. You can always say, 'I need to walk in a bit of wet sand.' 'Yeah, but you're fucking free from the Egyptians who are actually hunting you. So please just fucking go.'

Windy: Yeah. If Moses became Niklas, he would've said, 'Yeah, it is a little muddy. I'm gonna put it all back and see if I can try it again without the mud.'

Niklas: Yeah. And there's a weird expectation that, when you hit a certain level, like parting the Red Sea, you say, 'OK, no, no, no, I want perfection. Let's put it together again,' and then for some reason there's a thought that I can do this again and do it better, but there's nobody saying you can actually do the same thing again. You actually put this as a default mode, like, 'Of course I can do that,' and that's weird, actually, when I think about it.

Windy: Yeah.

Niklas: If that makes sense. I feel like my language is a little bit of a barrier right now.

Windy: No, it does make sense. So let's end up with you telling me what's the takeaways for you gonna be and how you're going to implement any takeaways you have.

Niklas: First of all, I'm gonna try my utmost to catch myself on these self-monitoring tendencies I have. Does it feel like I want to do this today? No. OK, but wait, what was it? Say, 'Fuck it to fuck it.' And what does that mean? Well, you need to work through the displeasure. Why? Because I actually want to do this. Because I want to turn this in. Because I want this Master thesis. Because I want everything that follows with it. So, for me, the most important thing is this … training in catching myself in this almost automatic habit of having a thought that has to feel right before I do it.

Windy: And, if you do that and respond to it, what do you think you'll do?

Niklas: Well, right now I'd probably turn in my paper on 1st June and pass, and that's basically what I've dreamt of the last six years. But … it's also gonna have a positive impact.

Windy: You can generalise what you're learning, in other words.

Niklas: Generalise, yes, that's the word.

Windy: Exactly. You can generalise that. So what we're gonna do is, I'm gonna send you the recording, I will send you the transcript and then you can actually learn from yourself and remind yourself what we've been talking about.

Niklas: Lovely.

Windy: That's fantastic. So let me just stop this.

Niklas' Reflections (01/08/23)

In early May, I had an insightful single session with my counsellor, Windy, where we addressed the issue of procrastination that had been plaguing me. The session turned out to be a positive experience that left a lasting impact on my approach to life and helped me gain a fresh perspective on tackling procrastination.

Right from the beginning, Windy created a comfortable and open space for me to share my struggles with procrastination. He listened actively and offered genuine empathy, guiding the conversation with thoughtful questions that prompted me to explore the underlying reasons behind my self-monitoring tendencies and perfectionist mindset.

During the session, Windy introduced me to a simple phrase that, despite its bold language, had a powerful message: 'Say fuck it to fuck it.' The idea behind this mantra was to let go of overthinking and self-doubt, allowing me to take action even when the circumstances weren't perfect. While it may not have been a groundbreaking concept, its practicality struck a chord with me.

Applying the principle of 'Say fuck it to fuck it' to my daily life brought about a noticeable change in my behaviour. I began approaching tasks with a newfound determination, choosing to act even when I didn't feel like it. This shift in mindset allowed me to break free from the clutches of procrastination and make meaningful progress on various fronts.

As I embraced this mantra, I noticed its positive influence in other aspects of my life beyond academics. It encouraged me to let go of the fear of imperfection and take more risks, fostering a sense of resilience and personal growth. The phrase reminded me that perfection is an unrealistic standard and that true progress lies in learning and adapting along the way.

In the weeks following our session, I observed a tangible improvement in my productivity and overall well-being. By prioritizing action over perfection, I became more forgiving of myself and less critical of my shortcomings. I found solace in the idea that discomfort is a natural part of growth and that embracing challenges can lead to personal development.

While the session itself may not have been life-changing, the mantra 'Say fuck it to fuck it' has undeniably played a positive role in my ongoing journey towards self-improvement. It serves as a powerful reminder to confront doubts and self-limiting beliefs with a simple 'So what?' and take the necessary steps forward.

In conclusion, the 'Dealing with Procrastination' session with Windy provided me with valuable insights into overcoming procrastination and embracing imperfection. The mantra 'Say fuck it to fuck it' became a practical tool for challenging my own self-defeating thoughts and taking action despite uncertainty. While it may not have been a miraculous transformation, it has undoubtedly contributed to a more proactive and growth-oriented mindset.

As I continue to implement the lessons learned from the session, I am excited about the possibilities for personal and academic growth that lie ahead. The journey is ongoing, and I am grateful for the support and guidance that have empowered me to say 'fuck it' to the barriers that once held me back.

11

'Avoid the Crusher' vs 'Crème Egg' Mindsets

Date: 05/05/23
Time: 41 minutes 39 secs

Windy: So, Mike, what's your understanding of the purpose of our conversation this afternoon?

Mike: I think it's to bring some aspects of procrastination in my life, and hopefully, you're going to teach me some techniques to deal with that.

Windy: Based on our collective understanding of the factors that account for your procrastination?

Mike: Yeah.

Windy: Otherwise, I'll be teaching you disembodied techniques that could apply to anybody.

Mike: That's true. Everybody's unique. I mean, I don't know how you're going to do it. Are you going to do some 'there and then' work looking at early examples and try and relate those to here and now.

Windy: Well, I'd invite you to think about something that you're procrastinating on now that you'd like to do, so that we can actually make it as current and as relevant as possible. We can go back and look at some past work and then apply that to the present, but I'll be guided by you on that one, Mike.

Mike: OK, so let's see where it goes, because I guess a psychotherapy session can meander.

Windy: Not a single-session therapy session. I'm going to focus you, not like you're in a strait jacket, but focus you. My goal is to help you to take something meaningful away from this.

[*Here I am helping Mike to understand that it is best if we bring a focus to the session rather than meander.*]

Mike: Yeah, sure.... So I feel that I am really busy all the time and I feel I have lots of things to do, and I find it hard to get stuck in, into stuff that I remain feeling is more important. So I am training to be a psychotherapist. I have an academic essay to write this term. I have a reflexive essay to write. In my Easter break I set myself a goal of writing the reflexive essay. I have, prior to this, been in jobs where I've had to write. I've been able to write. I think I write quite well. I want to write a novel – I procrastinate on that. I have a very good idea for a novel, but I'm stuck in the novel and I spend a lot of time thinking how to get over the obstacles of that novel. Then I've got car insurance problems to sort out, my daughter's university stuff to sort out, trying to get my son's GCSE revision sorted. I feel I've just got loads of stuff to do. Clearly, I need to write the essay and I want to do the novel.

Windy: So I've got a non-psychological solution for you. Do you want to hear it?

Mike: Mmm [yes].

Windy: Cloning.

Mike: … Right, OK.... I'm making some notes.

Windy: I said that with my tongue firmly in my cheek.

Mike: Oh.

[*My attempt at ironic humour was not identified.*]

Windy: We haven't got that technology yet. If you're a sheep, maybe we could do that. In other words, you sound very busy. Then, if there were five of you, maybe you could get all the stuff done.

Mike: Yeah.

Windy: We could look at this as a problem with procrastination because, if you take one thing that you are looking at in isolation, we could say that you are not doing something that you want to do. But, if we put it into a wider context, I'm hearing about a man who's got a lot on his plate and it sounds like you're doing more than you're putting off, in a way.

[*This a good example of setting out to understand the client's problem in context.*]

Mike: Interesting.... [*Pause*] Yeah.... [*Pause*] What I find myself doing, Windy, is... I'm not sure whether it's an aspect of I'm older now, I'm 56, I think my ability to concentrate's good. But let's say this reflexive essay, it's 1,000 words, it's based on a presentation I did last term, I'd really like to crack this one by the weekend, but I kind of keep putting that off. And I now think, 'Oh, I'll just see what's happening on the Guardian website. OK, what's happening on the local election results.' Do you know what I mean?

Windy: OK. So what I'm hearing, although you're busy – and you are busy, you've got a lot on – there is a window of time that you've got this weekend that you could do this reflexive essay, but you are delaying it by looking at some things which you are interested in or not interested in?

Mike: Yeah, I'm a news junkie. I read most papers from the *Guardian* to the *Telegraph*. I like reading political magazines.

Windy: And which do you put first, then? Are you putting the news before the essay?

Mike: I kind of gravitate to doing that. It's kind of like I guess an addiction or it makes me feel good. Then I wondered whether I gravitate towards activities that are anxiety-minimising as opposed to an activity like engaging in a piece of written work which is potentially anxiety-maximising because you'll inevitably go wrong at some point and, 'Oh God, I've got to rewrite that. I've got to find that reference. Ugh.' It's almost like it's just nicer to read the newspaper.

Windy: It is.

Mike: Do a Sudoku.

Windy: You're definitely right and I think that you're talking about the human condition here, Mike, that, given a choice between doing something that's anxiety-free or anxiety – using your words – maximising in any moment in time, then the human being would go for the anxiety-free activity, unless there is a reason to do the other activity. And is there a reason, Mike, for you to do your reflexive essay this weekend?

Mike: OK. No. There is a reason for me to do the essay. If I don't do it, I'll fail my MA. But there's not a reason for me to do that essay this weekend. Therefore, I put it off and procrastinate.

Windy: Could you create a reason to do it this weekend? Let me ask you, Mike, let's share definitions of procrastination – you show me yours first and then I'll show you mine. How do you define procrastination?

Mike: I see it as … well, this phrase comes to mind: 'procrastination is the thief of time'. I don't know why that comes to mind. Maybe I read it somewhere. Maybe it's a famous saying. I don't know.

Windy: It is a famous saying.

Mike: Yeah, 'procrastination is the thief of time'. I feel, for me in my Heideggerian being in the world, time is a precious commodity to me. I don't want the Mercedes, I don't want Hugo Boss clothing, I want to buy time. Time's important to me because I feel I'm busy.

Windy: You are busy.

Mike: I kind of feel procrastination, to me, is about a binary use of time.... If I'm not doing this essay, I am doing something else, but it's something else I need to be doing.

Windy: Yeah. So your definition of procrastination, what I can see, is quite focused on the immediate, the here and now. Is that right? 'Using time is important to me. I've got a choice whether I can do an essay which doesn't have to be done this weekend or I could read the *Guardian*, and, since that's a much more appealing use of time than the essay, I will do that.' That's what I'm hearing. Is that correct?

Mike: Yeah, but I kind of want to bring this word 'priority' in, because just before lunch I'm looking at my diary, I've got a two o'clock with you, I've then got a three o'clock, then I've got to go out tonight with two people at seven o'clock for a catch-up drink, and I'm thinking, 'I need to sort the car insurance out.' So that is an important thing I need to do, otherwise the car won't be insured, but somehow I've fitted that in, but that's gonna expire on 14th May, so that's more pressing. I just wonder whether procrastination to me is like you're trapped in a room and there's this great big thing across you – I'm trying to explain the metaphor. It's not an immediate pressure, the essay, at the moment, but I would like to get it out of the way. Like my colleagues have all said, 'Yeah, I've done the reflexive.' They don't have to worry about it anymore.

Windy: Yeah, but you could do that.

Mike: I guess I could do that, but I don't seem to be able to. Like I'm really looking forward to this session – I don't seem to be able to do that.

Windy: I think you are able to do that, because, if you didn't have the ability to do that, we could stop now. You don't have the ability to flap your wings and fly and, no matter how many sessions with Professor Dryden you'll have, that's still the case. But would you agree that you have the ability?

                   [*It is important that Mike acknowledges that he does have the ability to solve his problem.*]

Mike: Yes.

Windy: But you're not using the ability.

Mike: OK, that's good, yeah.

Windy: So here's my definition of procrastination. Procrastination is putting off doing something at a time when it is in your interest to do it, and doing something that is in your interest to do. So there's an element of the activity: is this something worth doing? In your case, it sounds like, with the essay it is because your overall goal is to train as a psychotherapist. Then presumably this will help you towards that because it will help you towards a qualification. I'm less convinced by the 'at a time when it is in your interest to do it', because, although you seem to be saying that you have a choice to either put it off to the last minute before you get crushed – Mike's writing away just before the crusher comes in. Or you can do it in a different mindset which says, 'I want to get this out of the way, so let me make an agreement with myself what my timeline is,' because at the moment you don't have a timeline other than to avoid the crusher, it seems to me, if I've understood you.

Mike: … Yes. With your definition – putting off doing something at a time when it's in your interest to do it and it's in your interest to do the task – it's certainly in my interest to do the task, but it doesn't fulfil that 'something at a time when it's in your interest to do it'. There isn't that immediate pressure.

Windy: Well, this is what I think you've done, Mike. I think you've trained yourself, as many, many people who procrastinate do, to avoid the crusher. Mike avoids the crusher. I'm not sure you've got an experience of actually working with a different mindset.

Mike: I agree. What you're saying is very liberating in a way because I think I waste a lot of energy on thinking about the procrastination.

Windy: Yeah, that's right, because then procrastination stops becoming a behaviour – which is an avoidance behaviour and I think you've hinted at certain things that you're avoiding which are anxiety-related – and it then becomes a stimulus to which you have feelings about: 'Oh, I'm procrastinating,' and then you start having feelings about procrastination, which, it sounds like to me, gets you further away from doing the task.

Let me ask you the question, Mike: would you like to experiment with a different mindset just to see what it feels like for a while? You could always go back to your old one. That's not going anywhere. A different mindset is, 'Because this is important to me, I'll do it early and get it out the way and confront the things that I would generally not confront, because I could always go to the Guardian website, and really grapple with that and see what that experience is like.'

Mike: Yeah, that will be good.

[Rather than engaging Mike is a struggle, I invite him to see a change in behaviour as an experiment.]

Windy: Yeah?

Mike: Yeah.

Windy: So it's a difference between saying, 'The motivation is to avoid the crusher versus the motivation is to do an important task earlier to confront what it is I would generally avoid, and deal with it, do the task and then have time for the Guardian website.' In other words, you would be using what I would call behavioural principles, in a way. You would be rewarding yourself with something enjoyable in terms of doing something which is important to you but less enjoyable, rather than going for the reward first.

So, if we were to take that stance, Mike, let's be really specific because one of the techniques I'm going to offer you is that, if you're really clear with yourself precisely when you're going to start a task, you'll be clear if you're procrastinating or not. So I'm going to ask you to nominate a starting time for this reflexive essay. When would be a good time for you to begin it this weekend?

Mike: I think four o'clock tomorrow, because I think I will be watching the telly because we're going to invite an 80-year-old lady round whose husband's a republican and she can't bear watching the coronation with him. So she's coming round and I'm going to be cooking roast beef and Yorkshire puddings and stuff. So I don't want to do it between ten and three tomorrow.

Windy: Fine, OK. So four o'clock. Now, where do you envisage doing the essay?

Mike: Here, where I am now in my office.

Windy: And is that an encouraging environment to work or a discouraging environment to work?

Mike: It's full of unfiled paper… everywhere because I haven't got round to it. A lot of those papers are to-do lists.

Windy: So it sounds like it may be something of a discouraging environment.

Mike: Well, yeah, because one of the things I've got to do, and I know this sounds crazy, is to go through all my to-do lists.

Windy: OK, but let's just stick to the task. Is it possible for you to cover up that for the purposes of doing the task, like a drape?

[*It is important for people with a problem with procrastination to make their working environment as conducive to beginning and continuing the task as possible. However, it is important for them to do this before getting down to the task at the time agreed with themself. Otherwise, they might use this strategy to procrastinate.*]

Mike: Yeah.

Windy: So that's what I suggest.

Mike: I'll just put it all in a bag.

Windy: Put it all in a bag. Just clear it out the way so your environment is working for you, not against you. That's one thing. So now it's four o'clock. Now, do you think having nominated that starting time, you would be able to start at that point or would you be tempted to put it off at that point?

Mike: … [*Pause*] Well, it's a very good question, isn't it? I mean, you're kindly helping me do this and it would seem somewhat churlish if tomorrow at four o'clock I said, 'Oh, I'd better go and load the dishwasher because of all the lunch stuff and put it off again.'

Windy: Would that be a temptation?

Mike: It would be, yeah, if I'm being honest. It made me think I almost want Windy there saying, 'I'm gonna chop one of your fingers off if you don't do it,' and make it painful.

Windy: I've heard of digital counselling but I think that is taking it a little bit too far, don't you think? But, in a way, what that shows me is that, left to your own devices when Windy or anybody else is not there, then it would be quite easy for you to think about doing the dishes and then actually doing the dishes. What ingredient would you think you needed to start the task rather than go to do the dishes?

Mike: I think what I just said actually might be the key to it which is, I don't know why this is, but it would be some form of pain or punishment, in a sort of kindly way. It wouldn't be, 'If you do this at four, I'll give you some Cadbury's Crème Eggs which I know you like, Mike, and are now impossible to buy.' Well, it could be that, actually. I think it would either have to be some reward or some punishment.

Windy: Well, what would you recommend a client to start with: the reward or the punishment?

Mike: Well, I think we should be on a reward basis for the client. I don't think you should be introducing negativity into it.

Windy: So what would be rewarding? What are we rewarding, by the way? Let's be clear about what we are rewarding.

Mike: Yes.

Windy: The start or the start continuing and finishing a certain chunk of work? What are we rewarding?

Mike: Well, I was gonna say it wasn't either of those. It was we're rewarding ... me not procrastinating, which is perhaps a different way of saying we're rewarding me starting. I see it more that I'm not procrastinating which is what the reward should be as opposed to the start.

Windy: So when would you reward yourself? If you're gonna start at four o'clock when would be a time when you would acknowledge, 'I am Mike and I am not procrastinating on this task.'

Mike: OK, good, I get that. So, rather than give the reward at four, 'Here's your Crème Egg,' I think you'd have to say, 'You get your reward at five after you've done an hour's work.'

Windy: OK. And what would that reward be, Mike?

Mike: I think it would be something I'd like – Crème Eggs.

Windy: But you said they're difficult to get.

Mike: No, I managed to get some, actually, at a fair we went to. I've got them in the freezer. I've got about three left.

Windy: So how long do they take to defrost?

Mike: When you've got them in your hands, they warm up. They're not melting.

Windy: So here's the situation: you are going to sit down, having put all the other stuff into a bag in your eyesight. You're going to sit down and you're going to say, 'OK, I'm going to experiment with a different mindset with working. Rather than wait for the crusher to come, I'm going to do it as agreed at four and I'm going to reward myself with a Crème Egg at five.' Now, can you picture yourself doing that in the mindset that we're talking about?

Mike: Yeah. I think it's a different way of conceptualising it. There's clear steps there.

Windy: OK. Now, in terms of the task itself, you did mention earlier that there were certain aspects of it that were anxiety-provoking? Did I understand you correctly?

Mike: Yeah. There's a tick box of five things you have to cover off in the essay and it's a very short piece of work and you've got to put in peer feedback, tutor feedback – I need to find that, four or five references perhaps, and knock it all to shape. I mean, it's essentially the length of a newspaper article.

Windy: So, as you hear yourself talking about it, is that something that you can do without my helping you to do it or do you think you might encounter an obstacle that I could help you with as you hear yourself talking about that?

Mike: No, I think I'm OK. I think I just have to knock it out, actually.

Windy: So let's compare the two situations. We'll call it the Crème Egg mindset versus the Avoid the Crusher mindset. Now, the Avoid the Crusher mindset is this: 'OK, I've got a lot on, I'm very busy. Yeah, I've got this task but there's no good reason to do it. I don't have to do it this weekend. I've got plenty of time and I'll get round to doing it to avoid the crusher.' And you don't need any help with that mindset, do you?

Mike: No.

Windy: This is something that you have rolled out. The Crème Egg mindset is saying this: 'OK, I could do that, but actually I want to develop a different way of being with regards to time. I want to do something earlier that's important to me so I can learn that the more something is important to me, the earlier perhaps I need to do it. And, in order to encourage myself, I'm going to reward myself after a period of time, in this case an hour, with something which I really like, which is a Crème Egg.' Now, can you see the differences between those two mindsets?

[This is another instance of me distilling two different ways forward – this time within the frame of the 'avoid the crusher' mindset vs the 'Crème Egg' mindset.]

Mike: Yeah, I can. I think it's good in that it delineates it and ... it allocates a piece of space/time for it as opposed to it being ambiguously in the future.

Windy: Yes, and it puts you at the point of agency.

Mike: Yeah.

Windy: You are in the centre of this and you are the person who chooses that you can access one or other of these mindsets.

Mike: Yeah.... [*Long pause*]

Windy: What are your thoughts about that?

Mike: Yeah, I like it. I'm gonna try it.

Windy: OK. So why don't you summarise what we've done and then we can talk about the takeaways and how you might be able to generalise that, because that's what I'm keen to help you to do? So why don't you summarise the work we've done today, Mike?

[*Once again, I encourage the client to summarise the work.*]

Mike: Well, I think we've discussed that there are two potential mindsets in respect of me and one is we call it the Crusher mindset and it's delaying things, not necessarily to the last minute but it involved a lot of energy thinking about all these things I have to do but delaying doing them and almost randomly choosing to do things on an ad hoc basis. Like here I can say, 'I have a book on something called Design Analysis and I want to read.' So, just because I see it out of the corner of my eye, I might think, 'Right, I'll get through another chapter of that.' So I think there's a lot of randomness and chaos to how I go about doing tasks.

So what you've created is a structure, on certain tasks that need to be done and do take quite a bit of time, I think it's to create a boundary around them. It's to create a boundary around them, to agree a time, to clear chaos and, once achieved, to give yourself a reward. That's how I see it.

Windy: Right. Now, can you see that you can generalise that to other situations other than the reflexive essay?

Mike: Yes, I was just thinking. I was thinking that book on Design Analysis, I've probably got a third of it to read, why don't I set myself a time, if that's a priority? It's not particularly a priority. It's a bit like the Guardian website, actually, that. But with things that are less leisure, let's call them things I need to create before I consume – I think that could be a way of looking at it – is to set these. The word 'rigid' is coming to mind, but there is a certain rigidity about it. But a kinder way of looking at that would be to say self-discipline.

Windy: Right. Rigid in what sense, Mike?

Mike: I'm not someone who naturally likes rules, but I am someone who understands you need to have a self-discipline in order to put in the effort to get the results. There's a bit of a conflict going on in my mind. I don't like rules. I agree with whoever it was who said 'good men don't obey the rules too well'. That might've been Disraeli, I can't remember. But I think, if you have too much chaos and anarchy, you're gonna end up in the crusher.

So … [*pause*] I can't remember what question I'm answering now.

Windy: Well, it's about generalising what you're learning to other aspects of your life. And I think one of the things that you're reacting against, and I don't see it as a rule, I see it as a mindset; I see it as a way of actually approaching something which is in your interests, which is the bit about procrastinating: it's in your interest to do this task because it's gonna help you to get your qualification. And we're talking about a different attitude towards at a time when it's in your interest to do it. We're experimenting and trying out the idea of actually not waiting until the crusher's around the corner but to actually put it into a frame of choosing to do something that's important to you earlier and to reward yourself along the way.

Mike: It's something that I've never, I don't think, done for a long time. I mean, I was talking to my daughter about doing A Levels and having a revision timetable, and I was explaining how I had a revision timetable and I stuck to it and, if someone came round to ask me to go out for a drink, I'd say, 'No, I'm sorry because I'm doing biology,' and I just wouldn't break the revision timetable. So, in a way, what you're saying is something akin to that.

Windy: What I'm saying, Mike, is I think you need to reacquaint yourself with that self.

[Mike indicates that he has had the experience of using the solution that we have developed, so I suggest that he reacquaint himself with his former self.]

Mike: Yeah.

Windy: Because you've got that in your repertoire. You very nicely articulated that you've actually got that in your repertoire, but you've lost touch with that part of yourself. You can say hello to that part of yourself and say, 'Actually, I've done it before. I can actually bring it into the present and help with doing it now.'

Mike: … *[Long pause]*

Windy: What's going through your mind right now?

Mike: … *[Pause]* I'm going to give this a go, actually, and then to roll it out. I have a friend who's very, very busy and he gives himself easy wins at the start of the day. He would make his bed and say, 'That's an easy win.' And then I think he'd proceed to difficult tasks and then he'd have tasks 8, 9 and 10 and would go back to easier tasks.

Windy: Do you think that might be of some help to you?

Mike: I think so, yeah.

Windy: I'm all for you learning from people who you know and who can be a bit of a role model to you at this point. So you can incorporate that one too. It's like the easy win helps you to build up ahead of steam, almost.

Mike: Yeah, but to have something that requires a lot of time and concentration but set a block of time for that.

Windy: Right, yeah.

Mike: Because I don't know how long it's gonna take to write it.

Windy: Right.

Mike: So it is a bit open-ended, but then it could be it's finished within an hour or it might be that you then have to do it again and say, 'I now need to allocate from six o'clock on Sunday night to finish it off.

Windy: Right, with another Crème Egg.

Mike: Yeah, or whatever. I might have a beer then because it's Sunday in the evening.

Windy: Sure. Is there anything else you wanna say about this before we finish or ask about this before we finish that you might think, 'Oh, I wish I'd mentioned that or asked that'?

Mike: Yeah. If you're happy to go on for a bit longer, yeah.

Windy: Sure.

Mike: We did talk at the beginning from a psychodynamic sense of everyone's unique, so, from a psychodynamic sense, is it useful to look at why people might procrastinate or is this something that's just a CBT activity to change somebody's behaviour, and we're not particularly interested in the causes of procrastination? I'm just interested in your theoretical underpinnings of it.

Windy: I kind of use Occam's Razor on this which means let's start off with the most simple approach and then see how we go, because, if you are going to be able to roll this out, as you say, then we don't need to look at the psychodynamics. But, if you're committed to rolling it out and you find that you don't and you keep not doing that, there's obviously some other factor that we have overlooked that we need to actually look at. But we don't know yet what that is. So why not take what you've got, put it into practice and see what happens?

Mike: Mmm [yes] … sure.

Windy: In fact, some people would say, looking at the psychodynamics of procrastination may be a form of procrastination, because it's putting off actually at the time when you need to do the task.

Mike: I mean, it's very much about action, isn't it?

Windy: Action and mindset, I think. I think the reason why you haven't solved your problem, apart from the fact the overall context is you do have a lot on, but, when we narrowed this thing down, once you said, 'Look, I could do this piece of work or I could read the *Guardian*,' I think you almost look in your environment and then, 'Oh, there's that book,' and you go to it rather than saying, 'Well, OK, I could go to that, but actually I've made this commitment.'

So it's a sense of actually behaviour based on a mindset. And I'm open to if a psychoanalytic explanation could add to the mindset, then that's fine, but we don't know whether that's the case with you or not.

Mike: No, and you're right, it's irrelevant, potentially.

Windy: And we also have evidence that Mike who was doing his A Levels was very organised, and that Mike is still there, he just needs to be brought into the present.

Mike: Yeah. ... [*Long pause*]

Windy: OK.

Mike: Thank you.

Windy: My pleasure. I'll send you the audio recording and then a little later on the transcript. I don't think we mentioned any names apart from your own, but feel free to change any that we have that I may have missed in there. Lovely to talk to you, Mike, and all the best.

Mike: Yeah, appreciate it. Thanks a lot, Windy.

Mike's Reflections (10-08-23)

Attending the 'How to Avoid Procrastination' session led by Windy was an illuminating experience that prompted me to re-evaluate my approach to tasks and time management. The session revolved myself and Windy discussing my struggles with procrastination over a course essay and my desire to overcome it. The key takeaways from the session provided valuable insights into how to address procrastination effectively and cultivate a more productive mindset.

The session highlighted the importance of understanding the underlying reasons behind procrastination. Windy emphasized the need to approach the issue based on individual circumstances rather than applying generic techniques. This perspective resonated with the idea that each person's challenges with procrastination can stem from unique sources, ranging from anxiety to disorganization. Windy's approach aimed to make the strategies directly applicable to my situation, avoiding a one-size-fits-all approach.

One central concept introduced during the session was the distinction between the 'Avoid the Crusher' mindset and the 'Crème Egg' mindset. The former referred to the tendency to postpone tasks until the last possible moment, driven by a sense of urgency or external pressure. The latter, exemplified by the metaphor of rewarding oneself with a Crème Egg after completing a task, represented a more proactive and structured approach to task completion. This concept encouraged me to establish specific starting times for tasks and incentivize my efforts with rewards. The Crème Egg mindset focused on taking ownership of one's time and prioritizing important tasks to foster a sense of accomplishment and self-discipline.

Windy's approach also delved into the significance of creating an optimal environment for work. By removing distractions and clutter, I could establish a conducive workspace that encouraged focused work. The session highlighted the importance of setting boundaries and creating a dedicated space for tasks, reflecting a broader principle applicable to enhancing productivity and focus.

Furthermore, the session underscored the importance of generalizing the strategies to various aspects of life beyond the immediate task. My realisation that I could apply similar techniques to other activities, such as reading and studying, showcased the versatility and practicality of the strategies discussed.

While the session primarily focused on behavioural strategies, the conversation briefly touched upon the relevance of psychodynamic perspectives. However, we decided that looking at causes in this way was actually a form of 'procrastination'. Therefore, the emphasis remained on actionable steps to address procrastination rather than delving into deeper underlying causes. This pragmatic approach aligned with the session's goal of equipping me with practical tools for immediate implementation.

In conclusion, the session was a thought-provoking exploration of strategies to overcome procrastination. The session offered a personalized and actionable approach tailored to my circumstances. The concept of adopting a 'Crème Egg' mindset, accompanied by creating an optimal work environment, setting boundaries, and generalizing the strategies, presented a comprehensive framework for addressing procrastination effectively. The session underscored the value of taking proactive steps to manage time and tasks, ultimately contributing to increased productivity and a more disciplined approach to work and life.

I'm now registered with BACP and got my MA – thanks to your session I did complete the assignment!

12

Attending to the Creative, Thinking and Organisational Aspects of Pottery

Date: 08/05/23
Time: 44 minutes 39 secs

Windy: So, Sharon, what's your understanding of the purpose of our conversation this afternoon?

Sharon: Well, it's a single session and it's dealing with an issue around procrastination.

Windy: And do you want to tell me what your issue to do with procrastination is?

Sharon: Yeah. Well, I was deliberating between a couple of issues, but I think this is the one that I've settled on for today. So I have a little online pottery business, and so I do counselling as well, and the pottery, I suppose it's more of a hobby but it's something that I've done for quite a long time, maybe ten years. And in a lot of aspects of the pottery business I do procrastinate, from most recently getting the website up and running and trying to decide which one to go for, and I just couldn't decide and I put it of and put it off. But I finally got that working. But even just getting things photographed to get uploaded onto the website and even getting up to make things and then getting them into the kiln and getting them glazed, every stage there seems to be a lot of procrastination. And, therefore, I feel like it stagnates; it never reaches its full potential because of that.

Windy: So you say you've been doing this for ten years?

Sharon: Yeah, about that.

Windy: And has there been a time with the pottery business that you would say that you weren't procrastinating?

Sharon: … [*Pause*] Probably not totally, but I do remember a time when the boundaries were totally blurred in terms of it had taken over my life and I was working at a dentist's at the time. And, so every evening I was doing pottery. So … yeah, I might've been procrastinating in some elements there … in terms of … [*long pause*] sharing things perhaps online. But … I think it was probably in the other extreme: I pushed myself too hard, I think.

Windy: Right, OK. So, although there was an element of procrastination in terms of sharing the work you were doing online, there was a time when you were actually, we can say, not procrastinating; you were actually working quite hard and you were pushing yourself, from what you were saying, too hard with that.

Sharon: Yeah, and I think part of that was perhaps a career transition. So I was working at a dentist's and I was planning to use the pottery to support whilst I was doing my counselling training. So there was an urgency then.

Windy: An urgency as experienced by whom?

Sharon: Well, I felt perhaps that was maybe driving me to create more pottery and to push the pottery business.

Windy: Because?

Sharon: Because I needed the income really from it in order to support the transition.

Windy: And that was important to you to do that, to have that transition?

Sharon: Yeah.

Windy: So, when we look back and look at a time when you were actually working quite hard at the pottery, we see that you did that because it was important to you to make the transition from being a dentist to a counsellor and that you needed to have the pottery work as a transition between one and the other. And, because you experienced that as being important to you, you didn't procrastinate.

Sharon: Yeah.

Windy: So we can say that, when you experience something that's important to you or what you experienced in this area, you didn't procrastinate.

Sharon: Yeah. I suppose I felt like I had to.

Windy: Like there wasn't a choice.

Sharon: Yeah, like I needed to make it work because I really wanted to be able to move.

Windy: So what I'm picking up there is there is a sense of determination.

Sharon: Yeah.

Windy: And commitment.

Sharon: Yeah.

Windy: So, when there was a sense of determination and commitment, you didn't procrastinate. Do you work as a counsellor now?

               [*I will use these ingredients because they have helped Sharon in the past not to procrastinate.*]

Sharon: Yeah.

Windy: For whom?

Sharon: Links Counselling.

Windy: So do you procrastinate in your counselling work?

Sharon: No.

Windy: Why?

Sharon: Well, I have a contract and ... yeah, I suppose I'm determined and committed. Perhaps there's an element where, when I need to contact a client, I will maybe put a phone call off in the day, but I always do it.

Windy: So, again, when there's a sense of determination and commitment, you don't put things off.

Sharon: Yeah. You see, I'm employed as a community counsellor. I guess I'm just curious, I wonder if I was a private therapist would I have a problem with procrastination.

Windy: And what's your sense?

Sharon: I don't know. I think the contract, it helps me to keep momentum because I'm expected to be in certain days and to see a certain number of clients per week.

Windy: Have you ever made a contract with yourself about anything?

Sharon: ... [*Pause*]

Windy: Not a formal thing that you had to sign, but I'm thinking about the thing with the experience that you had with the pottery where you, in a sense, made a contract with yourself to really push hard on the pottery because you wanted to make the transition. It sounded like there was a bit of a contract there between you and you.

Sharon: Yeah. Yes, I know what you mean. I would say I probably have made an unofficial contract with myself in different areas.

Windy: And when you do that what happens?

Sharon: Yeah, largely I can stick with it.

Windy: OK. Would it be possible for you to make a contract with yourself regarding the pottery in terms of where you are with it now, so that you did not procrastinate, having made that contract with yourself?

Sharon: Yeah. So I have had an intention. So I've tried to keep a Tuesday clear. I haven't officially made a contract with myself, but over the last number of months I think I have had that intention: I'll do pottery on a Tuesday.

                [Here I see the idea of Sharon making a contract with herself as another anti-procrastination ingredient.]

Windy: So what's the difference in your mind between making a contract with yourself and having an intention?

Sharon: Perhaps an intention is on a spectrum of good intentions. I'm more likely to procrastinate if it's just an intention.

Windy: So what would the difference be at this point where you are in your pottery business between having an intention and having a contract with yourself?

Sharon: More specific, perhaps. Maybe I need to do something more specific.

Windy: With that specificity, if you were to verbalise it, what would it sound like?

Sharon: So, in terms of what I would have in the contract?

Windy: Sure.

Sharon: ... So ... I'm gonna commit to... doing – I suppose it needs to be time ... I need to have a think about what specific task needs doing. Maybe I need to think ahead at times, because there's lots of different aspects of it from photographing to making to glazing.

Windy: Right. I'm wondering where you are in your pottery business. It's been with you for ten years. I don't know how you would describe it, whether it's on the up, just treading water, on the way down, in terms of where it is and where you'd like to see it.

Sharon: Yeah.... I did start the website last month.

Windy: What was the purpose of the website?

Sharon: Because I had made quite a few things and I had a lot of queries. I thought it would be easier to sell them through a website rather than through interactions with people, because that's quite time-consuming.

Windy: So you built your own website?

Sharon: Yeah.

Windy: Well, that takes some doing. And the purpose of doing that was because you've got quite a lot of stuff that you wanted to sell.

Sharon: Yeah.

Windy: And the purpose of selling it is what? Obviously financial, but what would you use the finances for. Beforehand you were using it to facilitate your transition from being a dentist to a counsellor.

Sharon: Yeah.

Windy: What would the purpose of it be now?

Sharon: Yeah. I hadn't really thought about it, but it's more for the family to help.

Windy: To help what?

Sharon: I suppose just to help with bills and things.

Windy: Is that important to you?

Sharon: We always seem to manage whether or not I do. Yeah, so I don't feel that pressure.

Windy: Right. So it sounds like there's a big difference between when you were doing the pottery in order to aid the transition and now, because you say, 'I did the website in order to sell more pots. Why do you sell more pots? Well, to make money for the bills. But we managed anyway.' So it sounds like, when we take a close look at it, I'm wondering what the real value this business has for you.

Sharon: Yeah. The motivation?

Windy: Well, I define procrastination as putting off something which is in your interest to do at a time when it's in your interest to do it. And I'm wondering at the moment is it in your interest to do much with the pottery because, certainly from a financial point of view, it's not making that big an impact. And I'm wondering if there are any other points of view, like creativity, anything else.

Sharon: Yes, it is the creativity. It's a really important part of me.

[*Money is not an important motivational factor for Sharon; creativity is.*]

Windy: So the idea would be then, 'OK, the finances don't really make a difference, but what is really important to me is actually being creative.'

Sharon: Yeah.

Windy: So the question is are you putting off on something that's really important to you?

Sharon: ... Yeah.

Windy: Because it enables you to express your creativity.

Sharon: Yeah.... Yeah, I know I do really miss it whenever I neglect it.

Windy: So what mindset would you have to be in to not neglect it, to go back to that part of you that wants to make a contract with herself vis-à-vis the pottery with the point of expressing your creativity?

Sharon: Perhaps maybe being more organised and giving it thought. I think maybe sometimes it's upstairs, it's out of the way, it's kind of out of sight, out of mind.

Windy: What is out of sight?

Sharon: My pottery room is upstairs and I don't go up there unless I really need to use it.

Windy: What about your creativity? That's not upstairs in a closet somewhere, is it?

Sharon: That's a good point, yeah. It's making space for that, perhaps. Prioritising.

Windy: Yeah, making space for an important part of yourself.

Sharon: Yeah.

Windy: What's your family life? Who's in the family?

Sharon: I've got three children aged 17, 15 and 12, and a husband.

Windy: I don't know what they're like, but, if you went to them and said, 'Look, I really need to commit myself more to my pottery because it enables me to express my creativity. Can I have your support in this?' what do you think they'd say to you?

[*Here, I am encouraging Sharon to make use of external resources.*]

Sharon: Yeah, I think they would all be supportive.

Windy: So the question is can you give yourself that support? Can you contract with yourself so that you don't neglect what sounds like an important part of you?

Sharon: Yeah, it is an important part of me and I do neglect it now and again, and then I always come back to it.

Windy: Yeah. So what would a contract sound like that would actually enable you to move forward without procrastinating, because we know that, when you make a contract, you don't procrastinate?

Sharon: Yeah.... [*Long pause*] What would the contract sound like? So I will set aside ... Tuesday morning to ... work on some aspect of the pottery.

Windy: OK. What does it feel like saying that, because you looked hesitant?

Sharon: Yeah. I guess I'm thinking of other demands and other things that push in and push that out of the way.

Windy: Do these things have a life of themselves?

Sharon: No, because I'm choosing. So I'm not prioritising.

Windy: I guess it comes down to the idea how much are you going to put yourself first, Sharon?

Sharon: It's a challenge.

Windy: Is it?

Sharon: … Yeah.

Windy: What's challenging about putting yourself first?

Sharon: … [*Pause*] Well, I do believe in self-care.

Windy: You mean as a theoretical concept that applies to other people or something that can be part of your lived experience?

Sharon: Yeah. No, I do believe and I have implemented it in different ways. Like I always make time for exercise.

Windy: But not for creativity.

Sharon: … Yeah.

Windy: What's the difference between exercise and creativity?

Sharon: Yeah, it's an important part of me, and I guess that's a good challenge.

Windy: I'm always a great believer in trying to bring things together, but I'm not sure how you'd combine exercise with pottery.

Sharon: Yeah. It has been done. I've done research whilst on the exercise bike.

Windy: Yeah, but I guess you can't do the actual creating of the pots while being on an exercise bike. I think you're going to have to stand back and ask yourself, 'Creativity is an important part of me, but, in order for me to turn that into regular action, maybe I need to make that contract with myself. Maybe I need to say the difference between: "I'll do it on a Tuesday unless other things crop up that are more important," to, "I'll do it on a Tuesday no matter what, unless the house is burning down or something really bad's happening to the kids or my husband,"' or something like that. 'That's my time. Tuesday morning is Sharon time.'

Sharon: Yeah, because I think you're right the way you have stated the current contract. I will set aside pottery unless other things… creep in. So I think that's probably as it stands. So it needs augmenting slightly.

Windy: Yeah, and also don't forget other things don't have a life of their own. They don't creep unless you've got snakes in the house – snakes will creep in, but tasks don't. Tasks are there and you get to choose whether to do it or not. What would happen if you made a contract with yourself, Sharon, which said, 'Look, creativity's really important to me and I do need to commit myself to doing that. So I'm going to devote myself every Tuesday morning to pottery, unless there's a real family emergency.' How does that sound?

Sharon: Yeah. Well, I can imagine if I did that, that I would make progress.

Windy: The way you say it: 'I imagine if I did that.' Can you experience some kind of obstacle that's around that will stop you from making that commitment?

Sharon: It's what I say yes and no to. I'm just thinking, I have a position in terms of a leadership role within a church and often ask to meet up or ask to have a chat, and I suppose the way I currently am managing that is that I see Tuesday as being that day where I could do that. So I'm not protecting that creativity time.

Windy: Yeah, so can you imagine when they want to have a chat and they say, 'Tuesday morning?' and you say, 'Actually, no, Tuesday mornings I'm not free'? Could you imagine saying that?

Sharon: Yeah, I could. Well, yeah.

Windy: What experience goes along with saying that to people?

Sharon: … [*Pause*] I think it's just something that's new to me. But I am aware that I have a limited amount of capacity and there could be other options for people if they do need me.

Windy: What other options are there?

Sharon: Other times during the week.

Windy: Yeah. In fact, you might want to organise a time for that as well.

Sharon: ... Yeah.

Windy: So, if you reminded yourself, 'Look, this is my time with pottery. If they wanna intrude upon that, I'm just saying, "No, I'm not available. This is when I am available." And so I'm gonna take charge of my life so that I can give myself the opportunity to express that part of myself which is important to me to express,' could you imagine doing that?

Sharon: Yeah. I mean, I'm thinking, something I've been considering lately is people pleasing and I suppose what's the driving force behind that.

Windy: Well, yes and no, Sharon, because it sounds like there's one person that you're not pleasing in all this.

Sharon: Mmm [yes].

Windy: Who's that?

Sharon: Yeah, that creative part of me.

Windy: Yeah, you. But the point is, let's suppose somebody says to you, 'Are you free, Sharon, on Tuesday morning?' and you say, 'No, I'm not, but I can see you on Thursday afternoon,' one is are they gonna be displeased by that?

Sharon: ... No. I think it's fair enough.

Windy: And, if they are gonna be displeased about that, how are you gonna view their displeasure?

Sharon: … Yeah, well, they're being a bit unreasonable if I'm offering them something.

Windy: That's right, yeah. So, if you offer them something within a boundary and a structure, and they are displeased about that, then, as you say, they're being unreasonable, because they're really saying, 'It's gotta be when I want it to be.'

Sharon: Yeah, I know.

Windy: It sounds like you've got a lot on in your life to balance, and I think that what you've done is, like many, many, many people have done is to edit out yourself in the picture. And now we're talking about bringing yourself back into the picture: making a contract with yourself, having a structure to support that, having a family to support that, recognising that, if people are displeased with that, then that's unreasonable; you don't have to please people who are unreasonable. You could but you don't have to. And then, if you turn that into more of a contract with yourself, would you still procrastinate, Sharon?

Sharon: … [*Long pause*] Well, I have contracted with myself in the past with certain things that are important to me, and have been able to protect them. So, yeah.

Windy: I don't think you've lost sight of that. It's a bit like saying, 'I like plants. I value plants but I'm not gonna feed them.'

Sharon: … [*Pause*] Yeah, my actions are not matching up.

Windy: That's right. So, if you wanna feed that plant of yours called creativity, what follows?

Sharon: Yeah, it's more likely to flourish.

Windy: If you feed it.

Sharon: That's a good point.

Windy: I'll take a line and change it around from my favourite film, *The Field of Dreams* – 'If you feed it, it will grow.'

Sharon: Yeah.

Windy: If you don't, it won't. And it sounds like you haven't been feeding it because I don't think you've really brought your creativity to the centre stage of why things are important to you. It didn't come out until we probed on it. What came out was money, but then you said it's not that important. So, it sounds like you have buried your creativity somewhere, and maybe you need to bring it out and really say, 'Look, this is important to me. If I don't tender it, it's not gonna grow. It's not gonna grow in the room upstairs with my other stuff where I think I temporarily left it.'

Sharon: Yeah. I like that imagery. And the funny thing is my daughters are very creative also, and I really encourage them in that aspect of them, but I guess I'm maybe not modelling that so well.

Windy: That's right, because if you model it, you're encouraging them. So modelling is not only doing something for yourself but also really showing your daughters that you can model by example, not by just encouragement without doing it.

[*Helping Sharon see that she encourages creativity in her daughters underscores the importance of creativity in and for herself.*]

Sharon: Yeah. And I'm wondering as well whether being disorganised is part of the issue as well.

Windy: Tell me about that.

Sharon: Well, it's just if I could have a clear plan of what I'm doing on a Tuesday. Sometimes it's just there's so much potential, you could do so many different things you could be working on, I almost don't know where to start.

Windy: How much are you prepared to give your pottery on a Tuesday morning? What's the time parameters?

Sharon: Well, I'm thinking from ten until lunchtime, perhaps.

Windy: Lunchtime being what? Half past eleven|? One o'clock? Two o'clock?

Sharon: Probably closer to 1:30 or so.

Windy: OK, 10 'til 1:30. OK, you've got three-and-a-half hours. So, we know that in that time you're gonna have to put some creativity because what else has got to go into that time? Organisation?

Sharon: Yeah, perhaps just even thinking time, 'What am I gonna do?'

Windy: Thinking time, organisation and creativity, OK?

Sharon: Yeah.

Windy: So, if you say, 'I've got to give expression to these three different facets,' then you can play around with what comes first and are you going to do the creativity first and then do the other stuff later, or what? You've got to figure out what works for you. But, if you really take that and say, 'I've got three-and-a-half hours here and I've got these tasks to do, then I can assign what time I'm gonna give it.' What do you think will happen if you actually bring your organisational skills? It sounds like to me that you do have organisational skills. Is that right?

Sharon: It's not my strength.

Windy: No, but how do you manage to express that in the family situation?

Sharon: With being organised.

Windy: Yeah.

Sharon: With meals and things like that.

Windy: Whatever you have to organise.

Sharon: Yeah, I do organise meals, I do organise getting the school lunches and things, I guess in comparison.

Windy: So you do have organisational skills which you are able to implement, right?

Sharon: Yeah. I just suppose we all have strengths and weaknesses, and it probably isn't my strength being an organised person.

Windy: Well, if you want to regard yourself as an organised person as opposed to a disorganised person, you can, but I would see it as, 'I'm a person who has got organisational skills and strengths which I express in this area, and I'm not expressing it in this area. So maybe I can learn from myself that is good at organising in this area and bring those capacities and strengths to this area.'

[What I am doing here is suggesting that organisation is a matter of transferable skills rather than identity.]

Sharon: Yeah.... Yeah. I guess it's just making time to attend to that.

Windy: When you say make time, what do you mean by 'make' time? Is this another part of pottery: you make a pot, you make some time? How does it work?

Sharon: That would be good.

Windy: Yeah. 'Here's some time I made earlier.'

Sharon: Everyone would want to buy it.

Windy: Exactly.

Sharon: Yeah.

Windy: What do you mean by make time?

Sharon: … [*Long pause*] I think I mean … thinking time, to sit down perhaps with a piece of paper.

Windy: Yeah. So it sounds like that is something that you can choose to do within the three-and-a-half hours on a Tuesday. You could say, 'What is the best time that I can devote to thinking time when it's me and the piece of paper? It's not me and a piece of pottery. It's me and a piece of paper. Not me and the website. It's me and a piece of paper.' You're not making time. You're actually choosing what to do within a time structure. You're choosing.

Sharon: Yeah…. [*Pause*] Yeah, that's a good point.

Windy: There are other ways of doing this. You might say, 'Because I'm not used to doing it, maybe I'll start off with this and then get into it, and then I might do it afterwards.' That's what I'm saying, you play around with the idea. You've got three activities to actually pay attention to within three-and-a-half hours. You don't have to make a commitment. You can start off with one and then the other and then the third. You can reverse the order. You can play around with it.

Sharon: Yeah. I'm also wondering if it would be wise – and I've thought of this before but it's never materialised – to make that thinking time perhaps on a Monday evening for even half an hour or 20 minutes.

Windy: OK. What time on a Monday evening, in terms of your lifestyle, would be the best time to actually have thinking time?

Sharon: Maybe about 9:30 or nine o'clock or so. I could try that.

Windy: One of the things about procrastination, if I think about procrastination as a plant, as we've done by, one thing it doesn't like is having a set time. It likes time to be open so we can procrastinate.

Sharon: Yeah.

Windy: So I think it might be useful to say, 'Well, look, wait a minute, what's better for me? Nine o'clock or 9:30?'

Sharon: Be more specific.

Windy: Yeah.

Sharon: Yeah.

Windy: What do you think?

Sharon: … I'll say nine.

Windy: OK. Then again you can experiment as well. So thinking time, it sounds like for you, you've got a pen and a piece of paper?

Sharon: Yeah. I actually even have bought a little notebook for this purpose, but it has remained empty.

Windy: What's it called?

Sharon: It doesn't have a name, I don't think. It's maybe just like a planning book. I got that at the start of the year.

Windy: Well, just taking the wording from what you were saying – I don't know whether you can write on it or just put something on it – 'Thinking time.'

Sharon: Yeah.

Windy: A notebook by Sharon.

Sharon: Yeah.

Windy: So can you imagine then just drawing upon what we're talking about? You approach the pottery with this mindset: 'I'm going to make a contract with myself that I am going to devote three-and-a-half hours on a Tuesday morning to pottery including the creativity aspect of pottery, the thinking aspect of pottery and the website aspect, and I'm gonna make sure that all three get attended to. I'm going to make a contract with myself because it is important to me to keep this going so that I get to, at the very least, express my creativity which is really important to me. And, to aid that process, I'm going to commit myself to thinking that for half an hour at nine o'clock to 9:30 – it may move to later but I'm going to start off at nine, to aid that particular process. And I am going to be clear with myself and other stakeholders, like the people who ask to see me, that I'm not available on Tuesday morning but I am available,' whatever other time you make up, so that people know that Sharon's not available on a Tuesday morning. And that your family's gonna support you in this. Now, can you imagine implementing that solution?

Sharon: Yeah. I think what I'll have to do is set a reminder on my phone, because what could happen is I could forget to think, and have that thinking time on Monday evening. But I suppose that's like with any new habit.

Windy: Yeah, exactly right. You need to actually have a technological support. So set that on your phone. Can you imagine setting it on your phone and then, 'Ah, wait a minute, thinking time,' and getting down to it?

                [I am framing this as an external resource that Sharon can use to help herself.]

Sharon: Yeah, I think I'll need to. I think I will forget if I don't do that.

Windy: Yeah. Again, this is something you can actually get your family to support you with.

Sharon: ... Yeah.... [*Pause*] Yeah, I'm starting to feel quite excited about it.

Windy: OK, good. So do you wanna summarise what we've talked about, particularly what you'll take away from this that's gonna make a difference to you?

Sharon: Yeah. I think I've just reminded myself that that part of me is really important and that it's been shrivelled because I haven't been watering it, so it's not getting a chance to flourish, it's not getting a chance to be nurtured and to grow. And, in order to do that, I need to make a contract with myself, which I have done in the past in other aspects of my life, but making it quite specific in order to protect that block of time on a Tuesday morning and also a Monday evening, a short period of time for thinking, which I think is gonna be between nine and 9:30, initially anyway. And try and set a reminder on my phone in order to do that. And ... yeah ... I'll not be available on a Tuesday between the hours of ten and 1:30 because this part of me is non-negotiable.... And ... yeah, so in that Tuesday morning it's gonna have an element where there's gonna be a little bit of organising and the creativity and then website, attending to that.

So, yeah, I think, if there is a contract there, it's that determination and commitment. I've written that down because I have had that in the past.

Windy: So is there anything else you want to mention before we finish or anything you wanna ask before we finish that you wish you may have asked or mentioned a little bit later?

Sharon: ... No. I like what you said about the procrastination plant doesn't like specificity.

Windy: Yeah.

Sharon: Because I never actually thought about that before
because I can be quite vague.

Windy: Yeah. Procrastination is loving hearing that and saying,
'Oh great, vague. We love vague.'

Sharon: Yeah. So, actually, that's really helpful because I know,
even in terms of Tuesday mornings, it's a vague idea
rather than a specific plan.

Windy: That's right, and you may need to bring the specifics to
each of those three activities that you mentioned. That
might be something that you can think about on the
Monday evening.

Sharon: Yeah. One other wee thing, Windy, and probably for me
I would normally write things down anyway because I
always journal, but would you say it's important to write
that contract and have a written contract?

Windy: Well, I always quote the wise person who says that a
verbal contract is not worth the paper it's not printed on.

Sharon: Yeah. Point taken. From someone like me, I need to write
things down anyway.

Windy: That's right. Good. Lovely to meet you, Sharon, and I'll
send you the recording soon and then the transcript will
follow after it's done, OK?

Sharon: OK. Thanks very much, Windy.

Windy: Thank you, bye-bye.

Sharon's Reflections (12-08-23)

I found the session so interesting and helpful. There were some key moments which I feel unlocked my 'stuckness' around this issue of procrastination in relation to the little pottery business which I have been running for the last ten years.

Firstly we looked at a time when I hadn't procrastinated. This reminded me that at one stage, when I was feeling very motivated I had spent a lot of time doing pottery, it became clear that my key motivation had changed, I now do pottery in order to nurture the creative part of who I am, rather than for financial reasons. This shift, on reflection, has meant that I am somehow less able to guard, protect and prioritise time to plan and to make pottery.

Until this moment I hadn't really thought of my pottery as being self-care. This challenged me because I am passionate about self-care for my clients and I do strongly feel that nurturing the creative part of us is an essential part of that! I hadn't realised that is not what I had been modelling.

Windy identified key strengths of determination and commitment within me in light of the way I had managed my pottery when I perceived it as being more important and also in my current job where I don't have problems with procrastination. This was enlightening, and very clever as subversively Windy was showing me that I had the required strengths, perhaps I had been choosing, perhaps I had more control than I realised. If this was true, I was not at the mercy of procrastination!

Suddenly I could see that I had been neglecting to nurture that part of my life. I used the language that other things 'creep in' and I found it funny when Windy challenged this. I was allowing things in!

I have been much better at managing to keep my pottery day free of appointments. a metaphor of a plant introduced by Windy with a quote: 'If you feed it it will grow' I actually love this quote and I began to think wow ... imagine what could happen if that creativity plant was nurtured and cared for properly, consistently over time. I began to get excited about what that could look like. I still do!

I now feel a responsibility to water my creativity plant! This has in turn unlocked my determination and commitment to do so.

Something else that I took away from the session is 'procrastination hates specifity'. That has influenced the way I plan things, for my pottery – but also for other things that are important to me. I am writing things down more. Making more lists and feeling more organised.

I had a view of myself that I was 'not a very organised person'. Windy challenged this very simply but clearly by putting an alternative view in front of me: 'You have organisation skills but you haven't been expressing them in this area!' I now see that my viewpoint was very black and white and unhelpful and actually when I considered what Windy had said – it was true, I had the capacity to be organised, there was evidence of that in other areas of my life. This has made a real difference to me! I sometimes had unfairly compared myself to other 'more organised' people and hadn't realised that it was not a fixed personality trait, that it was something I could work on.

The single session was incredibly helpful in many ways, some of them unexpected – it has built my confidence in my own strengths and ability to plan and organise.

The session shone a light on ways of thinking which were unhelpful and introduced flexibility into my mindset.

It was empowering, I am now better at setting boundaries, at protecting that which is important to me. I had a fresh revelation of how important creativity is to me. I realise I had neglected it. Now it is a priority – and my choices are now reflecting that!

Procrastination is becoming less of an issue.

I am so grateful that I took part in the session, it has had a lasting effect on me, more than I ever expected.

Thank you Windy!

13

Dealing with Procrastination by Putting My Stamp on Avoided Tasks

Date: 08/05/23
Time: 43 minutes 45 secs

Windy: So, James, what is your understanding of the purpose of our conversation today?

James: My understanding of the purpose of this conversation is to, as I say, get some understanding and hopefully understand myself a bit better to lead to some change about what I would call my chronic procrastination or pathological procrastination. Something like that where I feel like I do it in lots of areas and I feel like I know that it holds me back, I guess.

Windy: And that knowledge has what impact on you?

James: The knowledge of it holding me back?

Windy: Yeah.

James: Frustration. A huge amount of frustration on myself and... I suppose anger a little bit towards myself for procrastinating as bad. It's like I know what I have to do but then I just choose not to do it or don't do it until the last minute, and then it tends to get done. ... Things tend to go OK, sometimes not, but yes ... I know that I procrastinate and then ... yeah, pretty much that.

Windy: So what would you like to change in that scenario?

225

[*Here, I am asking James to set a goal.*]

James: … I think … the thing that I'd like to change is … [*pause*] – I don't know perhaps what I mean by this, but I'd like to get things done earlier. I'd like to not live in … a scenario – honestly, at this point I feel like I've accepted that I procrastinate, and then I'm like, 'Ah, but I'll do it later.' And then some things have happened recently where doing it later has cost me mental health or it's cost me a lot of money. So it's got to the point where I was like, 'You know, this is ridiculous. I can't just accept that I procrastinate. So I'd like to get things done earlier. I'd like to not put everything off.'

Windy: It sounds to me, and you correct me if I'm wrong, acceptance almost like resignation?

James: Yeah. Resignation's probably a better word, as if I can't do anything about it.

Windy: Because accepting can actually lead to some change, not just acceptance, but acceptance meaning that you acknowledge that you procrastinate, you recognise that you don't wanna procrastinate and that you need to understand the factors that lead to you to procrastinate so you can do something about it.

[*As I mentioned in Chapter 2, clarity is an important part of SST and in this case, I clarified that by acceptance, James meant resignation.*]

James: Yes. You're absolutely right, yeah. So I suppose it isn't just acceptance. Yeah, I've resigned myself to being a procrastinator like it's a title: James the Procrastinator, because…, you're right, if I've accepted it I'd also accept the fact that I need to do something about it. But I think … this weirdly is what that is, signing up for this session, and the reason I found out about this session was because I tried to find some training around procrastination and obviously your name came up and there was a recent meeting, so I joined that too.

Windy: James, it doesn't sound like you need any training on procrastination.

James: It doesn't?

Windy: It sounds like you're pretty good at it.

James: Yeah, fair enough. I'm very good at procrastinating and I'm actually very good at pretending that I'm not procrastinating as well.

Windy: Yeah, but that's an important ingredient. I'm glad you mentioned that, James, because it's like a self-deception. And I think that one of the things I'm gonna ask you to do with me in going forward is to be scrupulously honest with yourself so that you can actually be honest and say, 'Yeah, I'm procrastinating. Let's have a look what's going on,' as opposed to, 'Nah, I'm not really procrastinating,' that kind of thing.

So how do you define procrastination, by the way, James? Let's see if we're gonna be on the same page understanding what this concept is.

[Here, I invite James to be scrupulously honest with himself, since, as he notes he is good at self-deception. Also, I invite him to give me his definition of procrastination to ensure that we are on the same page concerning what we are discussing.]

James: So, for me, it's leaving things to the last moment ... *[pause]* knowing that I could do it sooner and that it would relieve me of pressure and guilt and worry if I did it sooner. And then finding a reason not to. But sometimes, honestly, I feel like I don't even need a reason. Sometimes I just tell myself, 'Oh, I'll do it later.'

Windy: Yeah, that's the self-deception, isn't it?

James: Yeah.

Windy: So would you like to hear my definition of procrastination?

James: Go for it.

Windy: So procrastination is putting off what is in your interest to do at a time when it's in your interest to do it.

James: Yeah.... Yeah, that is true. I agree cognitively, but part of me is screaming: by procrastinating I get to enjoy ... doing nothing now as well. I'm not taking that away. I know that that's correct. I know that's what you're saying.

Windy: No, that's one of the obstacles, isn't it, because it sounds like you value doing nothing for the moment.

James: A lot, yeah.

Windy: Right, OK. So that's important, I think, valuing doing nothing. But, again, it's a question of whether you can value doing nothing in a way that harms you or valuing doing nothing in a way that helps you.

James: Yeah. I don't know that I've ever done nothing and it's been helpful. Well, it is, but not really helpful.

Windy: Well, no. I can imagine, for example, a scenario. Let me paint it for you, see if you can see what I mean. You actually decide on a task – and we can talk about which one we're gonna talk about that you currently want to focus on with me, but you can actually decide to do a task and you do it and then, having done it, you choose to do nothing and enjoy it.

James: Yeah. Once I've done it I can actually relax rather than thinking about it for three days.

Windy: That's right. Actually, my sense is that, once you're doing nothing, there's a part of you that's not entirely happy with you doing nothing. Like, 'Oh my God, I should be doing this piece of work.'

James: Yes, every moment.

Windy: Yeah, exactly. So it's not as if you're enjoying doing nothing.

James: No, I don't enjoy it.

Windy: So, listen, since you value enjoying doing nothing, I'm gonna work with you so that you can enjoy doing nothing.

[Here, I am suggesting to James that as he values doing nothing, he can do so in a way that is healthy and not harmful for him.]

James: That would be great, yeah

Windy: OK. What do you do for a living, James, if you don't mind me asking?

James: So, I'm a mental health coach. That's a very broad term that's used. It's more of a support role for people that are facing current mental health…, like poor mental health in the primary care network. So, when the doctors refer, they've got a list of people that they can refer a patient to if they don't have the capacity to work with them or there's a specific piece of work that needs to be done. I will work with a range of people with a range of different mental health things and help them get to some level of feeling better or sorting out an issue.

Windy: What would you say your strengths are that you bring to that work?

James: Strengths? That's interesting. The strengths that I bring to that work are … *[pause]*, I trained as a counsellor, like I did a degree in counselling, and I think a lot of the… strengths that I use in counselling is what I bring to that role, like understanding and compassion, empathy ... but also being able to break things down for people or focus on a particular task. This is a weird one because sometimes people come to me and they'll be massively overwhelmed with whatever they're doing, and I can be very good at helping them break that down into a non-overwhelming sense. But I actually don't do that for myself very well.

Windy: Is that because you've tried and haven't managed it or because you don't try?

James: Well ... [*long pause*] wow! Honestly, I think ... I'm scared to try and it doesn't work.

Windy: OK. Scared to try. So, if we gave you a guarantee that it would work, what would you do?

James: ... [*Long pause*] Yeah, maybe that's not it then. Maybe I'm, again, resigning myself to being a procrastinator, but there's a part of me that doesn't believe I still do it; doesn't believe that I'd ... do the things that I'd need to do.

Windy: We're talking about you breaking things down, and you said that the reason you don't do that is because you don't think it's gonna work. And I'm saying, 'Well, let's give you a guarantee that it is gonna work,' would you then break things down?

James: Well, I suppose there's more to it than breaking it down. It's breaking it down into ... [*pause*], well, yeah, if I understood it well enough, yeah, I think I would be able to do that.

Windy: Are there things that you do in life, James, that you don't procrastinate on?

James: ... [*Long pause*] Wow, OK, hold on.... [*Long pause*] Not that many things. Maybe ... [*pause*]

Windy: So, for example, you always turn up late for work?

James: Oh no. I hate being late for stuff. I really hate being late for stuff, so I tend to get to places earlier, to be honest.

Windy: Why?

James: Because it's ... [*pause*] important to be reliable.

Windy: Reliable to who?

James: To other people, like the people I'm working with, bosses, partners, friends.

Windy: I think one of the things you tend to do, and I wanna check it out with you, and you actually used the term, 'I am a procrastinator,' and so do you see the danger of using that as a term towards yourself, James?

James: Yeah. Well, for me, it feels like, again what you said earlier, I just ... [*pause*] let myself be and don't challenge that idea.

Windy: Yeah, because it's your identity. Once you say, 'I am a procrastinator' – I found that out many years ago, if you don't mind me sharing something personal about myself to help shed light on this. I have a stammer which you may or may not notice, I don't know, but, when I was in my late teens I regarded myself as a stammerer. Then somebody pointed out to me that the dangers of that are, if you regard yourself as a stammerer, what does somebody who is a stammerer do? They stammer.

James: You have to, yeah.

Windy: That's right. So even then I reflected on it – actually, there are times in my life when I don't stammer. And, as we look at it, James, there are times in your life when you don't procrastinate. So one of the things you might think about is de-identifying yourself with the issue. Stop saying, 'I am a procrastinator.' Start regarding yourself as a person who procrastinates in certain areas in their life, and in other areas of their life they rack up early because they hate being late, because it's important to them to be reliable to other people.

[*Helping people to take the identity out of the problem is very important with all problems, and it is certainly important when the client's nominated problem is procrastination, and they regard themself as 'a procrastinator'. I often use self-disclosure to emphasise this point.*]

James: That's a good point. I looked back. Recently, procrastination cost me a lot of money, and I've tried to think back to the last time when I didn't procrastinate, and I could only think of work-based things or ... [*pause*] telling myself I'll work out or stop drinking.

Windy: But you neglect that every day you go to work and you turn up early.

James: Yeah. That's what I mean. I didn't even regard that as being something where I don't procrastinate. I genuinely think that's the first time where I say to myself, 'I didn't procrastinate or I don't procrastinate when I do that.' I'm late occasionally but I feel that's because of traffic.

Windy: Do you have a family, James?

James: No. I've got a partner and my mum and my brother, but not a young family or anything like that.

Windy: If you had a child and you had to pick them up from work, would you procrastinate on that and turn up late?

James: No, I don't think I would. ... Yeah, I definitely wouldn't want to be late for doing that.

Windy: Why not?

James: I don't know. I feel that, if they're a young child, it's dangerous. Even when my partner goes out and I'm picking her up from the train station, I'll always get there early to make sure that I'm there on time and she's not waiting about. It just feels dangerous to let a young child to be waiting on their own.

Windy: So, again, when there's a reason for it. It sounds like, when there's a good reason for you to do something and do something in a timely manner, you do it.

James: Yeah.... It almost feels like narcissistic at some points, but sometimes I procrastinate and I realise it's because I don't really care about the thing that I'm procrastinating over.

Windy: Well, yeah. That's why one of the factors of my definition is that procrastination is doing things at a time that's healthy for you and the task itself has got to be something that's in your interest to do, because, if it's not in your interest to do, then why do it? Even if you're talking about your tax return form, there's a reason to do it at a certain time. So maybe it's time for us to really focus on something that you would really like to start off the process of understanding and change in terms of a particular issue that you're procrastinating on, and then we can maybe learn from that and generalise it to other areas? Would that be a good way of going about things?

[Having had an opportunity to understand James's problem with procrastination in a general context, it is time to get specific.]

James: Yeah.

Windy: OK. So what are you currently procrastinating on?

James: ... [*Pause*] This one's like a big, grey cloud, I suppose. In my work, as like most work, we have to keep certain notes and update certain files and tick certain boxes for working with people. There'd been a bit of an admin issue on that side. So there was a long period of time where I wasn't able to update those things; I had to keep my own personal records and update them later. And, now that issue has resolved and I need to update all of those notes and all of the work that I'd done with people needs to be updated, and I've done some of it but I don't feel like I've done all of it. I'm trying to do small parts, but I tend to leave it until the last minute.

Windy: If we could actually create a third screen where you could see yourself acting in this area in a way that you wanna act, if you could see that what would you see and what would I see?

James: ... [*Pause*] If they were acting in a way that I wanna act?

Windy: No, if you were acting in that way. If you could see you acting in terms of these notes and stuff, what would you see yourself doing? So under the heading: 'James is acting in the way that he wants and he's not procrastinating,' what would we see?

James: We'd see me updating our system with client notes quickly and they'd be very detailed and understanding. And I think the thing as well is that I'd be doing it with a lot more confidence, I suppose.

Windy: Yeah, OK. But is that a picture that you'd like to see in reality?

James: ... [*Long pause*] Yeah, I think there is a part of me that would like to see that because I know that I have to do it and I know that it is something that I need to do. It doesn't interest me but it is in my best interest to do them.

Windy: Why is it in your best interest to do them?

James: Because working with people, if things happen there's a paper trail of the work, when it ended, when it started, and there's an expectation to have those notes up to date.

Windy: Why's that important to you?

James: ... [*Pause*] This is gonna sound weird, but I feel like it's important to me because I'm told that I have to do it by my bosses or whatever.

Windy: You can't see the value of doing it for yourself?

James: Not the notes that they want. In my private work as a counsellor I keep slightly different notes and I see the value in keeping those.... The sorts of notes that they expect aren't.

Windy: Do you procrastinate on notes in your private work?

James: No, I don't, actually.

Windy: So it sounds like to me that, when you can see the sense of something yourself and you can say, 'I can understand this. It makes sense to me. They are notes and I need to do it and, because it makes sense to me, I'll do it,' and you don't procrastinate.

James: Yeah.

Windy: But, when you're told to do something and you know that it's a good idea to keep the notes but it doesn't really make sense to you, there's a part of you that says what?

James: There's a part of me that says, 'This seems a bit pointless or futile or this isn't the most helpful way of keeping notes on people's cases or files.'

Windy: And therefore what? What's the conclusion?

James: I don't know. Like what's the point in doing it, almost.

Windy: Is there a bit of rebelliousness about that for you?

James: I had this conversation with my partner recently. I don't really see that but I'm starting to believe that there is a

part of me which is like doing something for 'doing it's
sake' ... [*pause*] if I feel that there's a way of doing it
better or more helpful, then I see the value in it. I don't
know what I'm trying to say. I suppose yes, but I also
don't really identify as being very rebellious at all.

Windy: But, if you could put your stamp on that in some way,
that although you don't necessarily agree with the bosses
in the way that they want you to do it, but that you can
put your stamp on it, the James stamp, would that make
a difference to you?

[*The idea of James putting his stamp on work that he has
to do but can't see the point of doing in the way requested
by his agency becomes an important theme as we shall
see.*]

James: ... I think it would, and I think it wouldn't even just be
the notes. I think even in the way that I work with people
and the boundaries that I have to keep and the boundaries
which they expect, which I think aren't helpful. If I could
have my stamp on it, but this is where I feel a bit big-
headed, but I feel like there are more helpful ways of
helping people in general that they allow or they don't
allow. And the notes come with that and the notes reflect
that. If I had my stamp, the notes would also reflect that.

[*James sees that putting his stamp on things can be
generalised.*]

Windy: Who is in charge of whether you have your stamp on
things, James?

James: I don't know. What do you mean by that?

Windy: Well, we're talking about an activity here, right?

James: Yeah.

Windy: That you know you've got to do. You understand the
reason for doing it, but you don't agree with the way they

want you to do it. And we're talking about you putting your stamp on that. So, even though you're saying, 'I wouldn't go that way about things, but I'm working for these people and therefore I have a certain obligation to do that. However, I'm gonna put my stamp on it.' And I'm saying who's in charge of whether you put your stamp on something or not?

James: Honestly ... I feel like it is me, to be honest. I feel like I'm responsible for that.... I feel it's like procrastination as well at this point. I feel like I could find a way of doing that, but then ... I don't know why I don't.

Windy: Well, have you thought about it and dismissed it or have you not thought about it?

James: No, I've thought about it and dismissed it.

Windy: What was the reason for dismissing it?

James: A part of me feels like, firstly, why would I know better than the system that's been in place already and what if it isn't more helpful? What if it goes wrong in some way or I end up making a mess of it or there's more work for me to do?

Windy: So, if we gave you a guarantee again that all of those conditions that you fear would not come to pass, that you putting your stamp on it is perfectly fine, that you're not going to balls things up, you're not going to make things worse for yourself, you're still not gonna like the way that they're doing it, and you can say that your stamp isn't a case of being big-headed, it's a question of actually expressing your individuality.

James: Wow.

Windy: So, if you knew all of those things, would that make a difference to you?

James: Yeah, I actually think it would.

Windy: So I think what's going on for you, James, is that you're saying, it seems to me and you correct me if I'm wrong, that, 'I will do this task but only under certain conditions: the conditions where I know in advance that things are gonna work out, that I'm not gonna make things worse for myself, I'm not gonna do that. And, unless I know that for sure, I ain't gonna do it.'

James: Yeah.

Windy: And also you were saying that beforehand: 'The other set of conditions are that I want to be confident at it. So I've got to be confident right from the start.'

               [*As in other sessions, I am outlining the conditions that James believes have to be in place before he begins the task at hand.*]

James: Yeah.

Windy: 'If I'm not confident at it, I'm gonna wait until I become confident at it, and then I'll do it.' So what do you make of that kind of take on your procrastination?

James: Yeah, honestly I think that's what it is. … Tell me if I'm getting what you're saying, but there's also a part of me that, the reason I end up doing the notes and doing the things at the last moment is because … what ends up happening is I get chased for it or whatever, and I do them at the last moment to keep the status quo, in a sense.

Windy: What's the status quo?

James: That I do the types of notes that they want and the type of admin that they want and the bare minimum when I do the work, and the work that they want, and I just live in that perpetual state of thinking that there's something better.

Windy: Yeah, because there's no room in that image for you putting your stamp on things.

James: Yeah.

Windy: The way you talk: 'It's them and me,' as opposed to, 'Yeah, they want me to do it this way. It doesn't make sense to me, but I'm gonna see if I can get as much meaning out of it as I can by putting my stamp on it. And I don't have to know that I'm not gonna get into trouble. I'll find that out later and deal with it. And, you know what, I may not get into trouble. But, if I do, then I can deal with it at the time.' So it's almost like you put things off because you wanna avoid the bad things that you conjure up in your mind from happening.

James: Yeah.

Windy: The alternative to doing that is what?

James: ... The alternative to doing?

Windy: By waiting for the conditions to exist first and then actually putting your stamp on it.

James: Yeah.... I suppose the alternative is ... [*pause*] I guess doing it early.

Windy: Yeah, but while reminding yourself of what? You need to remind yourself of creating a different set of conditions that will enable you to do something that's in your interest to do.

James: I guess a big part of me for me is trusting that, if those things do happen, like if I do balls it up or ... mess something up or create more work or get into trouble, that I can deal with that, because I don't feel like I do trust myself to get myself out of those scenarios. I have to feel like I am competent enough.

Windy: Well, partly, it sounds like you're trying to trust yourself to know how you'd respond in a vacuum, because you don't know if you put your stamp on it. I mean, you know your bosses. I don't. What are they likely to say? If there's gonna be any negative, what are they likely to say when they look at this thing and they recognise that James is putting his stamp on things?

James: And they look at it and there's a negative thing?

Windy: Yeah, what will they say.

James: Well, I think honestly they're not terrible people; they're actually quite nice people. But I think they'd ... firstly ask me to not do it that way or to work in a different way or to... do something slightly differently. Part of me is about squashing that ... individualness, if that makes sense.

Windy: But you're squashing it yourself at the beginning.

James: By not doing it?

Windy: Exactly, yeah.

James: Yeah.

Windy: In a way, it's almost like you're saying, 'Unless I know they're not gonna squash it, I ain't gonna do it. So I'm gonna squash it.'

James: Yeah.

Windy: 'We have met the individualised squasher and it is me.'

James: Yeah.

Windy: Whereas, if you could say, 'Actually, no, I'm gonna give expression to my individualism and these people are not bad people. Maybe we could have a dialogue about it.' Is that possible, have a conversation about it and then see what happens? 'Then the worst case scenario is that I'm gonna have to take my stamp out of it.' But you're taking your stamp out of it before you start.

James: Yeah.

Windy: So what about if we put that stamp back into it? Let me outline a particular scenario for you based on what we're talking about here, James. So you actually approach this task, you know, ideally, being asked to do it in a way that you don't necessarily fully agree with, and you say, 'OK, but I'm gonna put my stamp on it and I'm gonna see what happens when I put my stamp on it. I don't need to know before I start that this is gonna work out right. If it doesn't, we can have a dialogue about it because I'm working for reasonable people. And a worst case scenario is that I'm going to have to go back and do it their way. But, actually, the best case scenario is that I'll be able to do it with my stamp. So I don't need to have the answers to those questions at the beginning. I can start and then find out what happens later. And I don't have to be competent at doing these things right at the start. I can grow in competence later.' Can you imagine having that more flexible way of going about things, James?

James: Yeah. Weirdly, that sounds like a workplace paradise, that confidence.... Because I think having all those questions, I feel like I need the answers to those questions. I think that's why I go, 'Well, I have all these questions in my head. If I don't have the answers, why bother doing it?' So imagining a world where I do it my way or put my stamp on it, then, if it does go wrong, yeah, I can have a dialogue and figure out how it's gonna go there, that sounds right.

Windy: So who's in charge of which type of workplace environment on this issue that you can create?

James: Yeah, it's me.

Windy: So, based on that understanding, do you think that, if you took these things away with you and really reminded yourself of that when you come to the task, certain key things like, 'I'm gonna put my stamp on it. I don't need the answers to all my questions before I begin. I can find out later. I'm in charge of actually helping to create the workplace environment that I want.'

James: Yeah. That's a big one, I think ... because that's something that I don't think that I do feel: having the power to create the environment that I want.

Windy: But, again, you're wanting to feel it first and then create it.

James: Yeah. ... [*Pause*] Yeah, I guess I've always been a bit like that as well, to be fair. I've always waited for the feeling to come first.

Windy: But what about experimenting with the idea of actually going about it and saying, 'Look, I don't need the feeling to start first'? In a way, that's partly what procrastination is, isn't it? It's waiting for the feeling to do something and then you do it, as opposed to recognising, 'No, wait a minute, I don't need to feel like I wanna do it. I'm gonna do it because it's in my interest. I'm gonna put my stamp on this. I don't need the answers to my questions. I don't need to be competent. And then I'm gonna review, after doing that a few times, where I stand with my feelings.'

               [*Here, I invite James to experiment with doing things differently. This is to help himself edge into change without making a big deal out of it.*]

James: ... [*Pause*] Yeah.... [*Pause*] That would be a great way. A part of me is... [pause] wondering... how well I'd do that as well, honestly.

Windy: OK. I can answer that question for you. I can. Wait a minute. What do you see here?

James: A crystal ball.

Windy: A crystal ball. That's what you do. You ask questions which can only be answered after the fact, and you're demanding to have the answers before the fact. Then, because you don't get it, you don't take action.

James: ... I don't get anything done because of that, to be honest.

Windy: That's right. But you could actually bring a fundamental transformation in you by actually making that shift and see what it feels like later.

James: Yeah. And something you said as well earlier, just a second ago, I think I would enjoy work in some areas of life better if I did that. It feels like I'm taking a lot more control over my work, as I say previously, I haven't felt. So, I do see the value in that. If I said, 'Sod it,' and then did the work, put my stamp on it and created the environment that I wanted to work in, and then, if they had a problem with that – again, I feel like I'm still trying to rationalise it into feeling it before it happens.

Windy: But you can spot that. Just because this pattern of waiting for the feeling to come first has been with you for quite a while, so it's gonna pop up. So, actually, when it pops up, just acknowledge that it pops up and recognise that you have a choice to go along with it or to recognise, 'No, wait a minute, I'm gonna do something different. I'm gonna wait and the feeling will come later.' Do you work out in the gym at all?

James: No, because I said that I'd start and I didn't.

Windy: Have you ever?

James: Yes.

Windy: Did you wait for the muscles to come first and then work out or did you work out and then get the muscles later?

James: Yeah. Obviously, yeah, the fitness came after using the gym.

Windy: Well, that's all I'm saying. I'm actually saying that it's about your emotional muscles. Your emotional muscles are gonna grow when you need to give yourself a gym workout in this new way of going about things: 'I don't need the answers to these questions. I don't need these feelings to come first. I can focus on what I want to do or want to have done and then, having done it, I can relax and do nothing and not have anything on my mind other than the satisfaction that I've done things that have enabled me to bring about some change for myself.'

                  [*Here, I am helping James to see that he has had the experience, in a different context, of doing things to get a state rather than waiting for the state to exist before doing things.*]

James: Yeah.... [*Long pause*] I do actually agree, I think ... [*long pause*] because that would be a wonderful world to be. There's a part of me that is just registering – there is almost a strictness to that, like ... [*pause*] a conversation with myself.

Windy: Yeah, you could look at it as strictness, but you could actually bring your strengths of understanding, compassion, breaking things down, and bring those strengths to the table and recognise that the important thing is regularity: you can do this in a regular way, you don't have to be strict with yourself, as you do in other areas of your life in terms of turning up early at work.

                  [*Here, I am bringing to the discussion the strengths that James outlined much earlier in the session. It is important that the SST therapist holds the client's strengths in mind or make a note of them before introducing them into the conversation at a salient point.*]

James: Yeah, that's true.

Windy: You've got that in your repertoire. It's not as if we have to create it. It's there. It's a question of actually making use of it and bringing it into this area of your life.

James: Yeah. And it's doing it for me.

Windy: Yeah, but are you worth doing it for, James?

James: I'd like to say yes, but apparently I've not been actually doing that.

Windy: But, if you can remind yourself, 'I am worth doing it for,' and then doing it because you're worth doing it for, then you'll bring the behaviour and the attitude together more. Because at the moment I think you've got them separated. We have to finish in a minute, but I'm curious about what you're going to take away from this that's gonna make a difference to you.

James: Yeah, I think ... [*pause*] you used the word 'putting my individuality on it', and I think that's actually something that ... I've lost over a period of time, and that's actually something that I wanna strongly take away and ... realising that I actually do have – power feels like the wrong word, but I do have something, the ability to create that world and put my stamp on it more and that I am worth doing those things for and the individualities. I think that's something that's definitely gonna stick with me more.

Windy: We'll reach out to you in a couple of months and get your impressions of this session and what difference, if anything, it's made to you.

James: Brill, thank you.

Windy: My pleasure. Take care.

James's Reflections (31-08-23)

My experience of the single session therapy on procrastination with Windy was a helpful and pragmatic exploration of my personal procrastination. Starting broadly in the reasons why I might procrastinate and defining the procrastination problem before getting to the roots of why *I* specifically procrastinate. I initially reached out for the session after a particularly horrendous period of procrastination had started to affect me emotionally and financially. I decided that it was time to change but felt clueless as to how, as I had been a 'procrastinator' my whole life. The session helped me to understand procrastination and gave me a set of guidelines to exploring my own procrastination further in the future.

Much like most things in life, I view my journey out of severe procrastination as an ongoing process. I believe that the single session therapy was the start of that journey. I found the session provided orientation and direction which I still use to guide myself when I notice procrastination creeping back into areas of my life I would rather it not to be in.

The most notable difference between before and immediately after the SST was how much more capable I felt to deal with my procrastination habits. Procrastination was something I feared and hated about myself; I had resigned myself as being a procrastinator. I found Windy to have a sense of calm empowerment in being able to deal with my procrastination, an energy that said procrastination is a problem that needs to be understood and can overcome. The session was practical and direct, I took away a sense of strength and hope which I have fostered slowly over time. I use this strength to overcome the procrastination in the areas of my life that are affected the worst.

Whilst I still procrastinate regularly (evidenced by my sending this reflection on the date of deadline, sorry Windy!), the extent to which I procrastinate has lessened, particularly in the areas of life I deem as more important. The most important and helpful thing I have taken away from the single session is a deeper understanding of why I procrastinate. Windy helped me realise the things I tend to procrastinate sit unaligned with my values – even when I had told myself they did not! This realisation has been the biggest source of change as I realised often, I do not give myself a good enough reason to not procrastinate.

Using my new understanding of why I procrastinate and my new sense of direction I find it easier to encourage anti-procrastinatory techniques. Over the past few months since the session, I have chosen to think about my values regarding my procrastination and give myself explicit reasons to not procrastinate, and explicitly thinking about what it is I would value about having the 'work' done.

14

Choosing to Go on a Waiting List for an ADHD Assessment with God's Help

Date: 22/05/23
Time: 27 minutes 36 secs

Windy: So, Andrew, what's your understanding of the purpose of our conversation this afternoon?

Andrew: Just to ... [*pause*] I suppose guide me towards... overcoming my procrastination, to have a potential solution to overcoming it.

Windy: And what are you currently procrastinating on?

Andrew: So I'm a recently qualified CBT therapist. I work at the University of Glasgow as a wellbeing officer. I've been in the role recently. I am procrastinating over, I wonder if I have a neurodiversity – ADD, ADHD – just my attention in certain areas and completing tasks is difficult, and I'm procrastinating over whether I should go and get a private assessment for ADHD.

Windy: And can you give me a sense of what led you to making that decision about whether to or not?

Andrew: ... [*Long pause*] If I'm going down the right lines, what led me was ... I suppose I have a lot of indecision, I find it difficult to make decisions, I overthink things a lot, I seem to take a long time to sometimes process answers ... sometimes, if two or three people are speaking, I've got excellent hearing but I don't actually pick up on what people say if I'm distracted. So I'm very curious about it, and obviously I work in my field as well, so I wonder if it's affecting my ability to be effective in my job.

Windy: So what's the advantages of going for the assessment for you?

Andrew: I use a lot of self-help because I'm an overthinker. So I would use it to focus my self-help in terms of I would focus more on a neurodiverse pathway to help with my anxieties.

Windy: So, if you had the assessment and it came back, what do you anticipate the outcome being?

Andrew: I would be surprised if I don't have some attention deficit.

Windy: So, if it came back that you had, it sounds like you would add that dimension to the self-help. You would be looking for materials, not general materials but materials with an ADHD orientation, if you like.

Andrew: Yeah, and it would give me a clear understanding and a bit of peace if I do struggle to formulate something or if I've got competing tasks, if I'm getting overanxious.

Windy: When you say peace, what do you mean?

Andrew: When I'm working, if I get an emergency client and I'm triaging, and I'm doing consultations in the day, I get very quickly anxious, and I have a mini meltdown. Nothing too verbal, but I would have that. I use a lot of compassion work personally, so I could maybe use a lot of compassionate self-talk just to remind myself.

Windy: And what would that sound like?

Andrew: ... [*Pause*] I would say, 'It's understandable that you feel this way right now. Let's try and ground, let's try and bring ourselves into this current moment. And then let's try and address these issues one at a time and understand that you can cope.'

Windy: And, if you didn't have the ADHD diagnosis present or if you went and the result came back that said, 'Actually, you don't have ADHD,' what would happen to the compassion there?

Andrew: ... [*Pause*] If I didn't get something along the lines, I have this core belief of failure and being stupid, so I would probably be a bit self-critical.

Windy: So it sounds like with the ADHD assessment confirmed, you would actually make use of compassion, you wouldn't regard yourself as a failure because your responses were coloured by that ADHD. Without the ADHD it sounds like your core belief of, 'I'm a failure,' would actually come up.

Andrew: Yeah.

Windy: So that, for me, would be a strong reason to go for an assessment, and I'm wondering what's the bit of you that's actually reluctant to go for the assessment?

Andrew: I am fearful in case I'm not; I don't meet the criteria for a diagnosis.

Windy: So you'd rather not know than know that you're not?

Andrew: ... [*Pause*] At the moment that's my overriding fear, yeah. It's quite scary to get the diagnosis and not be, yeah.

Windy: So, if we gave you a guarantee and said, 'Look, Andrew, actually go for the diagnosis. It's definite you'll be ADHD,' what difference would that make to you?

Andrew: I could relax and just do it.

Windy: You wouldn't be procrastinating on it?

Andrew: No. I'd go straight for it.

Windy: So that's the condition that would lead you to deal with it: 'If I know for sure that I've got ADHD, then I'll relax and I'll go for it. But, if I go for it and I'm not ADHD, then I'm at the prey of my core belief that I'm a failure.'

Andrew: Yeah.

Windy: How have you dealt with that core belief before, Andrew?

Andrew: Until recently quite badly.

Windy: Until recently?

Andrew: Well, I've started practising compassion in the last few months.... I hadn't even really been aware of it until probably about December of this year. In the past, I've just been very self-critical and hard on myself and just been very anxious just to achieve the things that I've needed to achieve, and that's become quite exhausting.

Windy: What does the self-compassion sound like without the protection of the ADHD wrapped around you?

Andrew: It's developing. I'm developing a kind of approach.

Windy: What does that sound like?

Andrew: ... [*Long pause*] I suppose it sounds pretty much the same as if I had the diagnosis. I would be still able to be kind, to try and imagine a kinder version of me saying ... [*long pause*] – it's a little bit tricky. I would be trying to ... I suppose, soothe the inner critic, because I can almost feel it now shouting at me, almost saying, 'If you don't get that then you are a failure.' So it would be stronger. I'd feel I'd have to do more work.

Windy: A failure as what, Andrew?

Andrew: I suppose it comes from unlovable and a fear of being rejected. So I would just be a failure, I suppose, as a person.

Windy: So who would be rejecting you and who would be regarding you as unlovable?

Andrew: … [*Long pause*] Oh God.

Windy: God?

[*As will be seen, my response to what seemed at the time like a chance remark by Andrew marked a pivotal change in the session.*]

Andrew: No, definitely not God.

Windy: What would God say about you, by the way, interestingly enough?

Andrew: Yeah. I'm quite religious, so I believe.

Windy: What would God say about you, then?

Andrew: God would not want me to be as hard on myself. He would say I'm loved and accepted and … I'm a likeable, loveable kindly person.

Windy: Would God want you to say those things about yourself?

Andrew: Yes.

Windy: To yourself?

Andrew: Yes.

Windy: Or would God say, 'Listen, Mate, you can only say those things to yourself about yourself if you have ADHD'?

Andrew: Not at all.

Windy: No, OK.

Andrew: No, regardless, it's who I am as a person.

Windy: So, if you really went into this with the idea, 'Actually, I don't really need ADHD to show myself compassion and acceptance. I can do that at God's urging. Then whatever happens I'm gonna accept and love myself. Then the advantage is, at least if I know I've got ADHD, I can actually get the self-help books with the ADHD emphasis.' If you were able to do that then would you still procrastinate on going forward to actually go for an assessment for ADHD?

Andrew: ... Well ... [*long pause*] yeah. I mean, I certainly wouldn't procrastinate on it because I would feel ... with that view, more balanced.... I potentially wouldn't even have to pay for a private assessment because I could even just wait rather than spend £2,000 or something for a private assessment. I could just go on a waiting list and just see what happens.

Windy: And would God want you to get into that state of mind of acceptance first before you go for an assessment or would he encourage you to see it as a process that you can go forward while developing that attitude towards yourself?

Andrew: Yeah, it's a process. He would want me to develop the process. I need to have it in first before I do it.

Windy: Yeah, that's your inclination but, when you step back, is that how it works?

Andrew: No, not at all.

Windy: So, if you found yourself with that inclination, how could you respond to yourself?

Andrew: ... The inclination to act immediately?

Windy: No, the inclination to say, 'I need to accept myself and really show myself full compassion first before I go for the assessment.' If you find yourself thinking that way how can you respond to that?

Andrew: Well, I suppose just to say, 'I don't need to do that. It is a process. It's a journey. I'm already on the journey. I'm feeling benefit from it. I can just acknowledge and accept this impatient urge and maybe just tolerate the impatience more than anything.'

Windy: And you've got a real good supporter on your side.

Andrew: I know, it's true.

Windy: Just name the person or name the entity?

Andrew: God. Absolutely, yeah, 100%, I know. I was at church yesterday.

Windy: I think, in a way, sometimes it's about seeing opportunities to use what God has got to say and bringing it to the issue that we're talking about.

Andrew: Yeah. I know. Bringing it into the real.... We're always encouraged to do that in church as well.

Windy: Yeah. But I think it's about recognising that the inner critic is not gonna go away.

Andrew: No.

Windy: But you don't necessarily have to engage with it, because you can engage with God.

Andrew: Yeah, instead. I know.

Windy: You could recognise the inner critic is there but actually just say, 'No, I'm going to go along with God. God is encouraging me to regard myself as loveable and to accept myself, and that's good enough for me.'

Andrew: Yeah.

Windy: 'I don't need to feel it first but I can go forward as a process.'

Andrew: Yeah. I have started to learn that because I didn't even really notice the inner critic – I knew about it but I didn't notice it in me 'til about December time.... It's like a mindful process. It's just an intention to shift to the compassionate voice – my compassionate voice, God's compassionate voice. That's the one thing that's led me to think I may have an attention deficit because I feel like I shift and I shift and I shift and I shift, and I started to wonder is there something blocking this shift because, I don't know, my sense was it was seemingly to take longer than it maybe should do.

Windy: How long should it take?

Andrew: Five minutes I'd like to, but I don't know. That's the thing, how do we know? It's a journey, isn't it? I suppose, on reflection, compared from now 'til over the last six months, it definitely is going in the right direction. I suppose it's just my impatience is just willing it to be a lot quicker.

Windy: Your impatience to will what to be a lot quicker?

Andrew: To ... [*pause*] be able to ... be more compassionate to the inner critic, I suppose.

Windy: What does God have to say about patience in this respect?

Andrew: ... [*Pause*] Again, it's a journey. We sometimes have to tolerate and accept and, when we can do that, when we can notice that and tolerate that difficulty, it gets easier. Not resisting it.

Windy: Right. So maybe it's a question of recognising the impatient part of yourself and just acknowledging that it's there, but the question is which part of you do you want to be driving the bus.

Andrew: Yeah.

Windy: God or the impatient part of you?

Andrew: God, absolutely.

Windy: But that still means recognising that you are gonna have an impatient part of you, there is gonna be an inner critic, and I think we all have that. Part of the compassion is to recognise that you're not alone in this. We've all got impatience, we've all got critics. It's a question of how we relate to that. As I say, you've got a profound supporter. In single-session therapy we look for what external resources can help the person. I don't know why because you just said, 'Oh God,' and I just picked up on that. I have no idea why I picked up on that, but it proved to be very, very important to pick up on that.

[*It is interesting to reflect on the different ways in which working with parts of a person's self can be done in SST. With Andrew, I am advocating an approach based on him acknowledging the existence of a part of himself (impatience) that is problematic, to be compassionate to himself about that and realise that there is another part of himself (God) that he can access instead.*]

Andrew: Definitely, yeah. I didn't find it hard, in the early stages, to use God or Jesus as a compassionate role model, just almost a power. But that was a lot easier there.... It felt like I was a little bit more worthy of allowing that to happen in that sense.

Windy: Yeah, and I think any role model that will wash your feet is worth listening to.

Andrew: That's true, I know. I've never actually looked at it that way. Gosh.

Windy: I envy you, Andrew. I'm an atheist.

Andrew: Right, OK. I didn't know.

Windy: I wish I could believe, but I don't.

Andrew: The strange for me, that's a journey for me, my belief. I mean, I do believe in God but it's definitely a journey.

Windy: Yeah, sure.

Andrew: And it does ebb and flow as well.

Windy: Yeah. So, in a way, we're talking about a journey towards self-compassion and self-acceptance inspired and encouraged by God. A journey towards dealing with the impatient part of yourself and really recognise that you don't need a guarantee that you've got ADHD before you assess for it; you can actually go forward and you can accept yourself whatever happens and feel compassionate towards yourself whatever happens. But the knowledge will help you to choose which direction you've got to do your self-help future work on.

Andrew: Yes, I know. Whatever happens, I'd rather self-acceptance regardless, I suppose.

Windy: Yeah, but it is a journey.

Andrew: Hmm-mmm [yes]. It'd certainly help me with my decision-making, I think. Yes, I have. No, I'm going to be decisive. I'm just going to go on the waiting list and I'm gonna wait it out.

Windy: You've made your decision then?

Andrew: Yeah. Sorry, is that too soon?

Windy: No. The thing about single-session therapy is, if you've made your decision, to quote this: 'My work here is done.'

Andrew: Yeah.

Windy: Why don't you just summarise the work that we have done today, Andrew?

Andrew: OK, yeah. We worked on an area of procrastination that has been a specific difficulty for me. I suppose I explored … the ends of that decision: what would be helpful about it, what would be unhelpful about having an ADHD assessment, and that helped me, I suppose, realise that obviously… there could be some self-criticism in there. The reason I'm procrastinating is because, if I got a diagnosis and it was negative, then my self-critic would come on stronger than my compassionate self, and that led us onto exploring how I would address that compassionately either whether I got an assessment or I didn't get an assessment. And you helpfully brought in God … as the ultimate compassionate voice to help me with my concerns about self-acceptance and even impatience, and have a more tolerant perspective of who I am regardless of whether I'm diagnosed or not. And remind me that it's a journey and these things take time and there's bumps in the road…. And, yeah, it's about, I suppose, acknowledging and appreciating that journey. It helped me. It wasn't as specific, it was just going for the assessment in total, but my impatience was down to do I then pay for an expensive private assessment, which was a worry. And it's helped me come to the decision that actually I'll just go onto a waiting list and I'll just wait my time and go through that journey compassionately.

Windy: Yeah. Is there anything you wanna say about this that you haven't said yet or anything you wanna ask that you would say, 'I wish I'd asked this,' when you went home?

Andrew: There's nothing specific I'd want to ask about my process of today's session, I don't think…. No, there's nothing specific come up. I feel just being able to focus in on the problem was just super helpful for me.

Windy: Lovely to meet you, Andrew.

Andrew: Can I ask you a question?

Windy: Of course you can.

Andrew: It's related to grounding and mindfulness and focusing attention. You're a busy person. How do you shift your attention between competing tasks? I practise mindfulness quite a lot to help with my focus of attention. Do you have any tips or suggestions?

Windy: Well, for example, I do a lot of writing. So I'm writing a book at the moment and my aim is to write a thousand words a day. So I'll do about 250 in the morning and I'll do bits here and a bit there. When I've finished with you I'll do another 100 words or so. So I have my mind on the total. So that's what I'm going after; I'm aiming for the total. I don't struggle with going from one task to another. I don't know how I do it but it's more natural. So I'm not sure anything I've got to say is going to be of use to you. I think, for me, setting targets that I can achieve and know I can achieve is going to be useful, because then I'm ahead of the game rather than behind the game. That really is what helps me, but it may not help you.

Andrew: No, I like achievable, realistic targets, definitely. It's great. Because you can do that it means we get your books and we get the pleasure of reading them.

Windy: That's very kind of you.

Andrew: I'm very glad.

Andrew's Reflections (21/8/23)

My experience of the session with Windy was enlightening in that I didn't believe something that I had been procrastinating over for month's could be so effectively addressed in one session. Being able to focus my attention on the problem and ignore the emotion, inner critic, fear of failure etc was most helpful. In session introducing how a compassionate voice would sound and speak to me was useful and focused awareness upon myself.

Putting the strands of my beliefs, rules, and assumptions into perspective with a solution-focused approach, helped focus my thinking logically. On reflection it was helpful having Windy guide the session because I noticed going off at a tangent when listening to the recording. Windy effortlessly guided me back to attend to my problem.

From the session, I learned that I could use God as a compassionate role model. Previously, I have been unable to use God because of feeling unworthy. Working with Windy gave me permission to utilise God. Also, I learned by developing self-acceptance, I can still function effectively as a person whether I have an ADHD assessment or not. Reflecting further, I learned that I could make a conscious choice on which version of me is running my life, 'Who's driving the bus?'. I began to realise that overcoming impatience and self-criticism while developing acceptance is a timeless journey and at times without self-awareness, I'm at the mercy of my negative core beliefs. The inner critic won't go away but I don't have to engage with it, I can patiently engage with God (my compassionate side). It was so helpful when Windy asked me 'What does God have to say about patience'. Using the session to rationalise God as a compassionate other, Windy reminded me that any role model that washes your feet is worth listening to. This allowed me to feel worthy of using God in this context.

The difference this single session has made to me, is that I am now far less focused on being diagnosed with ADHD or other neurodiversity; I adopt a kinder attitude to myself when trying to process or rationalise competing tasks and I'm more consciously self-accepting and happy to wait however long it will take to receive an ADHD assessment. Finally, I notice more when I am procrastinating and that a kinder attitude helps overcome it. Ironically, I was aware of procrastinating when writing this reflection.

15

The Case of the Doubting Counsellor Who Went Forward, Not Back

Date: 22/05/23
Time: 29 minutes 11 secs

Windy: So, Peggy, what's the understanding of the purpose of our conversation this afternoon?

Peggy: It's a single session to help me with my procrastination that I'm going through at the moment and it's all part of the book and your research.

Windy: So can you tell me about your problem with procrastination?

Peggy: Yeah. I definitely seem to procrastinate. I never thought of it as procrastination, as something I just avoid, things I avoid doing. Specifically at the moment it's avoidance of getting back into counselling. Having qualified in 2021 I was lucky enough to be working with Mind at the time as a counsellor, but then got a job with a university supporting students with mental health problems as a mentor. And I want to get back into my counselling because I was in quite a different role. But I feel like things keep happening to stop me and I can't work out whether I'm almost creating that. I'm just avoiding.

Windy: Why is getting back into counselling important to you?

Peggy: Actually, do you know what, thinking about this session before we met, I did wonder that. Because previously I just had a huge interest in mental health, but, having qualified as a counsellor, I feel like I don't want to waste that qualification, although I'm not because I'm kind of using it because I couldn't do my role without it.

Windy: So, when you decided to train as a counsellor, what was your reasons for training?

Peggy: Over the last ten years I've recognised my interest in psychology, read lots about mental health, gone through my own mental health difficulties, realised I support friends and family quite a lot with their difficulties. So it was very much around I think I need to do something here. I've got a 22-year-old autistic son so I've not been able to work for many years. So it felt that was where I was being led in life.

Windy: Well, I get the bit where you were saying support people, but, as you said earlier on, there are different ways of supporting people: there's mentoring and there's counselling. So I haven't heard anything so far that has given me a sense that you wanted to train to be a counsellor for reasons that are clear, certainly to me.

Peggy: Yeah, that's true. Someone did say to me, 'Decide on what you like to do and find the quickest, easiest route.' I wouldn't say counselling's the quickest, easiest route to get there, but it was very enjoyable. I did love my counselling training and there's a large part of me that's just fascinated by the training and the learning and the research, which is why it's brilliant to be working in a university. So I can see what you're saying, but I think what I miss, I suppose if I did it the other way, I miss the counselling process. As a mentor it's quite different. It's more coaching, although I do use the counselling at times.

Windy: So what is it about the counselling process that you miss?

Peggy: … [*Pause*] With students I can't always sit and say, 'I notice this about your body language.' Do you know what I mean? It's that ability to be able to contract and to be able to say, 'These are the things I might do. These are the things we could work on.' Obviously, it's very collaborative. The way I work is collaborative, but I think I'm wearing a different hat. So I miss that ability to ... connect on a different level, I suppose.

Windy: And what is that level?

Peggy: It's a deeper level and it feels like it's a bit more effective. Obviously not always.

Windy: So there's a part of you that wants to do the work so that you can connect at a deeper level with your clients. And that's the part of you that is drawing you towards counselling. You say that you're avoiding. What are you avoiding?

Peggy: I'm avoiding putting myself out there because I think I go between, 'Do I sign up with agency, go back to somewhere like Mind? Do I put myself out there as an independent counsellor?' I think that's the bit I'm avoiding.

Windy: What, the putting yourself out there as an independent counsellor?

Peggy: Yeah.

Windy: So what conditions would have to exist, Peggy, for you to put yourself out there as an independent counsellor?

Peggy: The belief that I can do it, I think.

Windy: So, when you trained, did you actually work as a counsellor?

Peggy: Yeah, as a student counsellor with Mind and then, once I was qualified, I was called a counsellor, I suppose. The pandemic came along and we did all of our training in the second year. I did a year-and-a-half of my diploma online. I think there's some part of me that feels I'm not

Single-Session Therapy and Procrastination

qualified enough to sit in a room with people as a counsellor yet.

Windy: You mean if you had a couple more bits of paper on the wall you'd be OK?

Peggy: Not even that because I've obviously considered that and many of my colleagues went on to do a Level 5 or a degree or Master's.... This is where I'm going round in circles, isn't it, because I know that by getting back into counselling I will build up that confidence; I would have those experiences of counselling someone in a room in person. Eighty of my hours of counselling were all online. No, more – 90 were online.

Windy: Right, so you know that, but it sounds like you don't want to experience, if you like, the interim period where you have your doubts.

Peggy: Yeah.

Windy: And it's almost like you're waiting for the doubts to disappear and belief to take their place, even though intellectually you know that that's not the process.

[Again, in striving to understand Peggy's issue with procrastination, I am informed by ideas from REBT.]

Peggy: Yeah, you're absolutely right.

Windy: Experientially you have this idea that, 'I think I'll wait. I don't wanna feel doubtful.' Have you ever felt, Peggy, doubtful about doing anything in your life and you did it despite the doubts?

Peggy: Yeah. I've just got a new job. I'm doubtful about that. Yeah, definitely. Lots of things.

Windy: How did you deal with the feeling of doubt there?

Peggy: I overcame it by thinking, 'Well, they won't hire me anyway. I'll just go for the interview if I get an interview and it's a good learning process.'

Windy: So you overcame your doubts because you took it step by step, it sounds like.

Peggy: Yeah, true.

Windy: So what would taking it step by step once facing your doubts about working at this more deeper connection that the other part of you really wants to go forward with?

[Here, I ask Peggy if she could apply what she did with her new job to the issue that we are discussing.]

Peggy: I suppose it would be maybe going to an agency and asking if they wanted me to start under the umbrella of an agency.

Windy: Right. So it sounds like, if you can actually take a small step forward, then, even though you're doubtful, taking a small step forward will enable you to do what?

Peggy: ... To face the fear. That's what came over me then.

Windy: The fear of what, Peggy?

Peggy: ... Going back in a room with someone as a counsellor, is what came straight to my mind.

Windy: Yeah. 'Because, if I go back into the room as a counsellor, then what do I fear I might face?'

Peggy: ... *[Long pause]* Actually, putting it that way, I feel like sitting in the room that first session would be OK. I think it's the concern that, if I did the work that someone's core scores might not come down – effectiveness.

Windy: As judged by the core scores?

Peggy: Yeah.

Windy: What about if the person said they felt it was helpful?

Peggy: That would make all the difference. That would overcome any core scores.

Windy: Would it?

Peggy: Yeah.

Windy: So it sounds to me that, if you knew that you could be helpful to people by their own reckoning and that you actually took it step by step and you went to an agency rather than announced to the world, 'Peggy is now open for business.' So it's the having the sense that you can be effective.

Peggy: Yeah.

Windy: What about going forward with the idea that you can be effective and help some people and there may be some other people that you can't?

Peggy: … I had that experience in Mind and it sat OK with me, because we know from the research that counselling will only be effective for a certain percentage of people. Which is why it's a bit confusing about why I'm avoiding coming back. Yeah.

Windy: It sounds to me that you're avoiding the experience of it. The feeling of doubt, the feeling of, 'Maybe I'm not gonna be helpful,' and rather than sit with it and go forward and get the evidence that you can be and you can't be. It's like faced with a choice of a door called Doubt and Peggy goes through Doubt, sits down with a client, gets back to a sense of familiarity of doing that, recognising that she may be helpful or not; or looking at the door of Doubt and saying, 'No, actually I'm not going to go in there until I really believe I can do it and I can be effective.'

Peggy: Yeah.... I think the doubt perhaps as well is around ... the fear. My first client opened up and told me, within a couple of sessions, that she'd regularly took overdoses. I think the doubt is a bit of a fear of that as well.

Windy: Of what?

Peggy: ... [*Long pause*] I don't know. There's almost a blockage there, because I work with students; I've actually experienced quite a lot anyway with students, but, yeah, as a mentor you don't hold the risk.

Windy: So you would see with counselling you hold the risk?

Peggy: ... [*Pause*] Yeah, to some extent, I think it feels like that, and yet I know really, if I'm rational about it, it's not. ... I mean, that comes back to lots of the clients were under secondary mental health or primary mental healthcare teams, and knowing that the National Health Service isn't in the best of ways at the moment and that outside of our sessions ... it's hard to explain but the fear that they're not being fully supported.

Windy: Right, and what's the relevance of that to your fear about going back into counselling?

Peggy: It makes me feel like that hour I would have with them would be more important than ever, which sounds ridiculous because it would always be important.

Windy: And, if it's more important than ever, what's scary about that?

Peggy: ... It comes back to being effective for them, doesn't it?

Windy: Yeah. And it sounds like that you're saying that, 'I might be seeing clients for whom counselling is actually more important, and therefore almost like I have to know that I'm gonna be effective before I do the work,' as opposed to recognising, 'I'm going to do the work and see if it's effective.'

Peggy: Yes, this is true, and actually I think I've just realised where the doubt comes from.

Windy: Yeah.

Peggy: The doubt that I trained in the right modality.

Windy: The right modality for what?

Peggy: For being effective as a counsellor personally.

Windy: OK. And what modality was that?

Peggy: It was humanistic existentialism, and I think what happened was I recognised that it didn't always sit that well with me. In fact, when I came to your session and I went to a solution-focused two-day training as well before your training, and that felt to me more me. And I think, yeah, the doubt then is, 'Hang on, they're two quite vastly different modalities.'

Windy: So which one is more you? Which one feels more like Peggy?

Peggy: The solution-focused just made me think, 'This is how I could work.'

Windy: Right, OK. So I guess the choice would be to erase the humanistic existential bit or to build on it.

Peggy: Yeah, and there are links. I could definitely see the links.

Windy: Now, the question is can you build on it while doing the work, maybe dipping your toe into it rather than taking a leap into private practice or whatever, but maybe to recognise that, 'Yes, I need some more training, but in order to do the training I still need to see the clients. And maybe I can go forward with that idea: that I'm still training,' as opposed to, 'That's it. I'm now trained, and I doubt whether I've got everything I need but I can still go forward with the idea that I'm training. It's a process and I can actually do that and actually get some support in that way while taking some small steps forward.'

Peggy: No, you're absolutely right. I think I did feel that I wasn't fully qualified when I finished, and maybe it came from the fact that the modality ... I didn't quite connect with it. It works for so many people, but I didn't really know how to apply it as well. As you say, it's only when you're with clients you realise you're learning all the time and, with the right supervision, I think I could probably, and maybe further training.

Windy: Yeah, maybe a supervisor that might have both a humanistic understanding and a solution-focused that can help you to integrate those two ways of working.

Peggy: Yeah. That's definitely. That's what I was thinking, but I don't know where to find that one.

Windy: Well, I tell you something, it's not gonna knock on your door.

Peggy: No.

Windy: 'Hello, I understand, Peggy, that you're looking for a position where you can integrate humanistic and solution-focused work and still be a trainee. You're in luck.'

Peggy: No, you're absolutely right. Yeah.

Windy: So let's put these things together. So how would you put these things together then that we've been speaking about so far?

Peggy: Yeah, that door with doubt on is really clear to me. Fear is around that. But recognising that there's an opportunity to step in, do it by little steps where I'd be getting back in with clients into the room, using what I know already and trusting the process to develop in terms of taking some of the things I've learnt from solution-focused, because you can. I like the scaling.... There's partly some embodiment there, isn't there, in both modalities. So perhaps I just need to also read up and try and link the pieces together a bit alongside looking for a supervisor who might have both.

Windy: And allowing yourself to feel doubtful in going forward rather than to avoid the feeling of doubt.

Peggy: Yeah. OK. Yeah. Because doubt is probably what's holding me back, isn't it, and sitting with that feeling of doubt, yeah.

Windy: Well, actually what we're talking about is you having the experience of feeling the doubt from your humanistic existential part and then to see, 'OK, now I'll do it, what's the solution? Maybe I can take a couple of steps forward.' Do you see what I'm saying?

Peggy: Yeah.

Windy: It's almost like integrating what we've been talking about into the very solution that you're looking for.

Peggy: Yeah, of course, doing that for myself, how would I see. Yeah. Because I think perhaps naturally, when I've had personal therapy as part of my training and everything, I recognise that I am someone who solved a lot of my own problems. So ... yeah, you're absolutely right.... [*Pause*] I think the tricky thing about the existential side is that it's opened up everything for me around meaning and purpose.

Windy: In a way, I was asking you what the purpose of going back into counselling was, and you said, 'Because I wanna work at a deeper level with people and I want to help them because it's even more important given the fact that the NHS isn't providing as much as they used to.' So that's the reason to go into counselling. The doubt is partly, 'Can I integrate the different parts of myself?' and also, 'Can I get the belief first and then do it?'

Peggy: Yeah.

Windy: If you could figure out how to do that, that would be great, because then you could sell it to other people.

Peggy: Yeah.

Windy: 'Get belief first and then do something.'

Peggy: It's true, yeah. And even you telling me that back – because I want to get on a deeper level with people – I found my tummy clench because I think there's a conflict there, isn't there, of wanting to do the work but knowing that's risky work.

Windy: Yeah, and how do you manage risk?

Peggy: Yeah. Well, this is the thing. I think what came up straight away into my head then is trauma training. I feel like I haven't done enough in trauma. ... [*Pause*] So that keeps coming back up to the surface with me.

Windy: The difference for me between procrastination and non-procrastination in this sense is that procrastination would be, 'I'll do the solution-focused work and the trauma work first and then I'll go into doing it,' as opposed to, 'I'll do it while I'm doing the work because it's a process.'

Peggy: Yeah, OK.

Windy: Now, which one do you favour? Do you wanna wait until you've got the qualifications and maybe, who knows, you might even get the belief that you're looking for?

Peggy: No, you're absolutely right because then they'll be other things that come up, won't there: 'Oh, I need to just do that bit of training.'

Windy: 'I haven't got ADHD training.'

Peggy: Oh gosh. That's a big one at the moment, yeah, definitely I feel the need.

Windy: So I guess it's a choice. One scenario would be, 'When I experience doubt, I won't go anywhere near it. I'll wait until the doubt will melt away through my belief, and I'll get my belief through qualifications. The more courses I go on, the greater belief I'll have. And then I'll go through the door and, oh, there's no doubt anymore. There's a big B there which means Belief rather than D, Doubt.' That's one way forward. The other way forward is saying, 'Now, wait a minute, I'm gonna feel doubt, I'm gonna have that sense of maybe I'm not gonna be helpful, and I do recognise that I do need some further training, so I'll do both at the same time.'

Peggy: Yeah, I think you're absolutely right 'cos I'm just smiling to myself remembering how my CPD log looks at the moment – there's a ridiculous amount on there. I mean, part of that is because of my current role as a mentor needing that, but I recognise I think that's me trying to overcome the doubt.

Windy: Do you drive, Peggy?

Peggy: Yeah.

Windy: Do you remember the process of learning to drive?

Peggy: Hmm-mmm [yes].

Windy: And when you got into the car did you feel confident or belief?

Peggy: I remember saying, 'You only really truly learn when you're on your own and you've passed your test.'

Windy: Right. So you didn't think you had to take the history of the car first of all, you didn't think you had to take a qualification of the mechanics of the engine?

Peggy: No, although my dad did teach me how to check the tyre pressures and check the oil.

Windy: That's sensible. What's my point?

Peggy: Yeah, you're saying that you don't need all of that to be able to drive a car.

Windy: Yeah, because it's not gonna help you drive a car.

Peggy: No. Yeah, you're absolutely right. And, of course, until you're sat with a client knowing what they're bringing to you, you can't know anyway. And, of course, as a trainee, that's what you experience.

Windy: It's about going through the experience of doubt, allowing yourself to feel the doubt and do the work.

Peggy: Yeah.

Windy: As opposed to anticipating the doubt and changing the subject. Dealing with doubt is another qualification.

Peggy: You're absolutely right.

Windy: Do you wanna summarise the work we've done so far?

Peggy: Yeah, absolutely. So it's dealing with doubt and... sitting with that. Well, there's two choices, really, isn't there? There's doing all the training and getting more qualifications and then going into become a counsellor, which could end up being a long time away. Or there's accepting that we all have doubts about things and going and starting the counselling again and doing the training as and when is required, and working with a counsellor.

Windy: Yeah, and getting the supervision that will enable you to integrate the humanistic and the solution-focused ways of working.

Peggy: Yeah.

Windy: Do you feel any more inclined to go forward towards the counselling as a result of this conversation?

Peggy: Definitely because I was just thinking I think I was putting pressure on myself to start my own counselling independently and it's now made me think, no, I know what I need to do; I need to see if agencies would like me to start with them because that feels the best way forward.

Windy: Yeah, OK. Is there anything else you wanna ask or say before we finish?

Peggy: … [*Pause*] No, I think it's really good how you've really cleared the way for me and helped me see where my doubt and my beliefs were coming from. Thank you.

Windy: So what's the takeaway for you, would you say?

Peggy: The takeaway is I think I overthink things. I've been really, really overthinking everything. And confidence, definitely – the lack of confidence is creating that doubt.

Windy: Didn't you know, Peggy, that you can become confident through overthinking?

Peggy: Yeah, I was gonna say I don't think it's a bad thing not to be totally confident because lecturers used to say you never ever become complacent in our role. But the takeaway is, yeah, to take those little steps and the difference between the procrastination and to make sure you're not doing all the training and then waiting … but to start putting myself out there and accepting and sitting with the doubt.

Windy: Yeah.

Peggy: Going through that door.

Windy: I'll call you *The Case of the Doubting Counsellor Who Went Forward, Not Back.*

Peggy: Yes ... because I think it's important that I do.

Windy: Yeah, OK. Well, nice to meet you.

Peggy: Lovely to meet you, Windy.

Peggy's Reflections (14-08-23)

Knowing that I was meeting with Windy, and how highly regarded he is, I was already a little nervous, and then my laptop failed me!! The Zoom link didn't work, apparently I was due an update (great timing!). Cortisol levels rocketing, I waited helplessly for my technology to enable me to join our session. When we finally 'met', Windy's calm and non-judgmental manner was apparent which helped me settle down. His tone of voice and body language indicated a genuine warmth, and it was easy to forget that we weren't in a room together. I felt a rapport quite quickly as he used humour in his reflections, so I relaxed into the session, enjoying being the client for a change.

I am usually quite decisive, so my procrastination was bothering me. At one point, Windy highlighted – 'it's not going to knock on your door!'. Such humorous challenges and his analogies made me literally stop and think at times, provoking new insight into how and why I was avoiding working as a therapist. The natural, honest dialogue helped me see that I was doing more and more CPD in an attempt to overcome my lack of confidence, but that this was classic procrastination. There was a very clear theme of doubt and conflict being the obstacle for me moving forward. The session took me straight to the core of my concerns, which I now see is around not feeling qualified or experienced enough. It was very focused; listening back, I notice that Windy used open and yet direct questions to help me delve more deeply into the issues, and yet closed questions to substantiate things.

Prior to this session, my understanding of procrastination was avoidance of doing something, or being lazy, but I've now learnt that it was presenting as me actively doing other things to avoid the issue. This single session assisted me in unpicking the reasons behind my procrastination in less than an hour, yet this is something that I have pondered over for the last 18 months! It provided useful insights into what was happening for me, altering my perceptions. It enabled me to see that this doesn't require a massive change but is possible by taking small steps that feel manageable.

This session helped me explore the doubt and anxiety over my counselling competence. It motivated me to make a plan, and I have since gotten in touch with an agency to become a counsellor with them, making that first step towards becoming the therapist I trained to be. This experience taught me how procrastination could have potentially been detrimental to my well-being as the longer it went on, the more my beliefs were becoming skewed. It was exactly what I needed for clarity and to overcome my hesitation.

Thank you so much for giving me this opportunity, Windy!

16

Dealing with Procrastination by Being Truthful with Myself and Responding Constructively to Echoes from the Past

Date: 22/05/23
Time: 35 minutes 22 secs

Windy: OK, Hubert, so what's your understanding of the purpose of our conversation this afternoon?

Hubert: Well, I did ask you for help because I'm really struggling with procrastination, which is fading away for some reason somewhere, I didn't know, but for a long time it was really a huge problem, especially now when I'm trying to educate myself again … with all my essays. It's a huge problem.

Windy: Did you say that it was fading away?

Hubert: Yeah. I've got a feeling now, I don't know, but it maybe just temporary. It's still there, but I'm trying to accept myself with the procrastination on the place, but basically the problem is still there.

Windy: So you've been working towards accepting yourself for procrastinating and have you noticed a difference when you do that?

Hubert: … [*Pause*] Well, I was getting angry whenever it was this situation in my head telling me, 'OK, just leave it for now. You've got plenty of time,' and then we're coming to the end of the plenty of time which was in my head and I'm starting again being really even nasty to myself, like

277

blaming myself: 'You this, you that, you this,' and those voices in my head.

Windy: Right. And you've been working towards accepting yourself instead, is that what you're saying?

Hubert: Yes. Maybe I'll explain a little bit what my procrastination looks like.

Windy: Sure.

Hubert: So, basically, on the example of an essay, I had this essay 3,500 words to do, and now basically I said to myself, 'OK, Friday, I will do it all Friday. I've got enough time to do it, and Saturday and I've got Sunday will be free. So, Monday I will send them back.' And Friday came, I was sitting on the front of the computer, but I was switching to my Facebook – instead of concentrating I was switching to Facebook. And then I will start reading a book which is supposed to be on the subject of that, but basically, obviously, I overread and then I spent two hours reading the book, which is not bad, but basically, I did it instead of writing about that. And then I said to myself, 'OK, it's Friday night, what should I do? Maybe I'll leave it until tomorrow and I will sit down on Sunday as well, then Monday.' And that was on and on and on just like a ritual.

Windy: Right. And that happened last weekend?

Hubert: No. It begins. I can feel the pressure because I've got the last exam, now it's coming.

Windy: The last exam?

Hubert: Yeah, it's in the form of an essay, these seven questions to do, and I've really got enough time right now because it's more than 11 days, as far as I was counting before our session. But now I'm feeling pressure. And I said to myself, 'If I've got only option to talk to someone who professionally knows what to do, I will search for help instead of going into the same scenario I'm always going into.'

Windy: Right. So let's just have a look at the current situation. So what piece of work do you have right now that you're procrastinating on? Let's be clear about what that piece of work is?

Hubert: That's the BACP final exam because I'm studying therapeutic counselling right now, my last year.

Windy: And, so this is the BACP what?

Hubert: That's the final exam, BACP.

Windy: And it's in the form of short essays, is that right?

Hubert: Kind of. There are seven questions, I think, and in total there's supposed to be 3,500 words.

Windy: In total?

Hubert: Yes, in total.

Windy: So what's your goal on this? What would you like to do instead of procrastinating?

Hubert: So, going with the new technology, I put it in my diary, I've got until the 11th of next month, so June, which is about two weeks' time. So, instead of waiting until the last week, I've done for myself a date of 6th June, the note in my calendar saying, 'This is the final day to finish the exam for me.'

Windy: So when do you want to start this?

Hubert: In the case scenario, I'll explain it to you, I was starting last week. It's Monday today, nothing's been done.

Windy: OK. So let's see if we can at least see where we're going with this because it will help me to understand what's going on. So when would you like to sit down and start the work?

Hubert: ... [*Long pause*] The last day is this Friday, coming Friday.

Windy: That's the last day?

Hubert: Well, yeah. The last day when I'm supposed to start it, not the last day when I'm supposed to finish it. But on the Friday I've got Friday, Saturday and Sunday to do it.

Windy: So this coming Friday, right?

Hubert: This coming Friday, yes.

Windy: So what time on Friday are you going to sit down and start it?

[*As I have stated before, it is important for the person to set and agree with themself a specific time to begin the task. Otherwise, they will not know that they are procrastinating.*]

Hubert: ... [*Pause*] Three o'clock, in the evening?

Windy: Three o'clock in the afternoon?

Hubert: Afternoon, yes.

Windy: So is that going to work for you?

Hubert: Yeah, that's clear. All my things done.

Windy: OK. So how long are you gonna work for on the Friday?

Hubert: Let's say five hours.

Windy: Three o'clock to eight o'clock?
Hubert: Yeah.

Windy: And you've got 3,500 words in total to write, so how many words do you want to write in that five hours?

Hubert: At least 1,000.

Windy: And what's the question you're gonna tackle?

Hubert: … You mean in the level of hardness of the questions?

Windy: No, what's the title of the piece?

Hubert: The title of the piece? You're trying to do it that way. I reckon … I will concentrate on client work, on the structure…. I will choose my clients because there are a few clients I have to do the work about. I will choose the clients and then … it depends what the questions are. I didn't even see the questions. I know there will be a case study scenario.

Windy: So, when you say you haven't seen the questions, you mean you haven't looked at the questions?

Hubert: I did and then I just go through them and then I said, 'Oh, that's nothing special.'

Windy: Part of the problem is that you're not clear with yourself.

Hubert: I am not clear with myself, yeah.

Windy: So let's be clear about what you're gonna be doing between three o'clock and eight o'clock on Friday. And the more specific you can be the better. So what are you going to be doing on Friday between three and eight? Let's be really clear about that.

[Clarity and specificity are two very important factors that will help the person deal with the core of their problem with procrastination. As will be seen, I am encouraging Hubert to be very clear and specific.]

Hubert: So, if there are seven questions and 3,500 is maximum of them—

Windy: You're gonna do 1,000 on Friday.

Hubert: So I will start with doing two first questions, answer two first questions.

Windy: Let's be clear about what the questions are.

Hubert: ... I have to research them. The questions are, just for example: what agency I'm working for, because I'm doing the placement now. So what was the agency and what type of clients they are, they say serving.... That's pretty easy questions.

Windy: Right.

Hubert: ... [*Pause*] Maybe I'm wrong. I will check.... [*Long pause*] So the first question is context, boundaries and ethical framework.

Windy: So read me the question.

Hubert: 'Describe the context in which you work showing understanding of the boundaries and ethical framework with the agency.'

Windy: And that's one of seven, is it?

Hubert: It is one of seven questions, yes.

Windy: OK. So, if you divide it up, it's 500 words a question, isn't it?

Hubert: Roughly.

Windy: So you are going to be doing on Friday two of those. So you're going to be doing that and what else are you going to be doing?

Hubert: The next one in the row, so second question.

Windy: Read me the question, Hubert?

Hubert: 'Develop a counselling relationship that established in a user-centre environment for the work.'

Windy: And that's another 500?

Hubert: That's another 500.

Windy: Now, do you have to do any research on that or do you think you can do it with what you know already?

Hubert: I will properly support myself with some kind of research.

Windy: Here's a little tip: do the writing first and then support with the research later, OK?

[*I suggest this because looking up research first can be used as a procrastination strategy.*]

Hubert: OK.

Windy: So let's suppose that Friday comes at three o'clock. Now, how would you stop yourself from sitting down and doing the first question?

Hubert: … What can stop me?

Windy: Now, how would you stop yourself?

Hubert: Stop myself? I will find lots of stuff must be done here and now.

Windy: What's the purpose of finding that stuff to do in the here and now because there's always stuff to find?

Hubert: … [*Pause*] I think in one hand I'm getting bored with writing.

Windy: Well, you haven't written anything yet.

Hubert:　No, but I'm presuming that I will get bored.

Windy:　Oh, I see, that you'll get bored.

Hubert:　Yeah.

Windy:　So, if you start to get bored, what will you do?

Hubert:　What I've done for the last, as far as I remember: Facebooks, call someone.

Windy:　So you respond to boredom with distraction. Have I understood you correctly?

Hubert:　Yeah.

Windy:　Or not?

Hubert:　Yeah, but, you see, I'm not really understanding myself it that's getting bored or that's a typical fear, my fear.

Windy:　Of what?

Hubert:　Of that I'm not good enough.

Windy:　You're not good enough in what sense?

Hubert:　English is not my first language.

Windy:　What is your first language?

Hubert:　Polish. I'm from Poland. And always, even though I was really into psychology and stuff for a long time, but then I ... totally changed my life. After 20-something years I get back to this subject. But still I think there is lots of fear behind me somewhere.

Windy:　Yeah, but when you say you fear not being good enough, what do you mean? Good enough as what or at what?

Hubert:　... [*Long pause*] No idea. As a normal person, I would say?

Windy: So the fear is that you won't be good enough to be a normal person?

Hubert: Maybe not to be, but as a normal person. I had this dilemma what's normality of the person, a normal life. I'm supposed to say I'm a recovering alcoholic. So for 24 years I was in addiction and for the last seven years I'm sober and I'm getting back to my normal life, and I had no idea what normal life is.

Windy: But what's that got to do with the essay or the piece of work?

Hubert: I'm just pushing to the last minute. Then I'm feeling the pressure because it's a finish of time.

Windy: That's what you do, but presumably you don't want to do that.

Hubert: No, I don't.

Windy: So we've got two things there that are obstacles. One is, 'I might get bored,' and, 'I might not be good enough.'

[Here, I highlight from what Hubert has been saying the two adversities that exist when he procrastinates.]

Hubert: … Yeah. Not good enough – I reckon that's the main subject.

Windy: That's the main obstacle, is it?

Hubert: Yes.

Windy: Now, if I waved a magic wand, Hubert, so that at three o'clock on Friday you felt good enough, what's the difference between feeling good enough at three o'clock and not feeling good enough at three o'clock?

Hubert: … I would go with the plan. My vision of normality that is someone – I will project on someone, it's not me obviously, someone saying, 'Four o'clock – no phone calls, no distractions from anywhere. I'm just sitting down doing my work,' then that's the normality. But whatever I'm trying to do, I'm trying to disturb myself.

Windy: Right, OK. When you say you're 'trying to', what do you mean? You have to put in effort to distract yourself or it comes easily?

Hubert: My concentration just disappears.

Windy: Yeah, OK. But it sounds like, when you leave it to the last minute, what happens to your concentration then?

Hubert: I'm feeling fear, this kind of pressure.

Windy: But, when you leave it to the last minute, you then do it.

Hubert: Yeah. You see, that's the crazy thing about that. I'm always on time.

Windy: Yes. So, what you could do if you wanted to is you could say, 'OK, I'm going for a process. I'm gonna put it off and put if off until the last minute and then I'll do it on time because I've always done it that way. So I don't have to change anything. I could just go through that routine or, if I do want to change something and do things differently, then I'm gonna have to deal with some of the issues,' which I'm not totally clear about but it sounds like you have this idea that to do it at three o'clock and to not have any distractions is normality and it sounds like you have a tough time seeing yourself as within that normality. Is that right?

                [*Here, I indicate to Hubert that he can choose to leave things to the last minute as a consciously chosen strategy or do things differently.*]

Hubert: Yeah, it is right.
Windy: So the question is the two ways forward would be to feel normal first and then do it at three o'clock or to recognise

that normality will come later and that you can start even though part of you wants to go on Facebook, part of you wants to distract themself, but you don't have to go along that route even though it will be a struggle, because it's not a struggle to go on Facebook; it's quite easy. So I'm wondering if you are prepared to struggle.

Hubert: You see, I think you touched the much bigger problem, because after this college I'm studying to university and I don't want to struggle again. I know it's another year in uni and I know there will be struggle. There is much more work to do. Probably that is where the fear is coming from.

Windy: Fear of what?

Hubert: I'm not staying here and now.

Windy: Yeah, but what are you fearing?

Hubert: I'm not good enough, probably.

Windy: But you want to answer that question now and what answer do you want in order to start the work at three o'clock?

Hubert: ... [*Long pause*] I know there must be some easy answer to that somewhere, but I don't know.

Windy: Well, you could say, 'Well, actually, I don't need to know that I'm gonna be good enough in the future in order for me to start work now. I can start work now and then build up a habit of normality and do it that way and, if I did it that way, have I got more chance later on to feel good enough?'

[*As with several other volunteers in this project, Hubert is demanding the presence of certain desired conditions, in his case a feeling of normality, before beginning the task, rather than starting the task without this condition being present on the understanding that it will come once he has made beginning tasks on time the start of a new habit.*]

Hubert: I think the voice of saying 'not good enough' is left over after my addiction. That's why I mentioned it. Basically, I'm still dragging myself as someone who's overused substance because of another fear. But I'm not doing this anymore; I've got a totally new life and I don't want to do it again.

Windy: Yeah. So what you're saying is you've made a commitment to lead a new life and to be clean and free of substances, but it sounds like some of the old echoes of not being good enough are still around for you.

               [*Note that I say that the 'not good enough' voice is an echo from the past. I will use this concept of the 'echo' going forward.*]

Hubert: Exactly.

Windy: And you're trying to get rid of it through distraction or to convince yourself that later on you'll feel good enough, rather than to see those as echoes and to just get on with the work even though you have the echoes.

Hubert: Yeah, but I just realised that now.

Windy: Yeah. So do you think it's possible for you to say, 'Look, I'm gonna have the echoes because that's what happens with human beings – they have echoes in the past – and I can either wait for the echoes to go or distract myself from them or to convince myself that later on the echoes won't be there and then I'll start work, or I'll start work even though I've got the echoes.' And, if you start work even though you have the echoes and get into the work, what do you think will happen to the echoes?

Hubert: … [*Pause*] I don't know, but I hope they will disappear with time.

Windy: Right. There's only one way of finding that out.

Hubert: Yes.

Windy: What you're doing is what many people who struggling with procrastination want is the answers now to questions, the answers of which are in the future.

[*This is an important point to bear in mind when working with people who procrastinate.*]

Hubert: Yeah.

Windy: Whereas, if you say, 'Look, Hubert, I can start work at three o'clock, I can do these questions. I don't have to distract myself from the echoes. I can do it and recognise that the echoes are there but they are coming from the past.' It sounds like you've really been extraordinarily successful at freeing yourself from the substances. So you've got some strengths there as a person, haven't you?

[*Here, I am bring Hubert's strengths into the conversation.*]

Hubert: Everyone is saying that. Me, do I think that way? Yes, I do.

Windy: What strengths do you have as a person that enabled you to free yourself from the substances?

Hubert: Truth, honesty.

Windy: Right. What were you truthful and honest about?

Hubert: I'm honest about my problem. I had a huge problem. I was destroying my life.

Windy: And you decided to do something about it, right?
Hubert: Yes.

Windy: So you can bring the same process to procrastination: be truthful to yourself, 'Look, I have a problem with procrastination. I do want to tackle it. I can actually use the same process as I went through with the substances, which is to recognise that, yeah, I may want the substances but I don't have to have them, and I want to distract myself but I don't have to do that.' And presumably you still had the echoes when you were coming off of the substances, didn't you?

Hubert: Mmm [yes].

Windy: So you can actually do the same thing. You could, if you wanted to, say, 'OK, I can bring the same process to procrastination as I did when I tackled my substances, which is to be honest with myself, to recognise that I can do it even though there's a part of me that wants to engage in the substances and the distraction. And there are echoes when I came off of the substances, there'll be echoes even though I'm actually working to overcome my procrastination.'

[*Here, I am showing Hubert that he can bring strategies that he found effective when tacking his substance overuse to dealing with his procrastination problem.*]

Hubert: Yeah.... That's right.

Windy: What are you thinking?

Hubert: In general, I'm thinking I have to use my knowledge about that. I mean, I totally agree with what you said and I should know that, but, basically, I'm always in this... denial that there is no problem, probably because, for some reason, I end up being on this session. So, if I'm honest with myself, I start doing something with that.

Windy: Yeah. So I think in the same way that you had to be honest with yourself in facing up to your problems with substances, because presumably before that you weren't honest with yourself.

Hubert: No.

Windy: You can bring that real strength, that real character of honesty that you sound like you have and you can bring it to the same issue here with procrastination, if you chose to.

[*Here, I am stressing again that he can bring his strengths to dealing with procrastination.*]

Hubert: Yeah. Believe it or not, I really want to do it, and I will do it.

Windy: So you've got the honesty, you've got the determination, but there's still to manage the part of you that wants to quickly get away from echoes and any discomfort. And, if you recognise that they're like the urges that you presumably went through when overcoming your substances – did you have to deal with urges?

Hubert: Yeah, probably.

Windy: So it's the same thing. The urge to distract yourself, to go for the comfortable in the moment, but you don't have to do that. The urge to get rid of the echoes rather than allow the echoes to vanish once you really get involved with the work.

Hubert: Yeah.

Windy: So why don't you summarise what we've spoken about so far, Hubert?

Hubert: So we were going through a little bit of history of my life. All the time from the beginning I was trying to be as much honest as I can. I don't want to hide myself anywhere. And I said that I brought the problem of procrastination today to the session and, in a simple way and the simplest I can even imagine I just came to a realisation that I've got echo behind me and the voices saying that I'm not good enough, which is not the truth, because my truth is I am good enough and I'm just supposed to concentrate myself on working the here and now. And I've got the strength to do it.

Windy: And you'll see what happens to the echoes once you start the work. We don't know what's gonna happen to them because we can't predict the future, but you'll find out. All we know at the moment, Hubert, is that, when you get the echoes, you don't do the work.

Hubert: Yeah.

Windy: That's what we know. We don't know what's gonna happen if you accept the echoes, recognise that it is coming from the past but that, once you do the work, we'll see what happens to them.

Hubert: Yeah. Let's try then.

Windy: Do you think that really breaking things up into 500, doing two questions a day of 500 words each, 1,000 words a day and really start at three o'clock and doing it even though part of you wants to do Facebook and part of you wants to shut the echoes up first of all, but you're not gonna do either? You're gonna go forward even though there's echoes to the left of you and there's urges to the right of you, but there's you with your strength and determination in the middle? Can you imagine doing that?

Hubert: Yeah. Well, now... I've got this embraced to do it, the determination to do it even more, at the moment.

Windy: Yeah.

Hubert: As you said, the only way to find out is to check it and then start doing.

Windy: And you can start at three o'clock no matter what happens, unless the house burns down. I'll accept the burning of the house down as stopping you.

Hubert: Yeah.

Windy: So what are you gonna take away from our conversation today, Hubert, that's gonna help you go forward?

Hubert: Two things: single session is working, but the main subject is honesty with myself on the front of other person can help me to break through with my old concepts of myself.

Windy: Right. The real quality of honesty that you've got that was so important to you when you dealt with the substance issues you can bring to the table, literally to the table as you sit down and write.

Hubert: I can use this. I can always imagine if my fear is not to be in truth with myself. So, if I don't want to feel the fear, I have to be truthful with myself. My truth is what I said: at three o'clock I'm sitting down doing my stuff and then I'll see.

Windy: Yeah, 'That's my truth and I'll see what happens, when I sit down with my truth and I'm honest with myself. There are echoes, there are urges, but I have choices.

Hubert: Yeah.

Windy: Well, it'll be interesting to see what happens, Hubert.

Hubert: I'll let you know. Thank you very much, sir.

Hubert's Reflections (31-08-23)

Attending a single session with Windy Dryden was a mind-altering experience that revealed deep insights into my ongoing struggle with procrastination. I approached the session with a mixture of scepticism, shyness and confusion, articulating the root causes of my procrastination proved challenging. Windy skilfully led the session, his challenges and acceptance enabled me to delve into the factors that contributed to my procrastination. Through the session, it became visible how echoes of past experiences affect my current challenges.

This newfound awareness was transformative. I realised that my procrastination was linked to these echoes, perpetuating the cycle of self-doubt and avoidance. Windy's emphasis on getting a clear picture of the problem provided me with the skills to identify these triggers and understand their impact on my behaviour. During the session, Windy imparted some wisdom that spoke deeply to me: he helped me realise that my honesty in grappling with past experiences made me stronger. This perspective changed my understanding of vulnerability and resilience. Realising that sharing my struggles was not a sign of weakness, but rather a sign of my strength, allowed me to face my procrastination more courageously. Armed with this insight, I learned to challenge the negative echoes and confront my procrastination. By addressing the core of the problem and accepting my past struggles, I took concrete steps towards breaking the cycle of procrastination and experiencing true personal growth.

One of the key takeaways from the session was Windy's wise statement: 'I don't need to know if I will be good enough in the future to start working on my tasks now'. This simple but powerful idea resonated deeply with me. It highlighted that waiting for a guarantee of success in the future without taking action now is a counterproductive attitude and encouraged me to focus on taking action in the present, regardless of uncertainty about the future.

SST with Windy marked a transformational journey from shyness and chaos to self-discovery and empowerment. Realising the impact of the past fundamentally changed my perspective on procrastination. Windy's guidance, along with the recognition that honesty about past struggles builds strength, equipped me with the tools to overcome procrastination and cultivate productivity. As I write these words, I am already a qualified counsellor as I have passed the final exam.... on time.

17

Some Final Observations

In this final chapter, I will draw together some themes based on the submitted reflections of the volunteers that appear at the end of their respective chapters. Each of the volunteers (all therapists who signed up for a single session on their struggles with procrastination) agreed to provide their reflections on their particular session with me. In my letter to them, I wrote as follows:

> *I said that I would approach you at the end of July 2023 to ask you to provide a 500-word reflection on the single session we had concerning 'Dealing with Procrastination'. Your reflection will go at the end of the chapter, which will contain the transcript of our session. I am happy for you to structure the reflection in any way you wish. However, I think readers would be interested in what your experience was in having the session with me, what you took from the session and what difference it made to you I look forward to receiving the statement by no later than Thursday, 31st August 2023.*

I was thus asking for their views on the process of the session and its outcome. However, I also stressed that they were free to reflect on the session in whatever way made the most sense to them. As is my practice, I sent those who had not submitted their reflections by 24 August 2023, a reminder and, again, where relevant, the day before the piece was due.

Expectations

Although not asked to address the issue of what they expected from the session, six volunteers did so. These volunteers had what I would call modest expectations concerning what they thought they would get from the session. Thus:

295

- Sofia said that she was not expecting a 'quick fix'.
- Hubert approached the session with scepticism.
- Both Dee and James saw it as the start of a process (Dee) or the beginning of a journey (James).
- Andrew did not think that procrastination could be so efficiently addressed in one session, and
- Bella was not sure what to expect.

Outcome

All thirteen volunteers met the deadline for their reflections. Usually, when I edit a book, several contributing authors fail to meet the deadline or ask for extensions. From this perspective, while four of the thirteen volunteers left submitting their reflections to the last minute, none of them were late with their submissions. This is perhaps one way of gauging the effectiveness of the session.

As I gave volunteers between three and four months to write their reflections after their session with me, sufficient time had elapsed therefore for them to gauge what difference the session made to them if they chose to address themselves to this issue. Here is what they said about what they had achieved.[17]

1. Two volunteers reported that they had achieved their professional qualifications as a result of their session with me.
    - Hubert said that he had passed his final exam on time and was now a professional counsellor.
    - Mike said that he registered with the BACP and got his MA thanks to the session.

2. Most of the other volunteers reported varying degrees of progress in addressing their issue with procrastination.
    - Niklas said that the session had a lasting impact on him, and this led to a more proactive, growth-oriented mindset.
    - Sofia had not yet completed the task she had agreed to do but was almost there.
    - Belle had gained the confidence to stop procrastinating and 'maybe even go for it'.

---

[17] In this chapter, I employed the words that volunteers used to describe the process and outcome of their sessions with me.

- Jane said that she left the session in a hopeful frame of mind and had stuck to her weekly schedule and, in doing so, was able to prioritise her needs.
- Sharon was able to keep her pottery day free of other appointments and said that, in general, procrastination is becoming less of a problem for her.
- Peggy had contacted an agency to work as a counsellor for them, something that she had been putting off.
- Moon had been getting on with things and reported that the block was not there anymore.
- James felt more able to deal with procrastination. He reported that he was still procrastinating, but less so in important areas.
- Andrew was able to notice when he procrastinates and adopts a kinder attitude to overcome it.
- Dee said that the change had not been immediate but slow and steady.

3. Margo

I took from Margo's reflections on the session and what happened afterwards that she benefitted least from her conversation with me. She did say that she derived some benefit but that it fluctuated. As she said in her reflection. 'I have a lot more to work on than just my procrastination. I think this was highlighted to me when I started mentioning everything else in my session, i.e., my relationship with my husband. In my opinion, this means that I could not stay focused because I am not processing what I am going through.' This meant that Margo was not as focused in the session on the issue of procrastination as she might have been if this was her only issue. In addition, she was distracted by my mispronunciation of her name, which also made it harder to focus on the issue of procrastination.

Process

Volunteers referenced several process issues when offering their reflections on their single sessions with me. I take these to be largely positive experiences that they have taken from the session and that have stayed with them concerning what it 'felt like' to have a single session with me. The first group of such process reflections referred to my therapeutic style.

WD's Therapeutic Style

Several volunteers referred to my therapeutic style in their reflections.

My Use of Questions

- Jane, Niklas and Sofia mentioned my use of questions that helped them to focus during the session.
- Andrew also mentioned my helping him to focus in the session as something that was helpful to him. Helping clients to focus in SST when clients seek help for specific issues is a key feature of the work.

Therapeutic Atmosphere

The therapeutic atmosphere or climate that I developed was referred to by several volunteers.

- Belle said that I helped her to facilitate her process in the session.
- Niklas mentioned that I helped him feel comfortable and set an open space where I demonstrated active listening and empathy.
- Peggy said that I was calm, showed genuine warmth and was non-judgemental in my manner, and also used humour.
- Moon referred to my calm demeanour.
- James mentioned 'calm empowerment' when referring to my therapeutic style.

Challenge and Bluntness

Two people mentioned a different aspect of my therapeutic style.

- Hubert referred to my challenges but from an attitude of acceptance.
- Belle referred to my bluntness and said that she found its challenge useful to her.

Therapeutic Factors

The second group of process reflections referred more to therapeutic factors that volunteers gained in and from the session.

- Sofia said that she was helped to focus and put things into a new frame. The session helped her to sit with her feelings and to leave with a sense of hope and empowerment.
- Andrew also mentioned being helped to focus and to see that he could make a conscious choice as therapeutic factors, as well as being encouraged to see that he could use God as a compassionate voice with himself.
- Dee said that focusing on one incident was helpful, as was setting clear objectives.
- Belle, Sharon, Hubert and James mentioned being helped to identify their strengths in the session as being therapeutic. This is a major feature of SST which is strengths-based in its orientation towards the work.
- Jane mentioned being helped to understand her goal, the obstacles that need to be addressed and being helped to develop an achievable plan as particularly helpful. She also mentioned that it was useful to be reminded that procrastination was unaligned with her values. Lastly, she said that our conversation helped her to develop an image of a sunflower, which reminded her of the difference between having a good reason to delay versus a rationalisation.
- Sharon pointed to the idea of pottery as self-care and the importance of developing a growth, flexible mindset as helpful ideas.
- Peggy mentioned being helped to get to the core of her concerns as well as the insights she developed from my humorous challenges valuable.
- Mike pointed to the individual approach that I took to his issue as particularly valuable. As he said: 'The session offered a personalized and actionable approach, tailored to my own circumstances, The concept of adopting a 'Crème Egg' mindset (see Chapter 11) accompanied by creating an optimal work environment, setting boundaries and generalizing the strategies, presented a comprehensive framework for addressing procrastination effectively.

Memorable Phrases

It is a feature of my SST work that I endeavour to help clients to distil points that we have discussed into short memorable phrases. Three volunteers made reference to such phrases in their reflections.[18]

- Sharon: 'If you feed it, it will grow' and 'procrastination hates specificity'
- Niklas: 'Say fuck it to fuck it' and 'Discomfort is a natural part of growth'
- Hubert: 'I don't need to know if I will be good enough in the future to start working on my tasks now'

Conclusion

In conclusion, it is my view that a single session of therapy focused on a person's struggles with procrastination can be useful and that volunteers found salient aspects of the practical applications of the single-session mindset to be therapeutic and helped most of them to achieve a positive outcome from the session.

---

[18] See the respective chapters for the context of these phrases.

References

Cannistrà, F. (2022). The single session therapy mindset: Fourteen principles gained through an analysis of the literature. *International Journal of Brief Therapy and Family Science, 12* (1), 1–26.

Dryden, W. (2012). Dealing with procrastination: The REBT approach and a demonstration session. *Journal of Rational-Emotive & Cognitive-Behavior Therapy, 30,* 264–281.

Dryden, W. (2022a). *Single-Session Therapy: Responses to Frequently Asked Questions.* Abingdon, Oxon: Routledge.

Dryden, W. (2022b). Skills in single-session therapy. Part 2: Ways of Beginning the Session. *European Journal of Counselling Theory, Research and Practice, 6* (3), 1–4.

Dryden, W. (2023a). *Single-Session Therapy: 100 Key Points and Techniques.* Abingdon, Oxon: Routledge.

Dryden, W. (2023b). *ONEplus Therapy: Help at the Point of Need.* Sheffield: Onlinevents.

Frank, J. D. (1961). *Persuasion and Healing: A Comprehensive Study of Psychotherapy.* Baltimore, MD: The Johns Hopkins Press.

Hamley, D. (2015), *Colonel Mustard in the Library with the Candlestick.* Joslin Books.

Hoyt, M. F. & Talmon, M. F. (2014). What the literature says: An annotated bibliography. In M. F. Hoyt & M. Talmon (eds), *Capturing the Moment: Single Session Therapy and Walk-In Services* (pp. 487–516). Bethel, CT: Crown House Publishing.

Ratner, H., George, E. & Iveson, C. (2012). *Solution Focused Brief Therapy: 100 Key Points and Techniques.* Hove, East Sussex: Routledge.

Simon, G. E., Imel, Z. E., Ludman, E. J. & Steinfeld, B. J. (2012). Is dropout after a first psychotherapy visit always a bad outcome? *Psychiatric Services, 63* (7), 705–707.

Slive, A. & Bobele, M. (2018). The three top reasons why walk-in single sessions make perfect sense. In M. F. Hoyt, M. Bobele, A. Slive, J. Young & M. Talmon (eds), *Single-Session Therapy by Walk-In or Appointment: Administrative, Clinical, and Supervisory Aspects of One-at-a Time Services* (pp. 27–39). New York: Routledge.

Index

Index

Index

www.ingramcontent.com/pod-product-compliance
Lightning Source LLC
Chambersburg PA
CBHW072112270326
41931CB00010B/1530